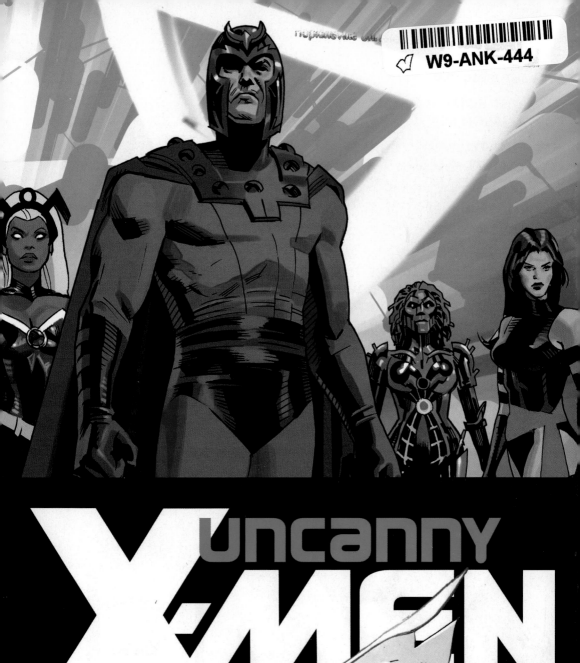

UNCANNY X-MEN

WRITER: **KIERON GILLEN**

#15-17 ARTIST: **DANIEL ACUÑA** WITH **MIKE DEL MUNDO** (#17)
ART ASSIST: **DIEGO OLMOS** (#17)

#18 ARTIST: **RON GARNEY**
COLORS: **JASON KEITH** & **MORRY HOLLOWELL**

#19 ARTIST: **DALE EAGLESHAM**
COLORS: **MATT MILLA**

#20 PENCILER: **CARLOS PACHECO**
INKS: **ROGER BONET** • COLORS: **GURU-eFX**

LETTERS: **VC'S JOE CARAMAGNA** • COVER ART: **DANIEL ACUÑA** (#15-16), **MIKE DEL MUNDO** (#17), **RON GARNEY** & **MATT MILLA** (#18-19); AND **CARLOS PACHECO, ROGER BONET** & **GURU-eFX** (#20)
ASSISTANT EDITOR: **JORDAN D. WHITE**
ASSOCIATE EDITOR: **DANIEL KETCHUM** • EDITOR: **NICK LOWE**

COLLECTION EDITOR: **JENNIFER GRÜNWALD** • ASSISTANT EDITORS: **ALEX STARBUCK** & **NELSON RIBEIR**
EDITOR, SPECIAL PROJECTS: **MARK D. BEAZLEY** • SENIOR EDITOR, SPECIAL PROJECTS: **JEFF YOUNGQUIS**
SENIOR VICE PRESIDENT OF SALES: **DAVID GABRIEL**
SVP OF BRAND PLANNING & COMMUNICATIONS: **MICHAEL PASCIULLO**
BOOK DESIGNER: **RODOLFO MURAGUCHI**

EDITOR IN CHIEF: **AXEL ALONSO** • CHIEF CREATIVE OFFICER: **JOE QUESADA**
PUBLISHER: **DAN BUCKLEY** • EXECUTIVE PRODUCER: **ALAN FINE**

UNCANNY X-MEN

UNCANNY X-MEN BY KIERON GILLEN VOL. 4. Contains material originally published in magazine form as UNCANNY X-MEN #15-20. First printing 2012. Hardcover ISBN# 978-0-7851-6529-3. Softcover ISBN# 0-7851-6530-9. Published by MARVEL WORLDWIDE, INC., a subsidiary of MARVEL ENTERTAINMENT, LLC. OFFICE OF PUBLICATION: 135 West 50th Street, New York, NY 10020. Copyright © 2012 and 2013 Ma Characters, Inc. All rights reserved. Hardcover: $24.99 per copy in the U.S. and $27.99 in Canada (GST #R127032852). Softcover: $19.99 per copy in the U.S. and $21.99 in Canada (GST #R127032852). Cana Agreement #40668537. All characters featured in this issue and the distinctive names and likenesses thereof, and all related indicia are trademarks of Marvel Characters, Inc. No similarity between any of the na characters, persons, and/or institutions in this magazine with those of any living or dead person or institution is intended, and any such similarity which may exist is purely coincidental. **Printed in the U.S.A.** A FINE, EVP - Office of the President, Marvel Worldwide, Inc. and EVP & CMO Marvel Characters B.V.; DAN BUCKLEY, Publisher & President - Print, Animation & Digital Divisions; JOE QUESADA, Chief Creative Officer; BREVOORT, SVP of Publishing; DAVID BOGART, SVP of Operations & Procurement, Publishing; RUWAN JAYATILLEKE, SVP & Associate Publisher, Publishing; C.B. CEBULSKI, SVP of Creator & Content Development; D. GABRIEL, SVP of Publishing Sales & Circulation; MICHAEL PASCIULLO, SVP of Brand Planning & Communications; JIM O'KEEFE, VP of Operations & Logistics; DAN CARR, Executive Director of Publishing Technol SUSAN CRESPI, Editorial Operations Manager; ALEX MORALES, Publishing Operations Manager; STAN LEE, Chairman Emeritus. For information regarding advertising in Marvel Comics or on Marvel.com, please cor Niza Disla, Director of Marvel Partnerships, at ndisla@marvel.com. For Marvel subscription inquiries, please call 800-217-9158. **Manufactured between 10/1/2012 and 11/12/2012 (hardcover), and 10/1/2012 5/6/2013 (softcover), by R.R. DONNELLEY, INC., SALEM, VA, USA.**
10 9 8 7 6 5 4 3 2 1

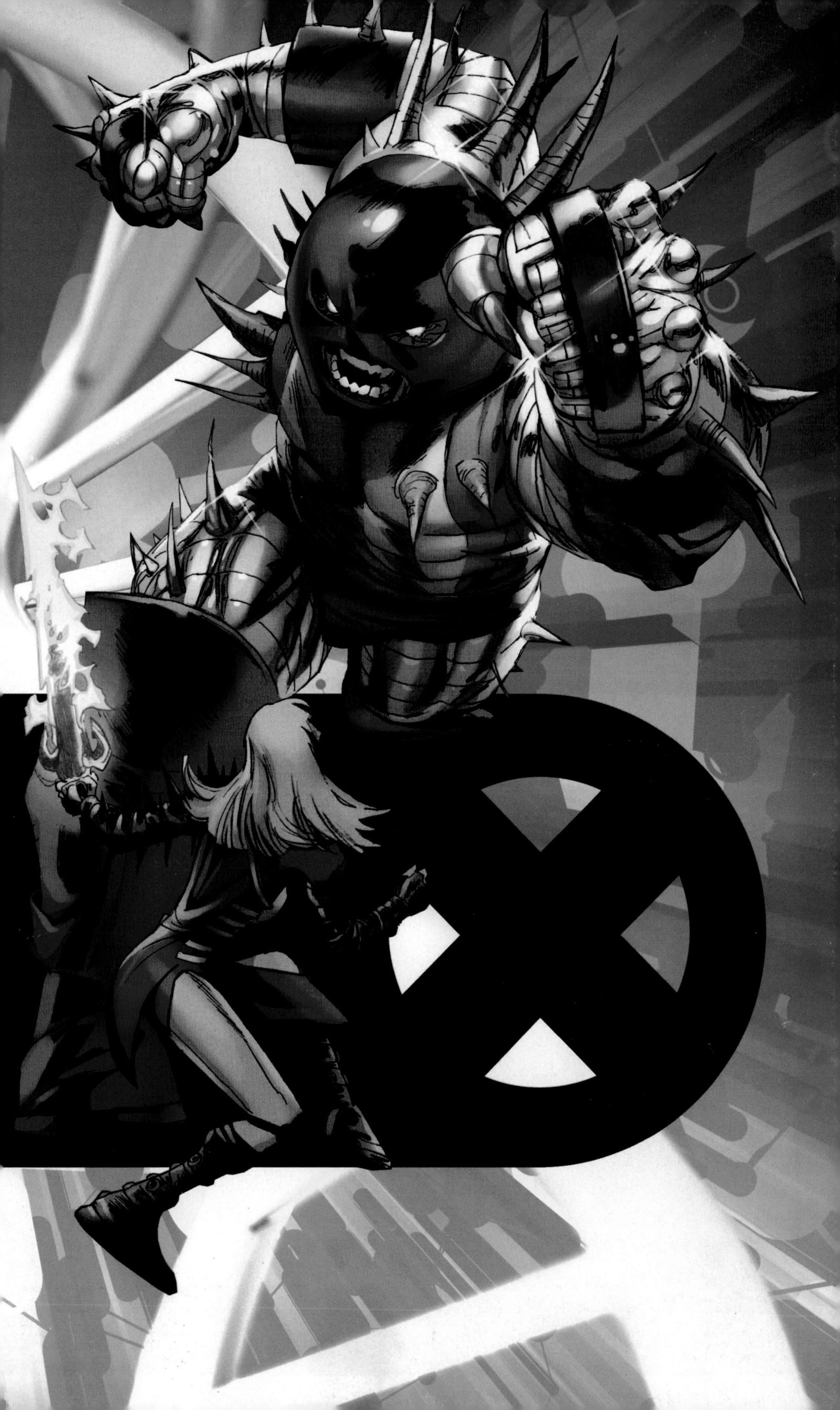

rn with powers and
ities beyond those of
rmal humans, mutantkind
s long been hated and
red by those they sought
protect. Now, from their
nd nation of Utopia, Cyclops
ds the most powerful group
mutants ever assembled
protect what is left of
dwindling species.
ed and feared? When
are as powerful as
Uncanny X-Men,
es it matter?

UNCANNY X-MEN

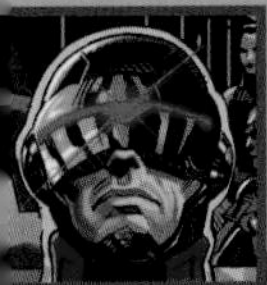

CYCLOPS
-blasting leader

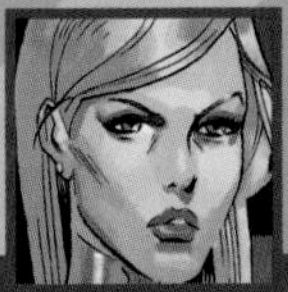

EMMA FROST
telepath with diamond form

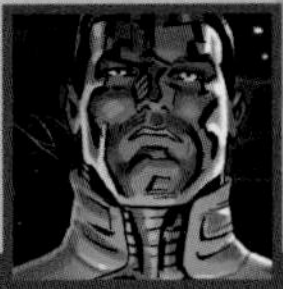

COLOSSUS
steel-skinned juggernaut

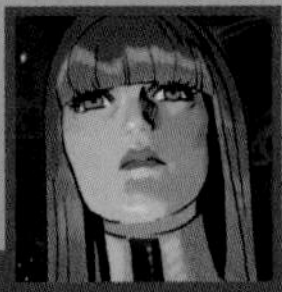

MAGIK
magic-using teleporter

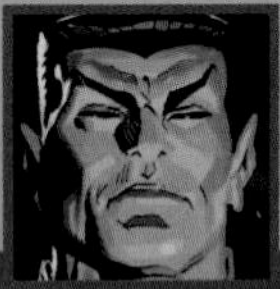

NAMOR
king of Atlantis

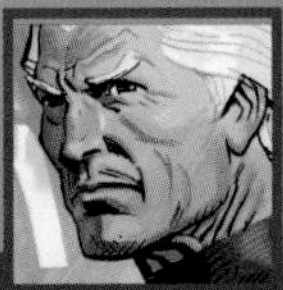

MAGNETO
master of magnetism

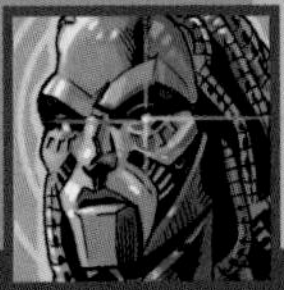

DANGER
light-shaping AI

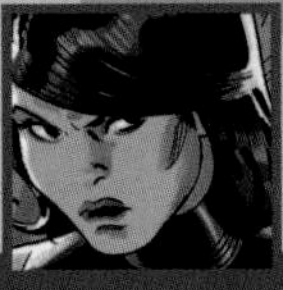

PSYLOCKE
telepathic ninja

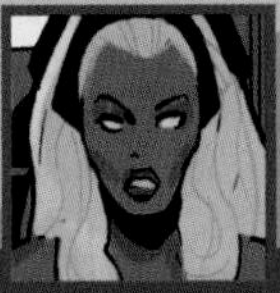

STORM
weather witch

REVIOUSLY

Mutantkind's ascension has begun. Following a battle with The Avengers, e Phoenix Force has been split into five separate parts, each one bonding with a member of the X-Men: Cyclops, Emma Frost, Colossus, Namor and Magik. Utilizing this power, they are rebuilding the world, solving its problems and building a better future.

anwhile, Mister Sinister has begun a new course of action against the X-Men. e has created an entire species of himself, all genetically perfect and identical ster clones. From his underground kingdom of Sinister London, he anticipates the X-Men's every move and eagerly awaits their attentions.

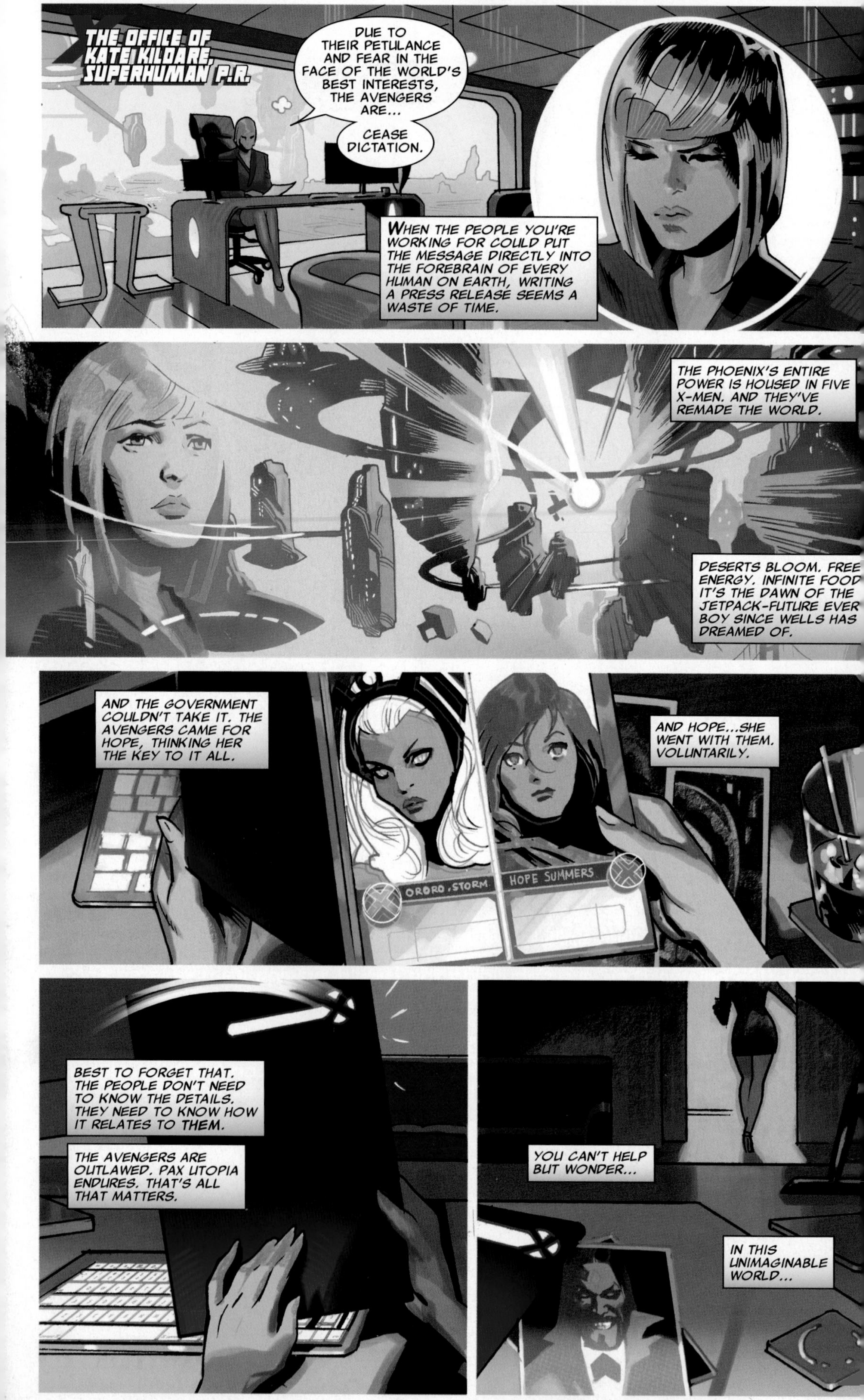
THE OFFICE OF KATE KILDARE, SUPERHUMAN P.R.
DUE TO THEIR PETULANCE AND FEAR IN THE FACE OF THE WORLD'S BEST INTERESTS, THE AVENGERS ARE...
CEASE DICTATION.
WHEN THE PEOPLE YOU'RE WORKING FOR COULD PUT THE MESSAGE DIRECTLY INTO THE FOREBRAIN OF EVERY HUMAN ON EARTH, WRITING A PRESS RELEASE SEEMS A WASTE OF TIME.
THE PHOENIX'S ENTIRE POWER IS HOUSED IN FIVE X-MEN. AND THEY'VE REMADE THE WORLD.
DESERTS BLOOM. FREE ENERGY. INFINITE FOOD IT'S THE DAWN OF THE JETPACK-FUTURE EVER BOY SINCE WELLS HAS DREAMED OF.
AND THE GOVERNMENT COULDN'T TAKE IT. THE AVENGERS CAME FOR HOPE, THINKING HER THE KEY TO IT ALL.
ORORO STORM
HOPE SUMMERS
AND HOPE...SHE WENT WITH THEM. VOLUNTARILY.
BEST TO FORGET THAT. THE PEOPLE DON'T NEED TO KNOW THE DETAILS. THEY NEED TO KNOW HOW IT RELATES TO THEM.
THE AVENGERS ARE OUTLAWED. PAX UTOPIA ENDURES. THAT'S ALL THAT MATTERS.
YOU CAN'T HELP BUT WONDER...
IN THIS UNIMAGINABLE WORLD...

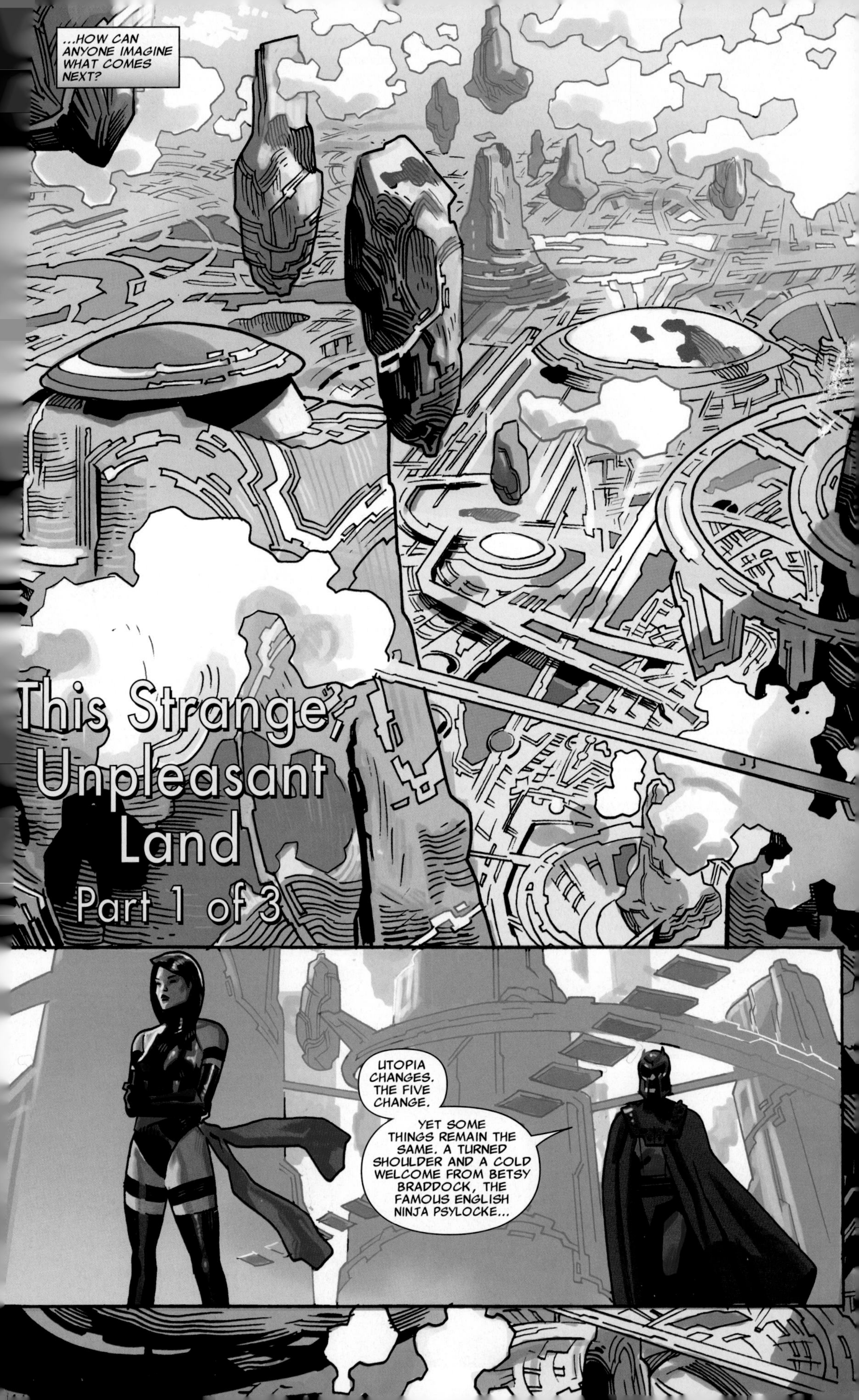
...HOW CAN ANYONE IMAGINE WHAT COMES NEXT?
This Strange, Unpleasant Land
Part 1 of 3
UTOPIA CHANGES. THE FIVE CHANGE.
YET SOME THINGS REMAIN THE SAME. A TURNED SHOULDER AND A COLD WELCOME FROM BETSY BRADDOCK, THE FAMOUS ENGLISH NINJA PSYLOCKE...

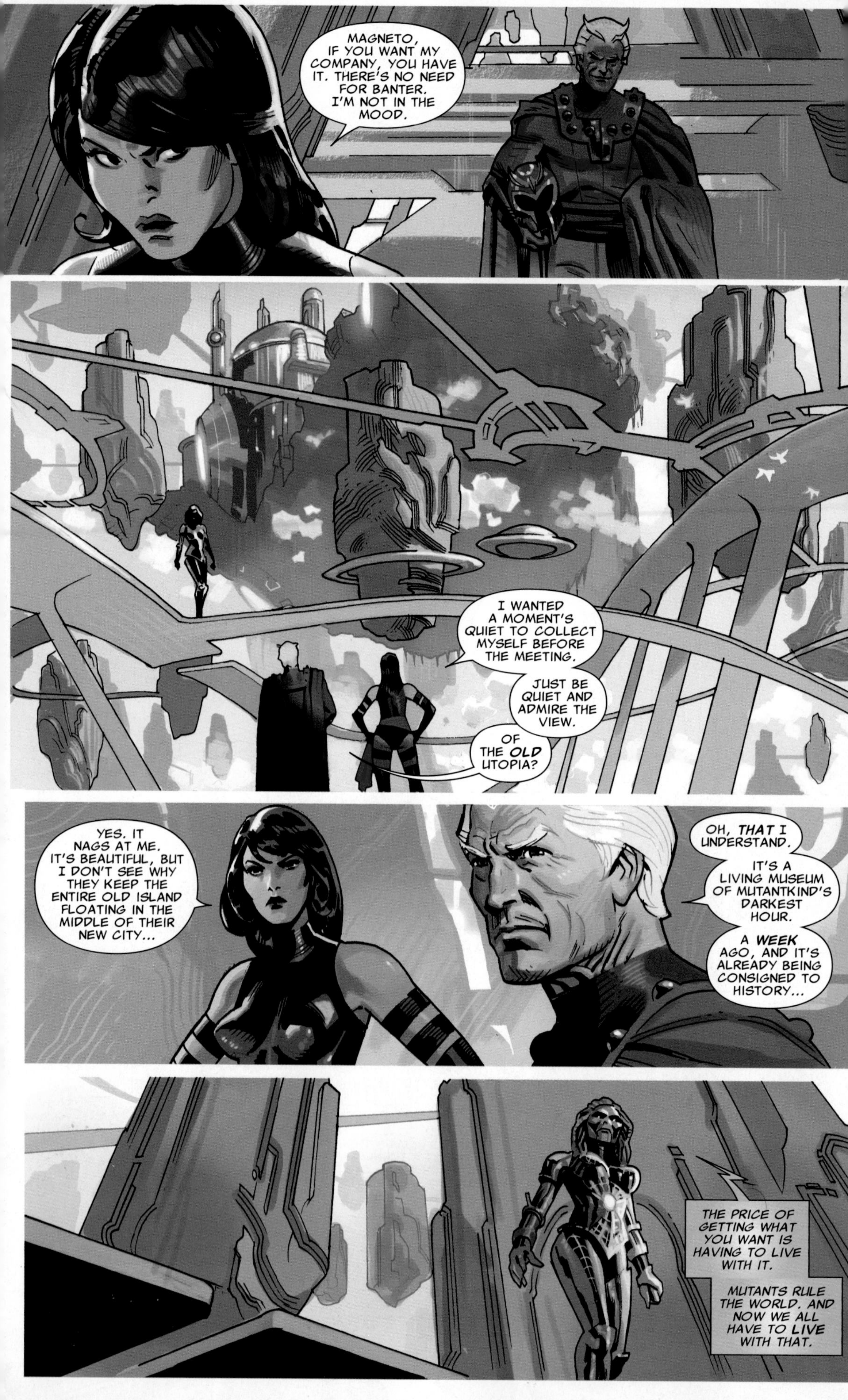
MAGNETO, IF YOU WANT MY COMPANY, YOU HAVE IT. THERE'S NO NEED FOR BANTER. I'M NOT IN THE MOOD.
I WANTED A MOMENT'S QUIET TO COLLECT MYSELF BEFORE THE MEETING.
JUST BE QUIET AND ADMIRE THE VIEW.
OF THE *OLD* UTOPIA?
YES. IT NAGS AT ME. IT'S BEAUTIFUL, BUT I DON'T SEE WHY THEY KEEP THE ENTIRE OLD ISLAND FLOATING IN THE MIDDLE OF THEIR NEW CITY...
OH, *THAT* I UNDERSTAND.
IT'S A LIVING MUSEUM OF MUTANTKIND'S DARKEST HOUR.
A *WEEK* AGO, AND IT'S ALREADY BEING CONSIGNED TO HISTORY...
THE PRICE OF GETTING WHAT YOU WANT IS HAVING TO LIVE WITH IT.
MUTANTS RULE THE WORLD. AND NOW WE ALL HAVE TO *LIVE* WITH THAT.

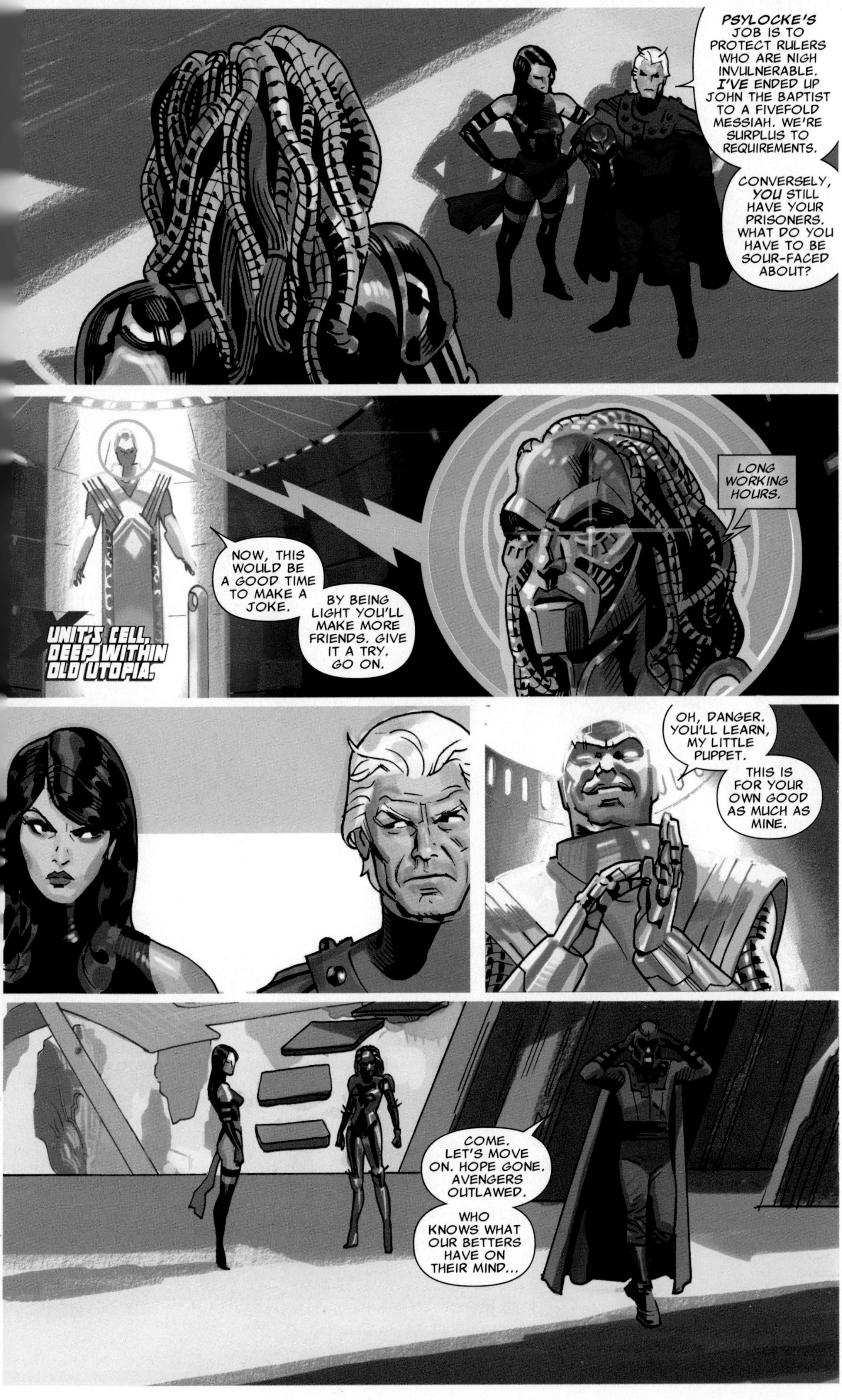
PSYLOCKE'S JOB IS TO PROTECT RULERS WHO ARE NIGH INVULNERABLE. I'VE ENDED UP JOHN THE BAPTIST TO A FIVEFOLD MESSIAH. WE'RE SURPLUS TO REQUIREMENTS.
CONVERSELY, YOU STILL HAVE YOUR PRISONERS. WHAT DO YOU HAVE TO BE SOUR-FACED ABOUT?
UNIT'S CELL, DEEP WITHIN OLD UTOPIA.
LONG WORKING HOURS.
NOW, THIS WOULD BE A GOOD TIME TO MAKE A JOKE.
BY BEING LIGHT YOU'LL MAKE MORE FRIENDS. GIVE IT A TRY. GO ON.
OH, DANGER. YOU'LL LEARN, MY LITTLE PUPPET.
THIS IS FOR YOUR OWN GOOD AS MUCH AS MINE.
COME. LET'S MOVE ON. HOPE GONE. AVENGERS OUTLAWED.
WHO KNOWS WHAT OUR BETTERS HAVE ON THEIR MIND...

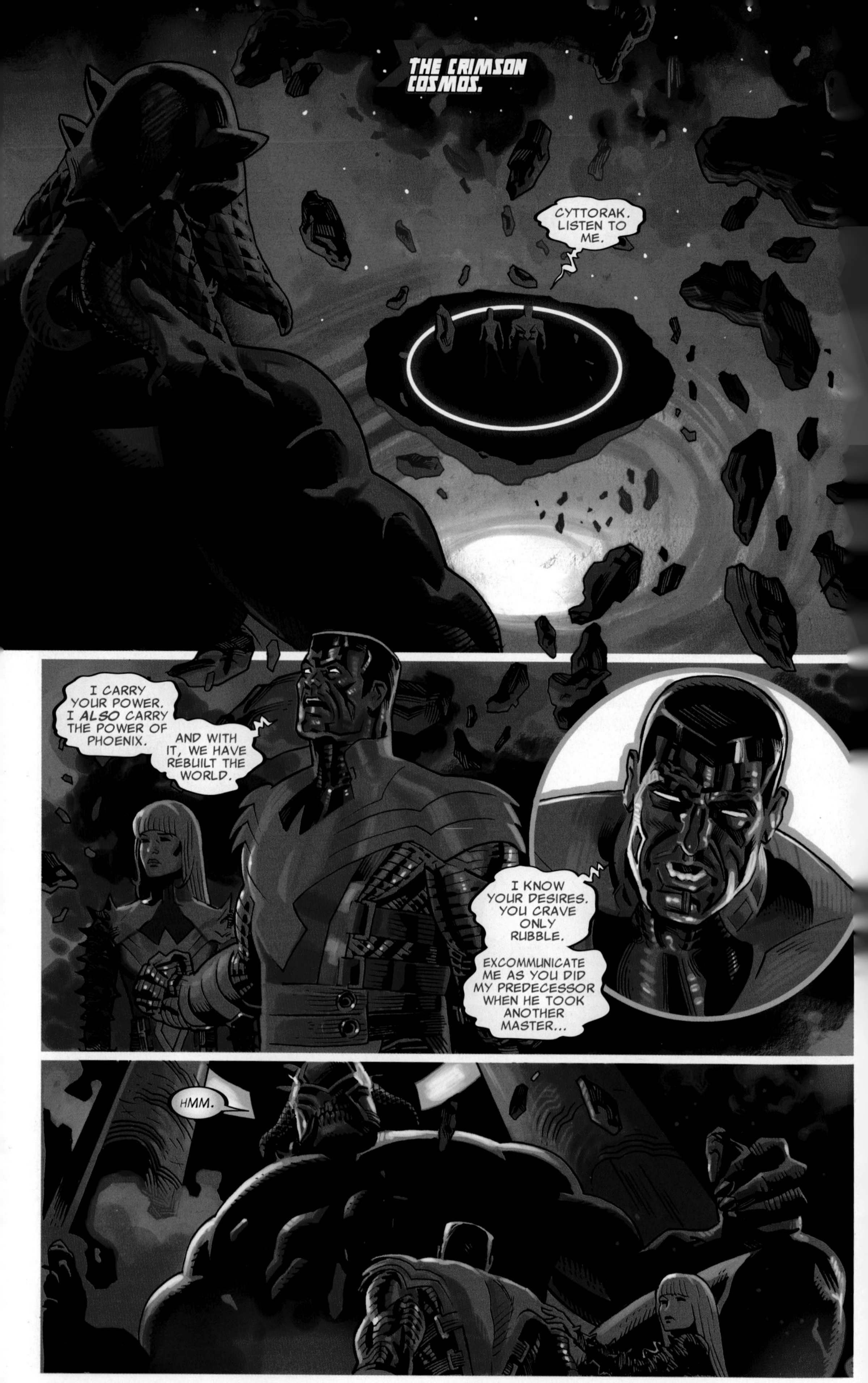
THE CRIMSON COSMOS.
CYTTORAK. LISTEN TO ME.
I CARRY YOUR POWER. I ALSO CARRY THE POWER OF PHOENIX.
AND WITH IT, WE HAVE REBUILT THE WORLD.
I KNOW YOUR DESIRES. YOU CRAVE ONLY RUBBLE.
EXCOMMUNICATE ME AS YOU DID MY PREDECESSOR WHEN HE TOOK ANOTHER MASTER...
HMM.

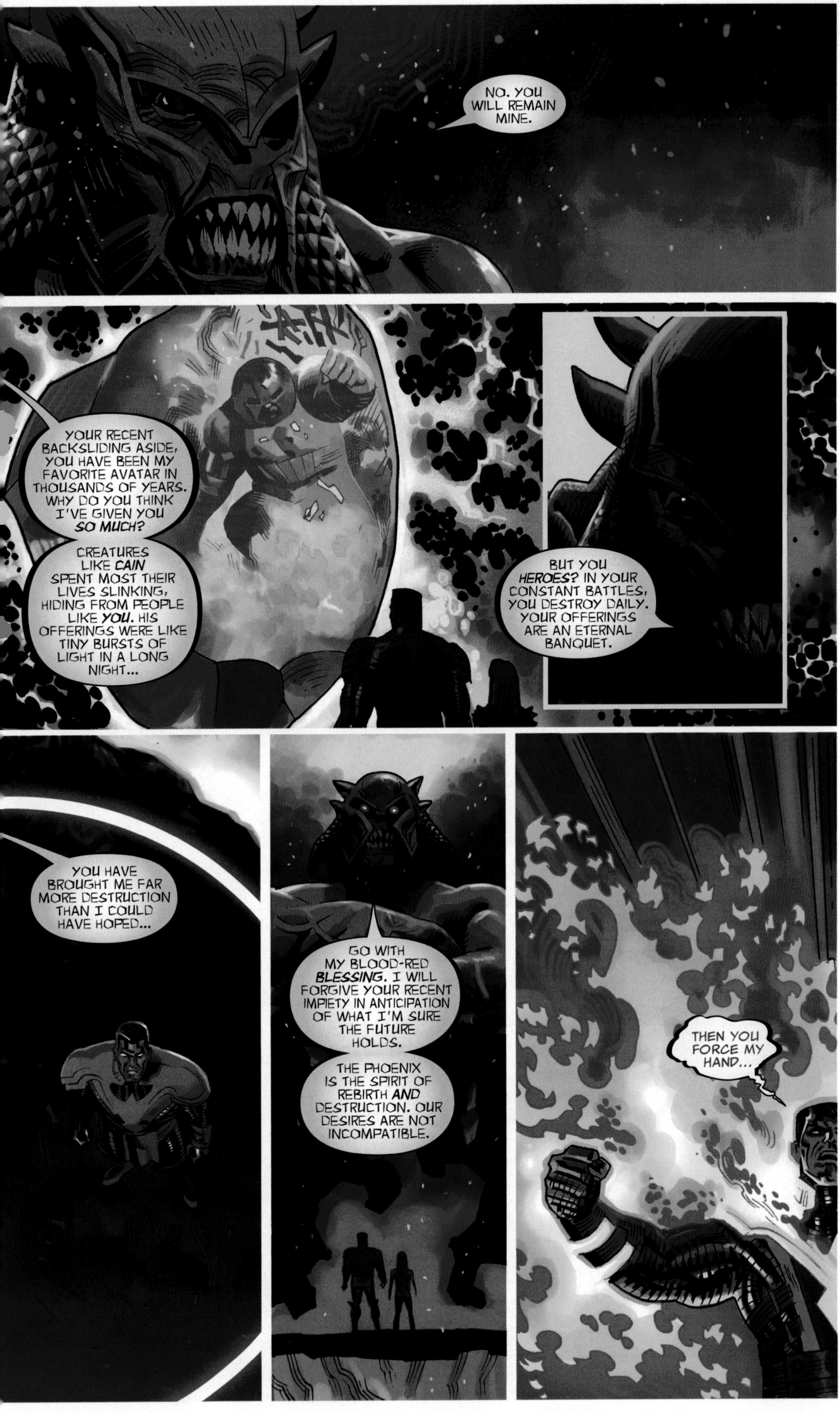
NO. YOU WILL REMAIN MINE.
YOUR RECENT BACKSLIDING ASIDE, YOU HAVE BEEN MY FAVORITE AVATAR IN THOUSANDS OF YEARS. WHY DO YOU THINK I'VE GIVEN YOU SO MUCH?
CREATURES LIKE CAIN SPENT MOST THEIR LIVES SLINKING, HIDING FROM PEOPLE LIKE YOU. HIS OFFERINGS WERE LIKE TINY BURSTS OF LIGHT IN A LONG NIGHT...
BUT YOU HEROES? IN YOUR CONSTANT BATTLES, YOU DESTROY DAILY. YOUR OFFERINGS ARE AN ETERNAL BANQUET.
YOU HAVE BROUGHT ME FAR MORE DESTRUCTION THAN I COULD HAVE HOPED...
GO WITH MY BLOOD-RED BLESSING. I WILL FORGIVE YOUR RECENT IMPIETY IN ANTICIPATION OF WHAT I'M SURE THE FUTURE HOLDS.
THE PHOENIX IS THE SPIRIT OF REBIRTH AND DESTRUCTION. OUR DESIRES ARE NOT INCOMPATIBLE.
THEN YOU FORCE MY HAND...

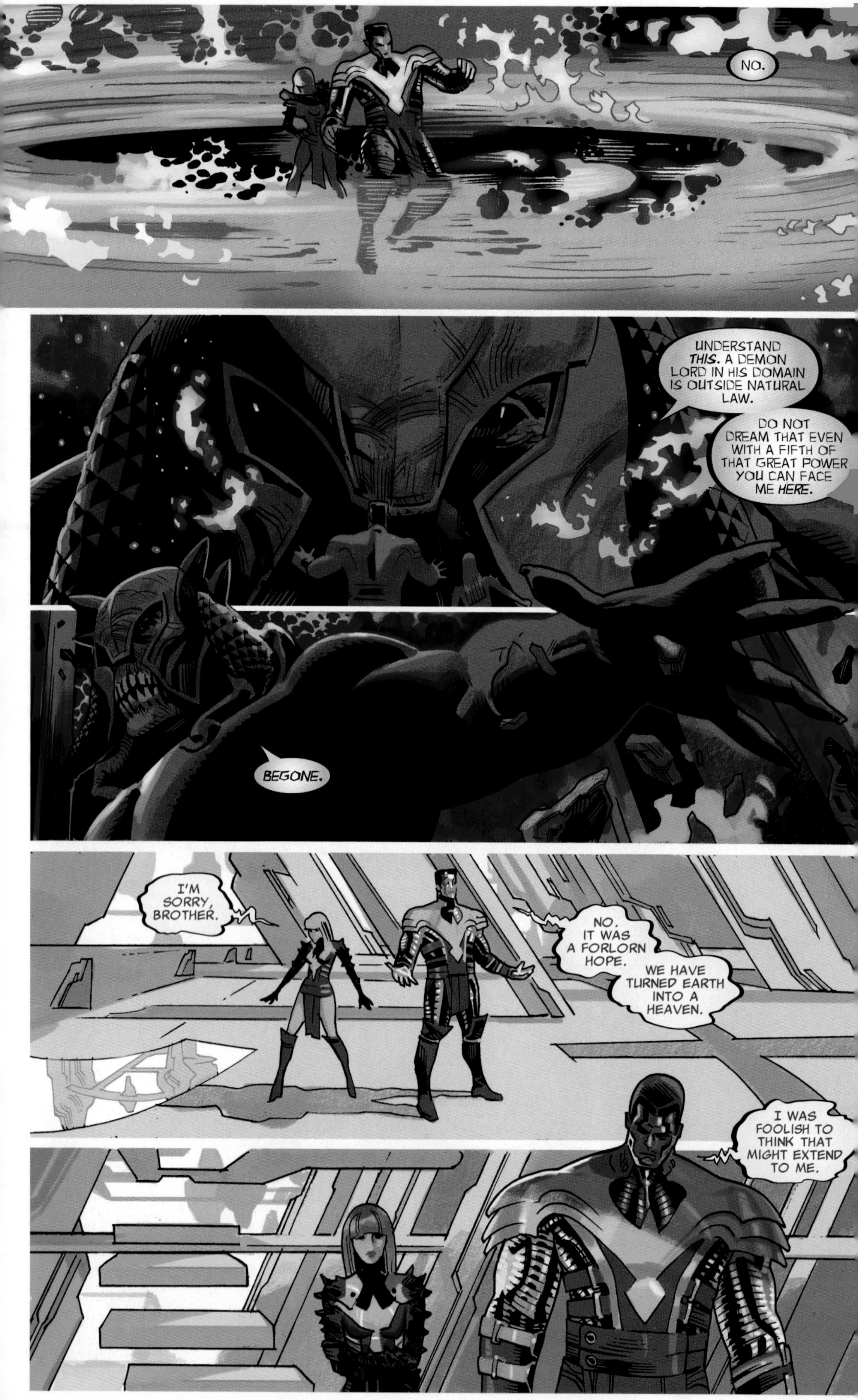
NO.
UNDERSTAND THIS. A DEMON LORD IN HIS DOMAIN IS OUTSIDE NATURAL LAW.
DO NOT DREAM THAT EVEN WITH A FIFTH OF THAT GREAT POWER YOU CAN FACE ME HERE.
BEGONE.
I'M SORRY, BROTHER.
NO. IT WAS A FORLORN HOPE.
WE HAVE TURNED EARTH INTO A HEAVEN.
I WAS FOOLISH TO THINK THAT MIGHT EXTEND TO ME.

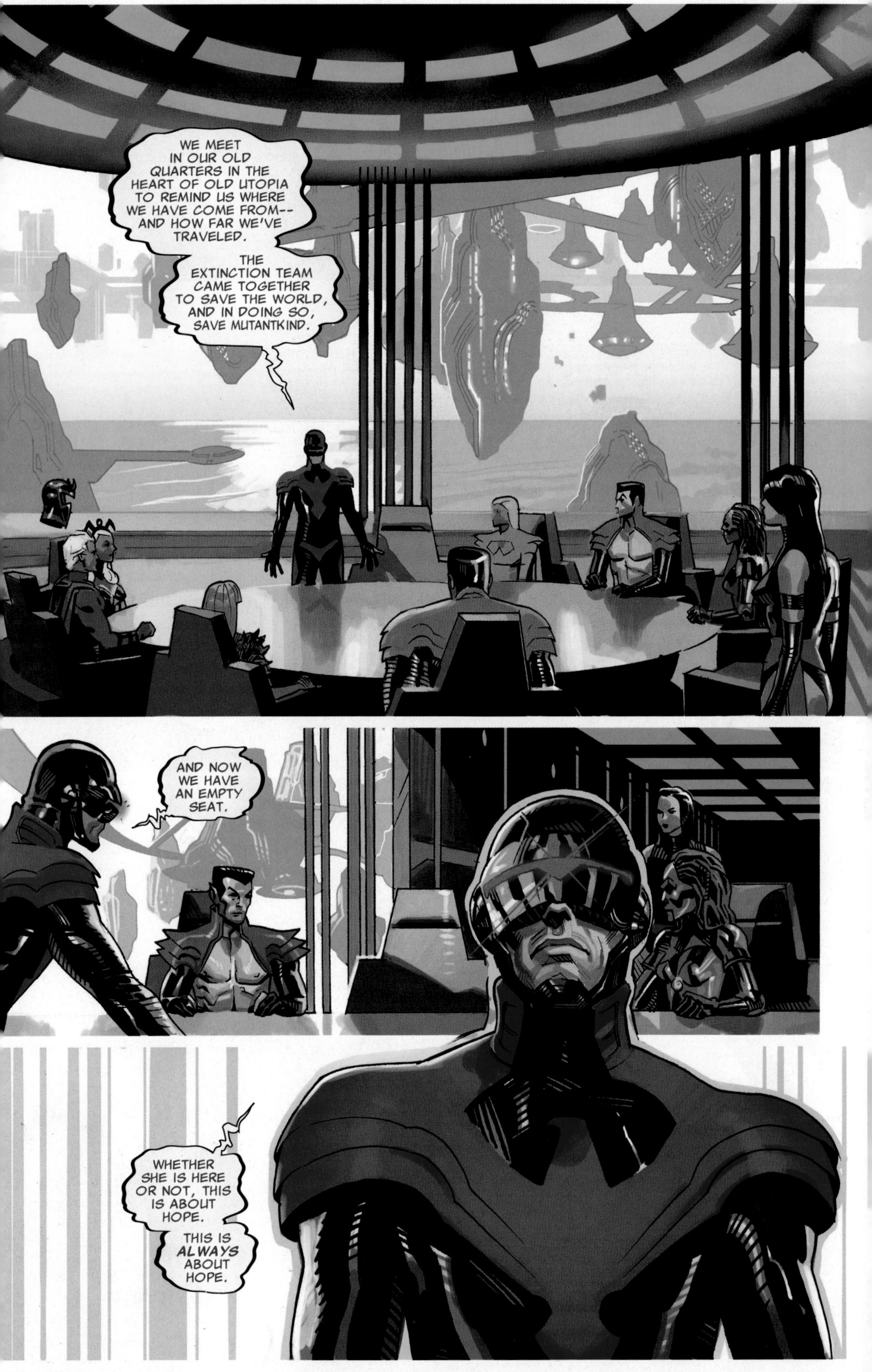
WE MEET IN OUR OLD QUARTERS IN THE HEART OF OLD UTOPIA TO REMIND US WHERE WE HAVE COME FROM-- AND HOW FAR WE'VE TRAVELED.
THE EXTINCTION TEAM CAME TOGETHER TO SAVE THE WORLD, AND IN DOING SO, SAVE MUTANTKIND.
AND NOW WE HAVE AN EMPTY SEAT.
WHETHER SHE IS HERE OR NOT, THIS IS ABOUT HOPE.
THIS IS *ALWAYS* ABOUT HOPE.

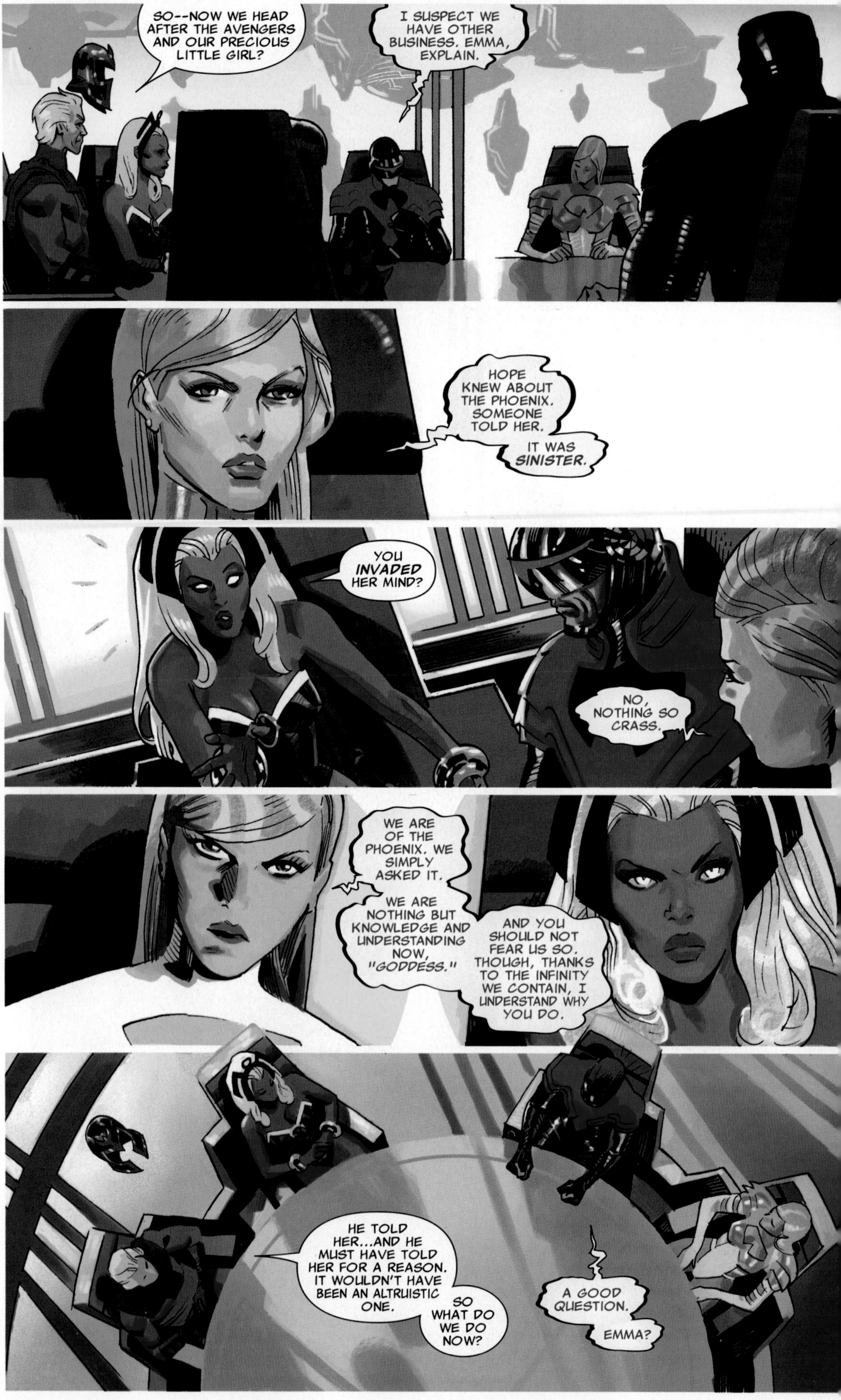
SO--NOW WE HEAD AFTER THE AVENGERS AND OUR PRECIOUS LITTLE GIRL?
I SUSPECT WE HAVE OTHER BUSINESS. EMMA, EXPLAIN.
HOPE KNEW ABOUT THE PHOENIX. SOMEONE TOLD HER.
IT WAS SINISTER.
YOU INVADED HER MIND?
NO, NOTHING SO CRASS.
WE ARE OF THE PHOENIX. WE SIMPLY ASKED IT.
WE ARE NOTHING BUT KNOWLEDGE AND UNDERSTANDING NOW, "GODDESS."
AND YOU SHOULD NOT FEAR US SO. THOUGH, THANKS TO THE INFINITY WE CONTAIN, I UNDERSTAND WHY YOU DO.
HE TOLD HER...AND HE MUST HAVE TOLD HER FOR A REASON. IT WOULDN'T HAVE BEEN AN ALTRUISTIC ONE.
SO WHAT DO WE DO NOW?
A GOOD QUESTION.
EMMA?

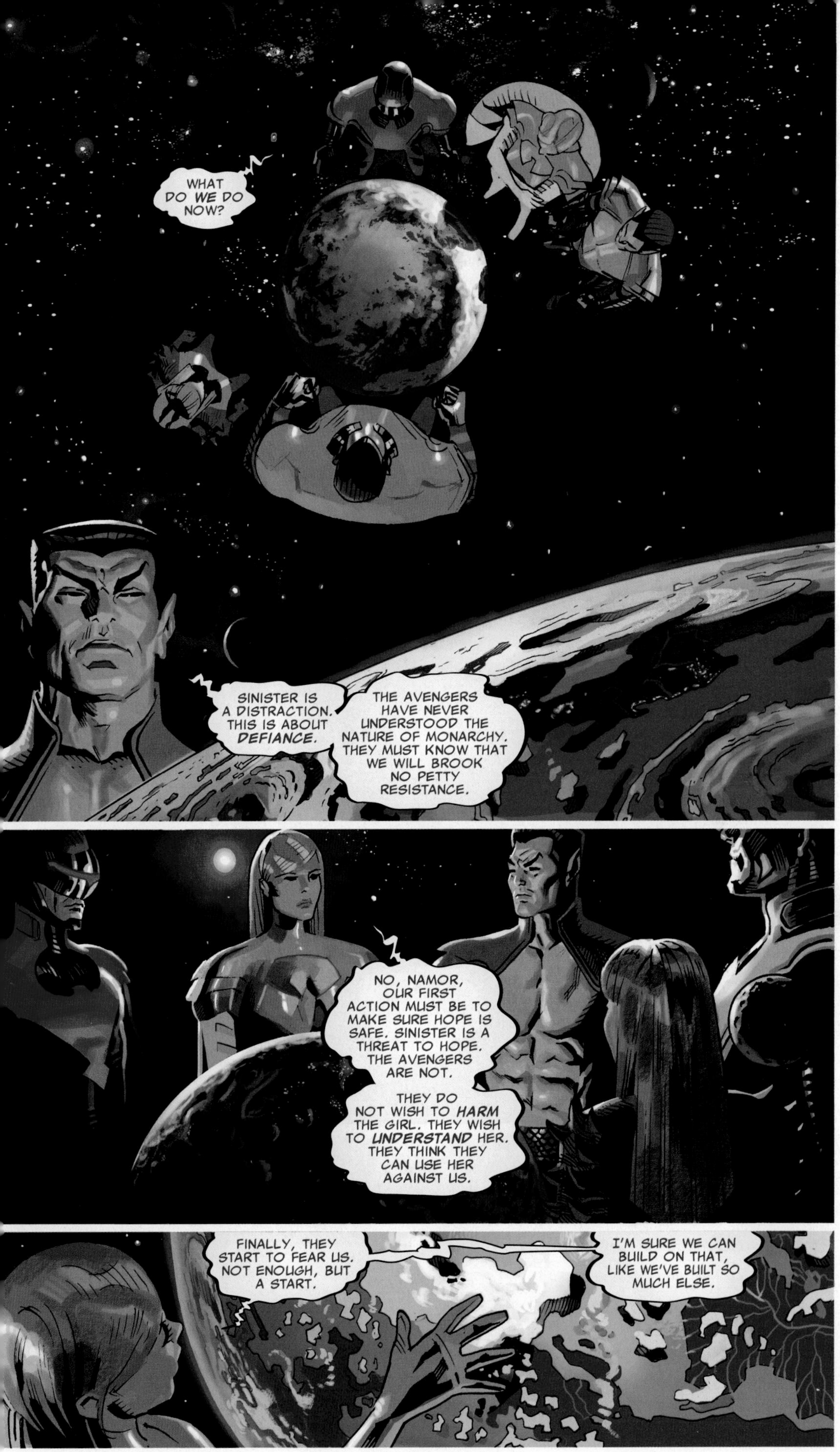
WHAT DO WE DO NOW?
SINISTER IS A DISTRACTION. THIS IS ABOUT DEFIANCE.
THE AVENGERS HAVE NEVER UNDERSTOOD THE NATURE OF MONARCHY. THEY MUST KNOW THAT WE WILL BROOK NO PETTY RESISTANCE.
NO, NAMOR, OUR FIRST ACTION MUST BE TO MAKE SURE HOPE IS SAFE. SINISTER IS A THREAT TO HOPE. THE AVENGERS ARE NOT.
THEY DO NOT WISH TO HARM THE GIRL. THEY WISH TO UNDERSTAND HER. THEY THINK THEY CAN USE HER AGAINST US.
FINALLY, THEY START TO FEAR US. NOT ENOUGH, BUT A START.
I'M SURE WE CAN BUILD ON THAT, LIKE WE'VE BUILT SO MUCH ELSE.

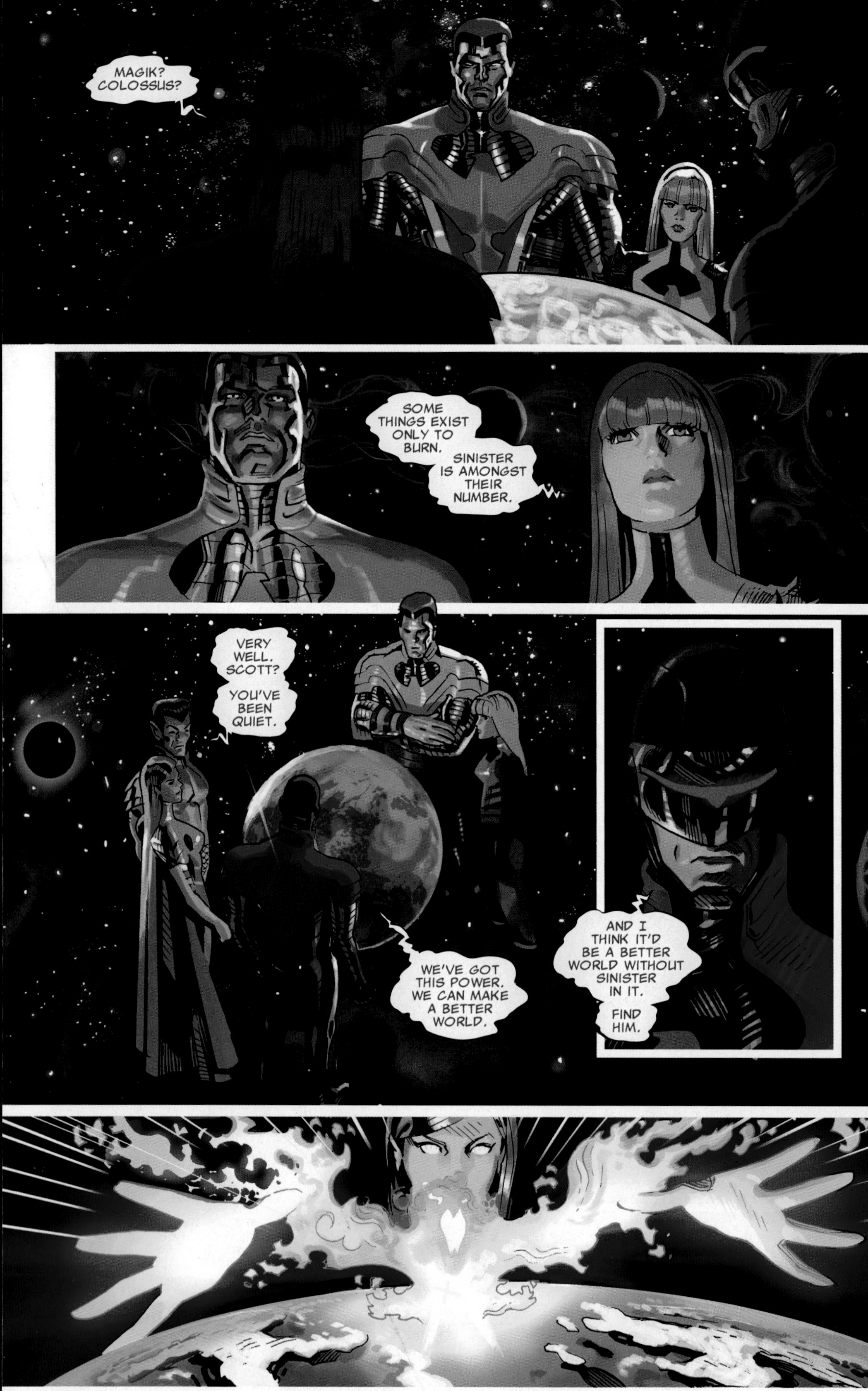
MAGIK? COLOSSUS?
SOME THINGS EXIST ONLY TO BURN.
SINISTER IS AMONGST THEIR NUMBER.
VERY WELL. SCOTT?
YOU'VE BEEN QUIET.
WE'VE GOT THIS POWER. WE CAN MAKE A BETTER WORLD.
AND I THINK IT'D BE A BETTER WORLD WITHOUT SINISTER IN IT.
FIND HIM.

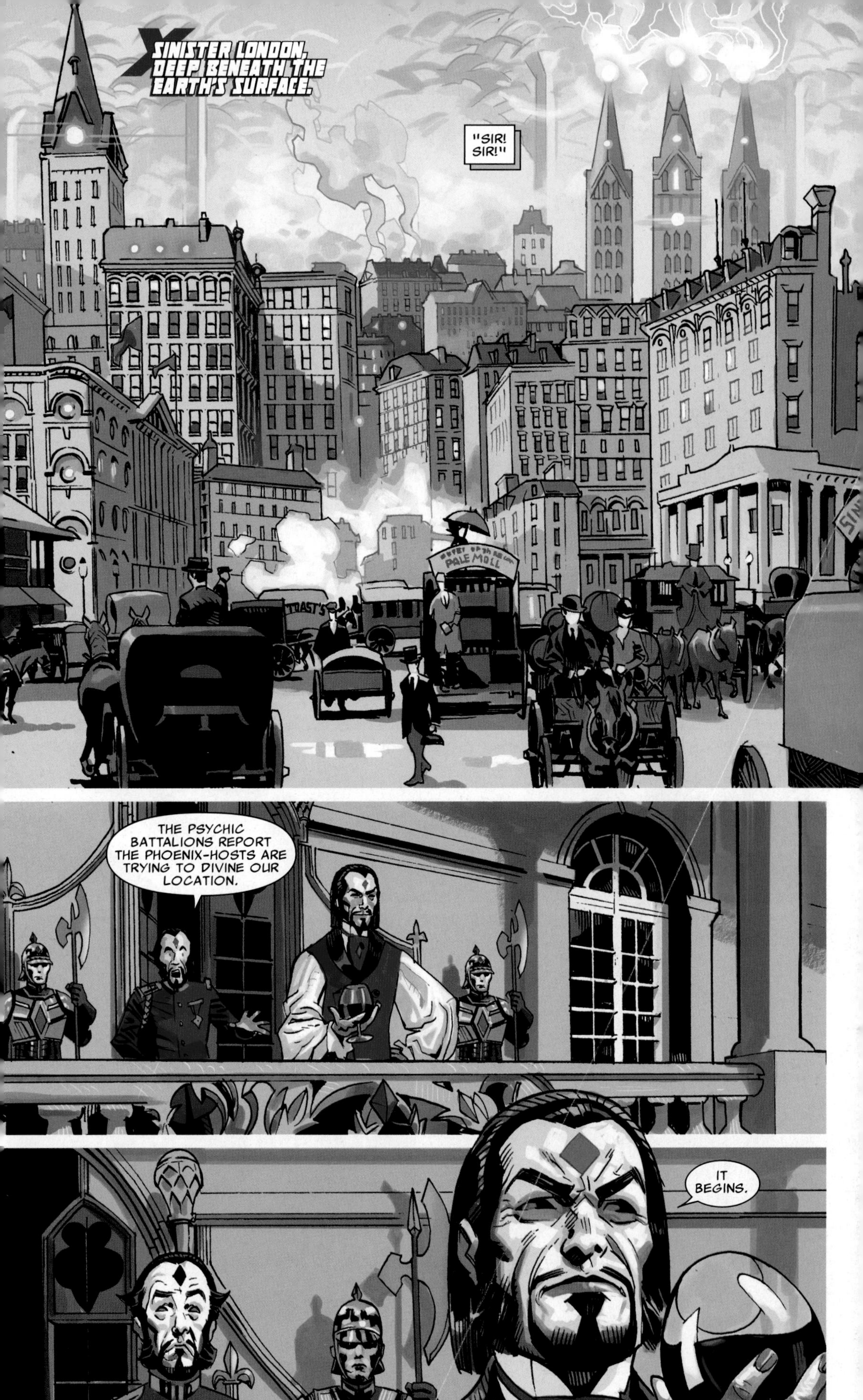
SINISTER LONDON, DEEP BENEATH THE EARTH'S SURFACE.
"SIR! SIR!"
PALE MOLL
TOAST'S
THE PSYCHIC BATTALIONS REPORT THE PHOENIX-HOSTS ARE TRYING TO DIVINE OUR LOCATION.
IT BEGINS.

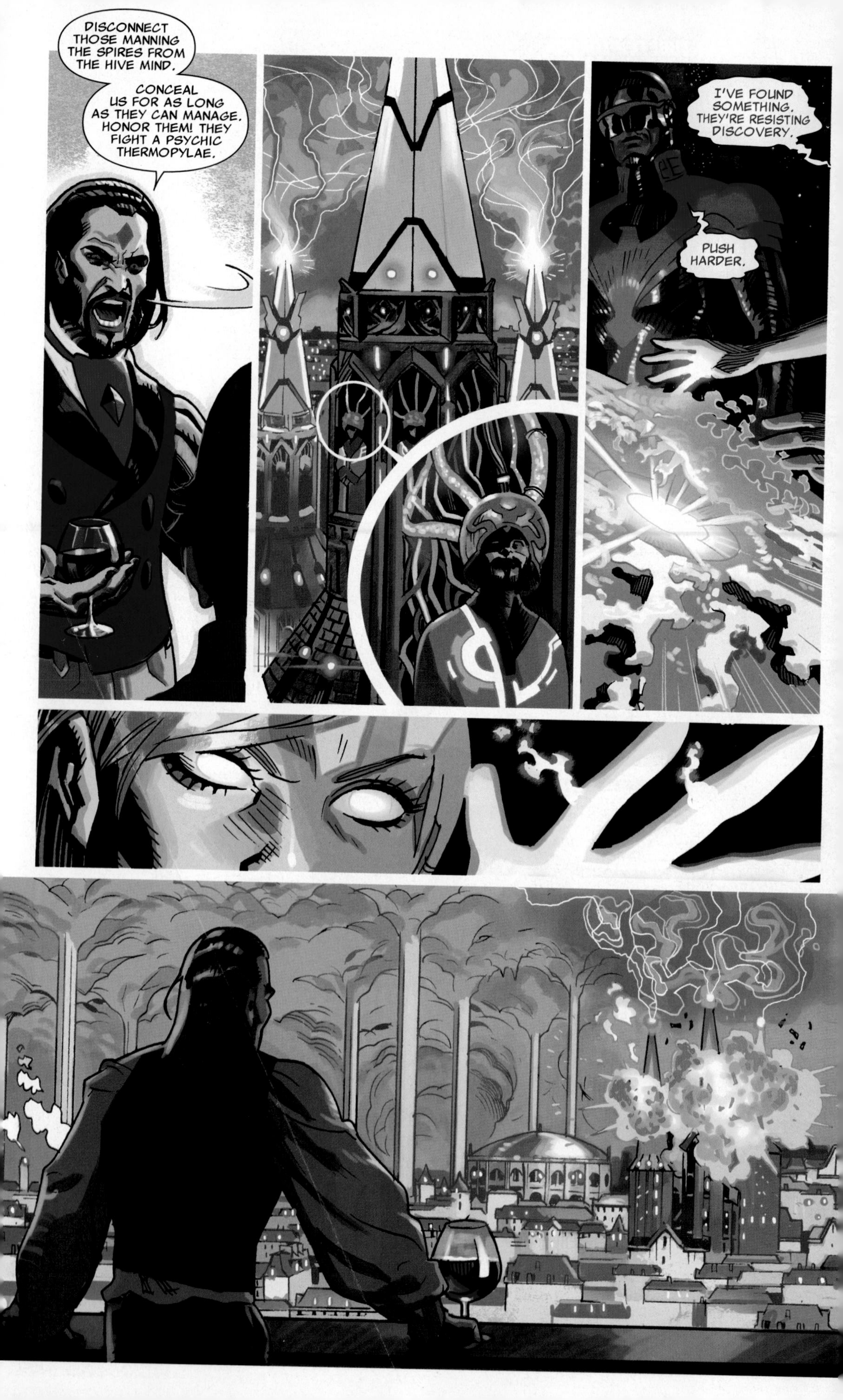
DISCONNECT THOSE MANNING THE SPIRES FROM THE HIVE MIND.
CONCEAL US FOR AS LONG AS THEY CAN MANAGE. HONOR THEM! THEY FIGHT A PSYCHIC THERMOPYLAE.
I'VE FOUND SOMETHING. THEY'RE RESISTING DISCOVERY.
PUSH HARDER.

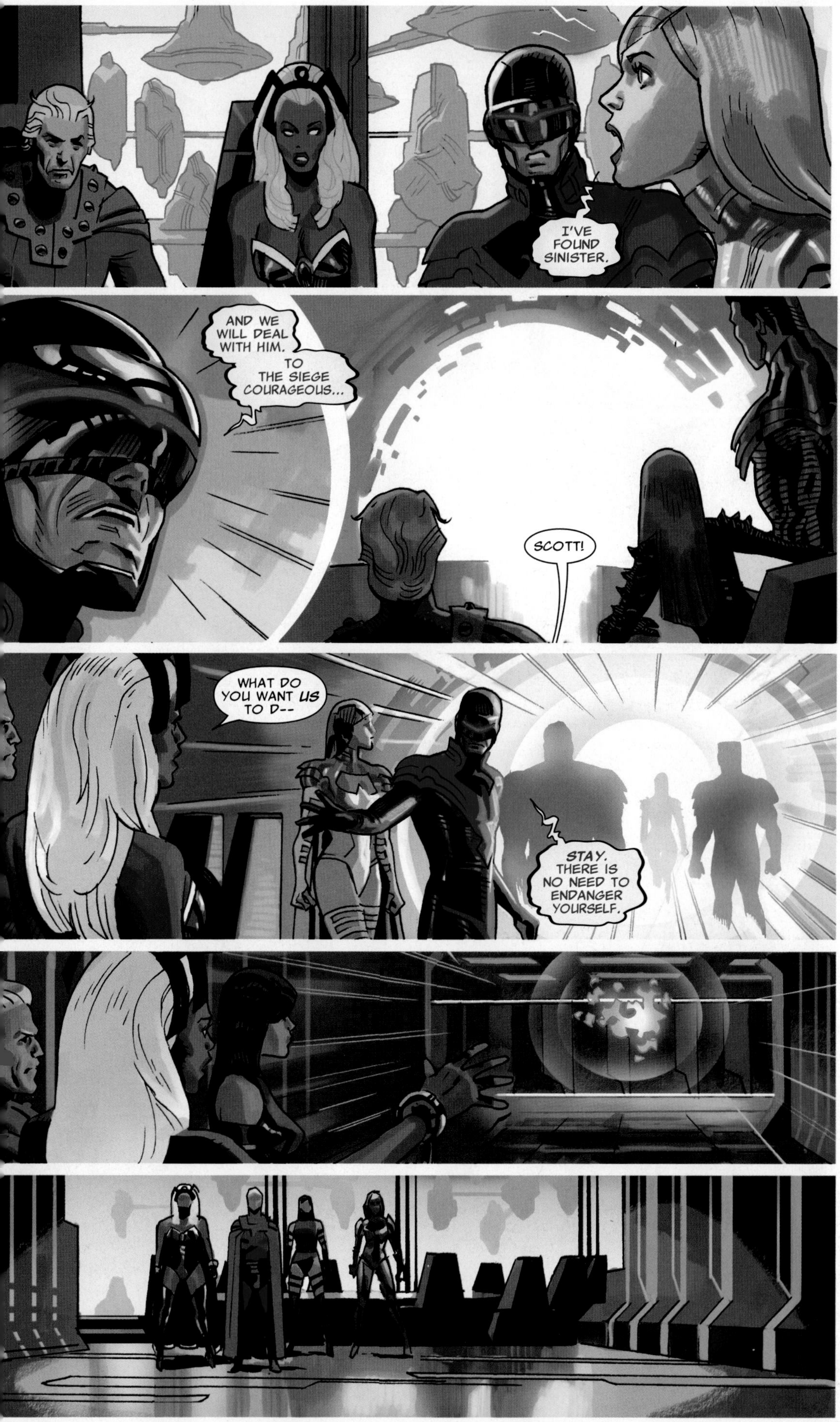
I'VE FOUND SINISTER.
AND WE WILL DEAL WITH HIM.
TO THE SIEGE COURAGEOUS...
SCOTT!
WHAT DO YOU WANT US TO D--
STAY. THERE IS NO NEED TO ENDANGER YOURSELF.

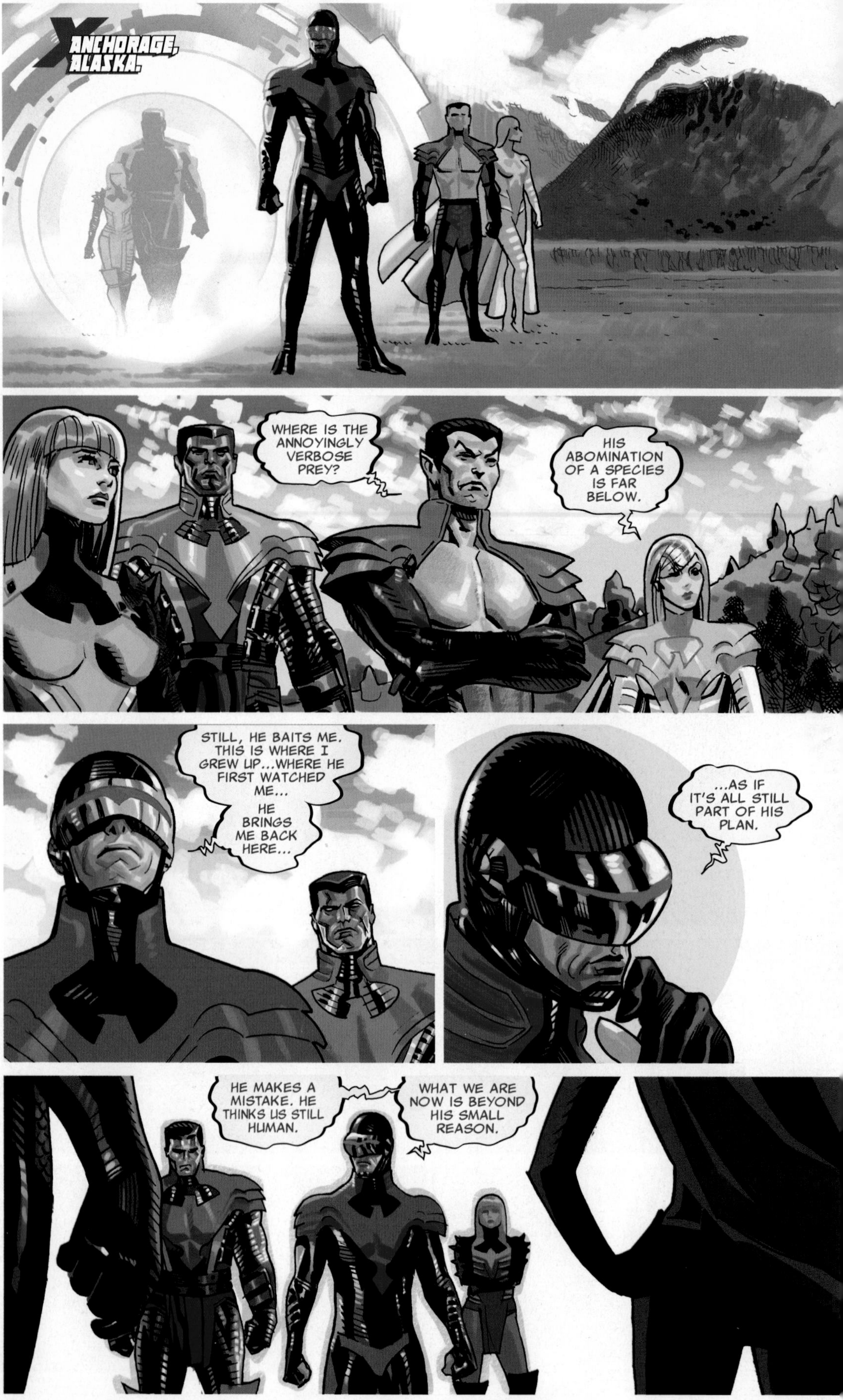

ANCHORAGE, ALASKA.
WHERE IS THE ANNOYINGLY VERBOSE PREY?
HIS ABOMINATION OF A SPECIES IS FAR BELOW.
STILL, HE BAITS ME. THIS IS WHERE I GREW UP...WHERE HE FIRST WATCHED ME...
HE BRINGS ME BACK HERE...
...AS IF IT'S ALL STILL PART OF HIS PLAN.
HE MAKES A MISTAKE. HE THINKS US STILL HUMAN.
WHAT WE ARE NOW IS BEYOND HIS SMALL REASON.

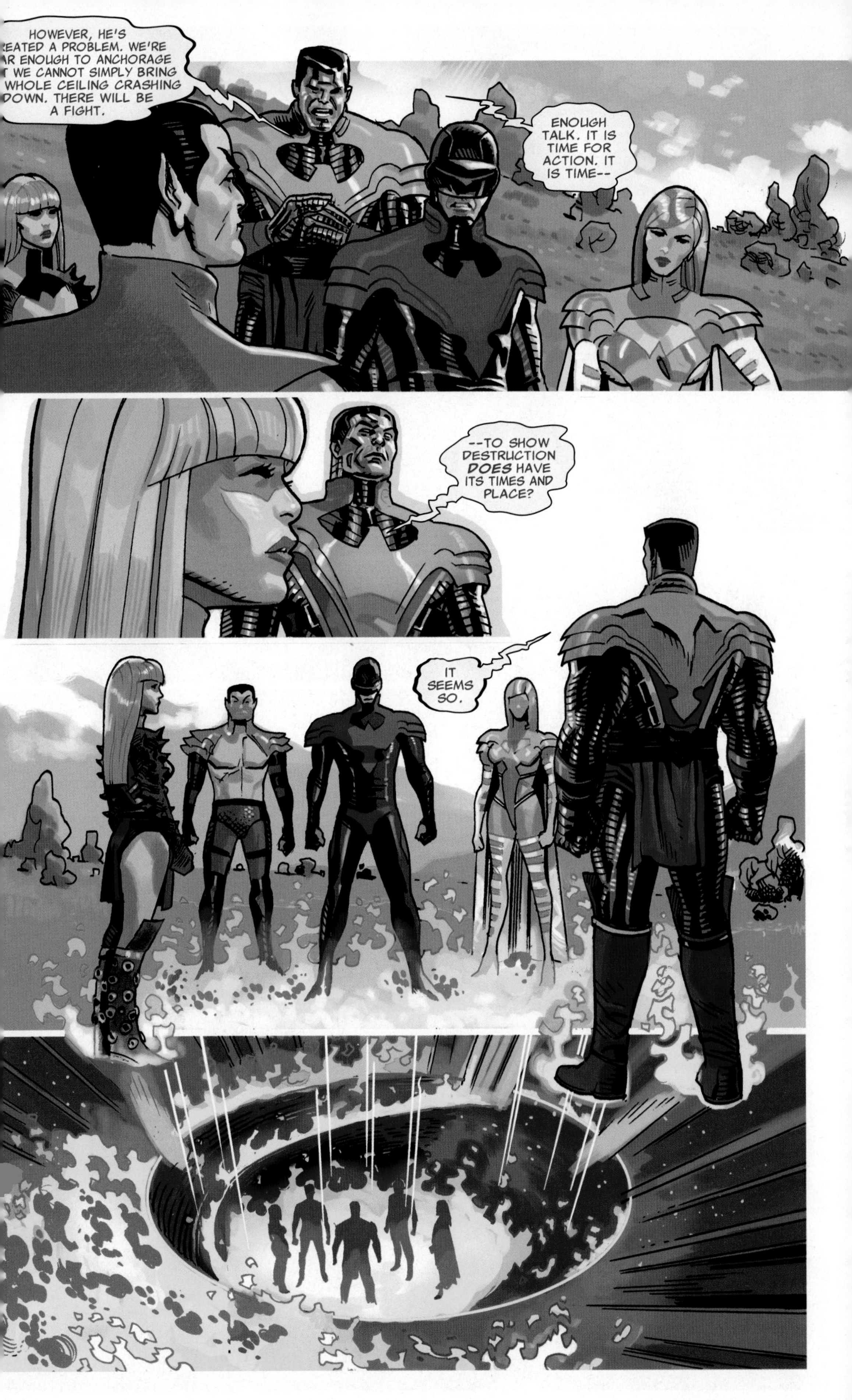
HOWEVER, HE'S
EATED A PROBLEM. WE'RE
AR ENOUGH TO ANCHORAGE
T WE CANNOT SIMPLY BRING
WHOLE CEILING CRASHING
DOWN. THERE WILL BE
A FIGHT.
ENOUGH TALK. IT IS TIME FOR ACTION. IT IS TIME--
--TO SHOW DESTRUCTION DOES HAVE ITS TIMES AND PLACE?
IT SEEMS SO.

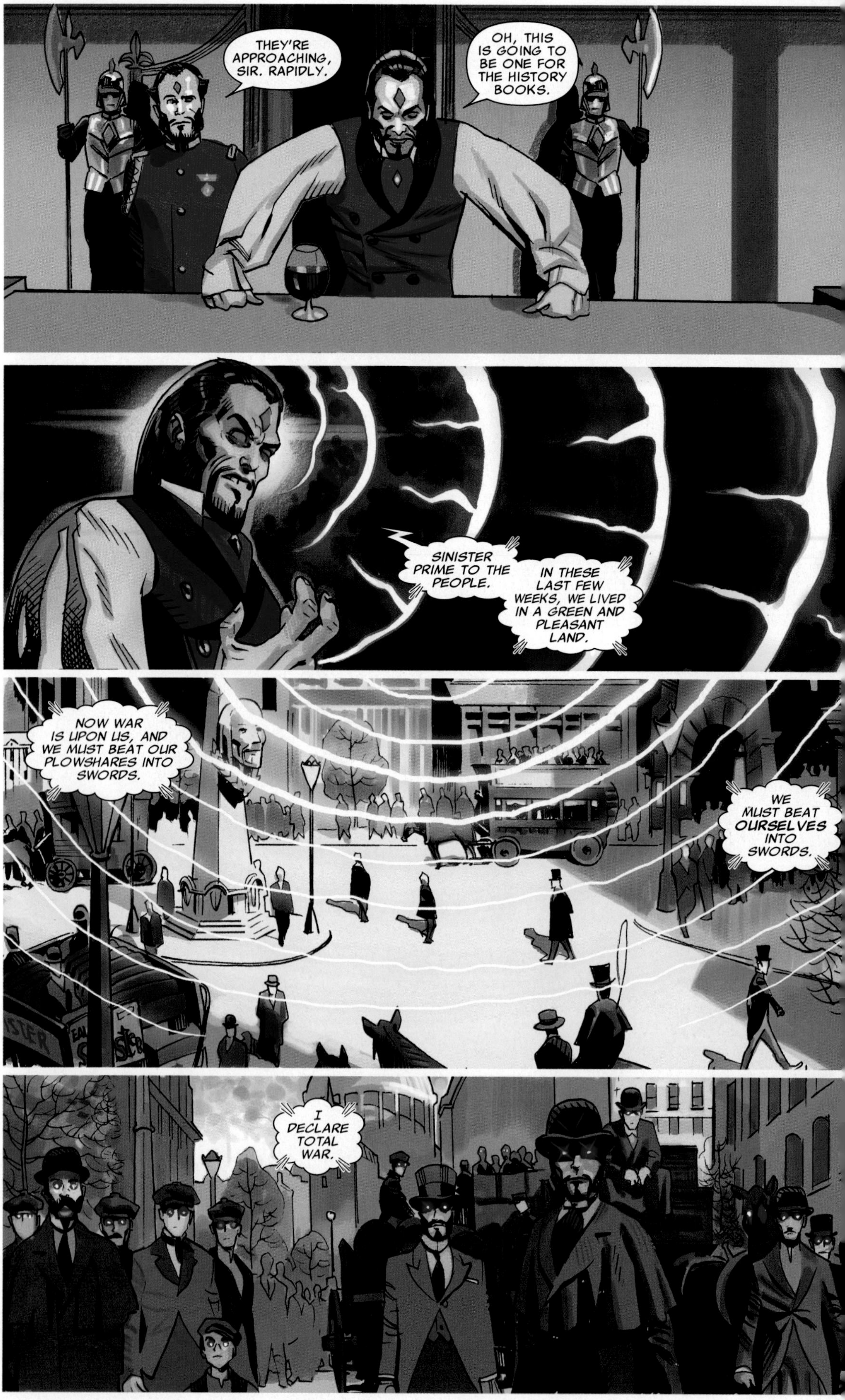
THEY'RE APPROACHING, SIR. RAPIDLY.
OH, THIS IS GOING TO BE ONE FOR THE HISTORY BOOKS.
SINISTER PRIME TO THE PEOPLE.
IN THESE LAST FEW WEEKS, WE LIVED IN A GREEN AND PLEASANT LAND.
NOW WAR IS UPON US, AND WE MUST BEAT OUR PLOWSHARES INTO SWORDS.
WE MUST BEAT OURSELVES INTO SWORDS.
I DECLARE TOTAL WAR.

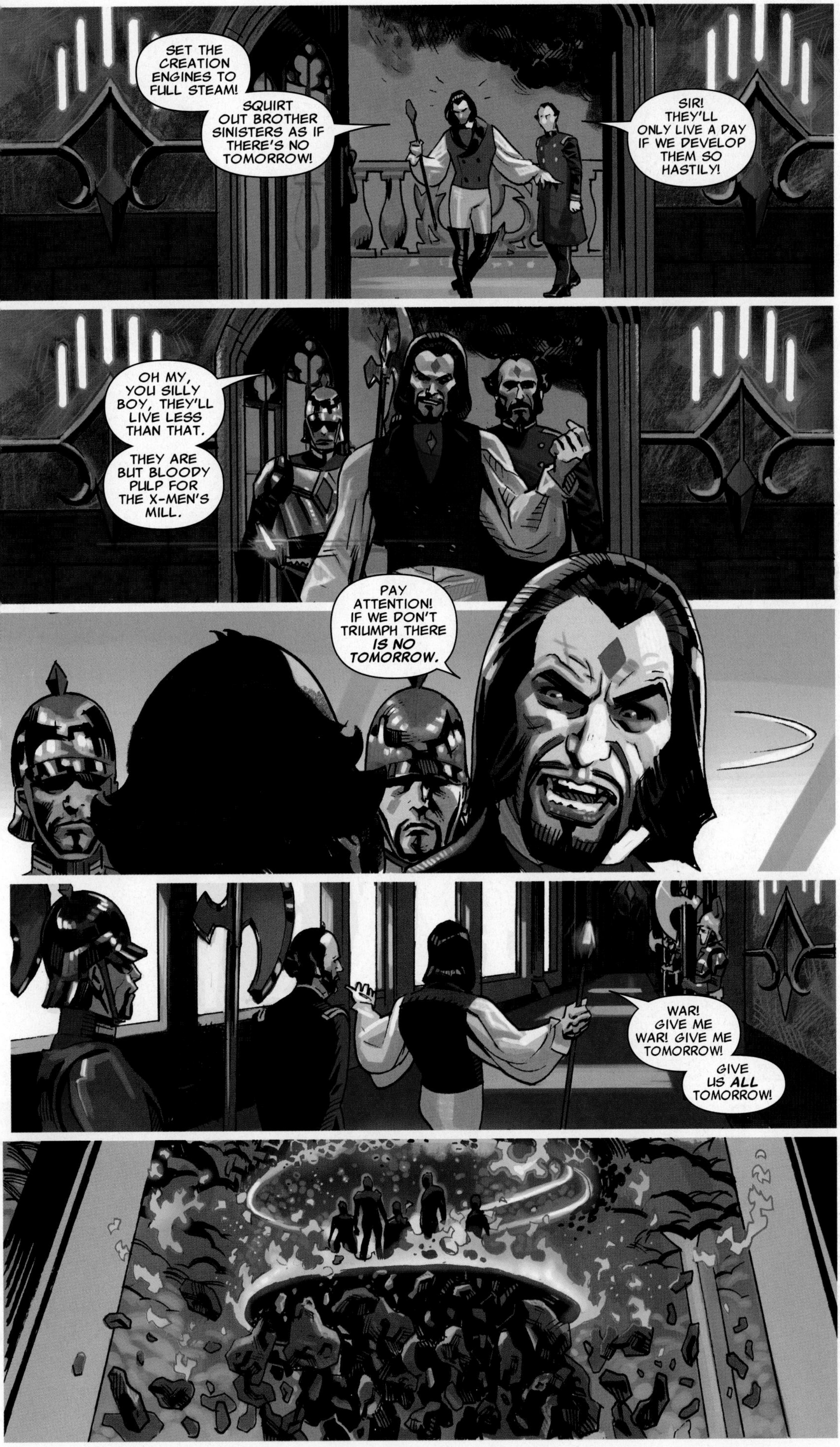

SET THE CREATION ENGINES TO FULL STEAM!
SQUIRT OUT BROTHER SINISTERS AS IF THERE'S NO TOMORROW!
SIR! THEY'LL ONLY LIVE A DAY IF WE DEVELOP THEM SO HASTILY!
OH MY, YOU SILLY BOY, THEY'LL LIVE LESS THAN THAT.
THEY ARE BUT BLOODY PULP FOR THE X-MEN'S MILL.
PAY ATTENTION! IF WE DON'T TRIUMPH THERE *IS NO TOMORROW.*
WAR! GIVE ME WAR! GIVE ME TOMORROW!
GIVE US **ALL** TOMORROW!

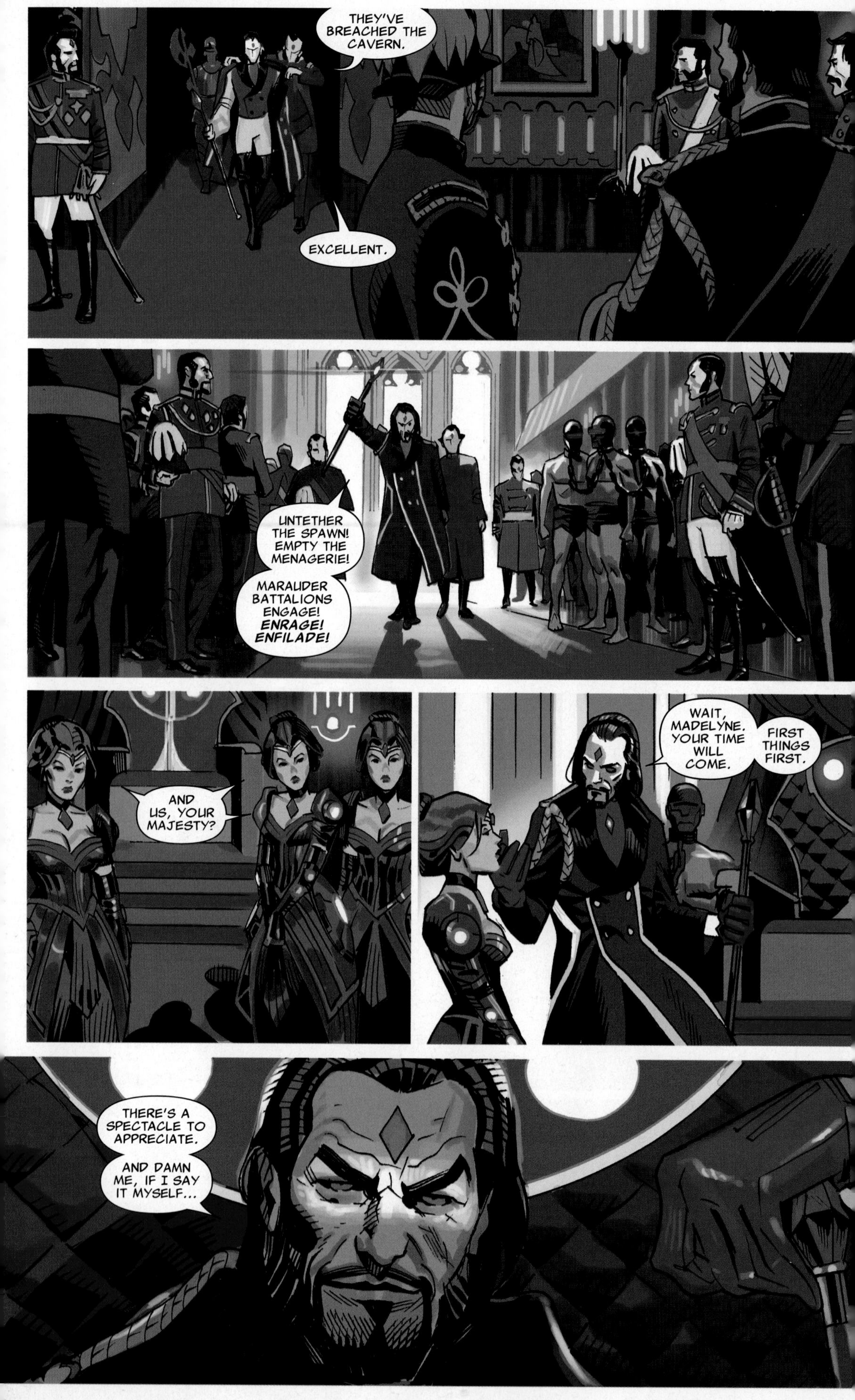
THEY'VE BREACHED THE CAVERN.
EXCELLENT.
UNTETHER THE SPAWN! EMPTY THE MENAGERIE!
MARAUDER BATTALIONS ENGAGE! ENRAGE! ENFILADE!
AND US, YOUR MAJESTY?
WAIT, MADELYNE. YOUR TIME WILL COME.
FIRST THINGS FIRST.
THERE'S A SPECTACLE TO APPRECIATE.
AND DAMN ME, IF I SAY IT MYSELF...

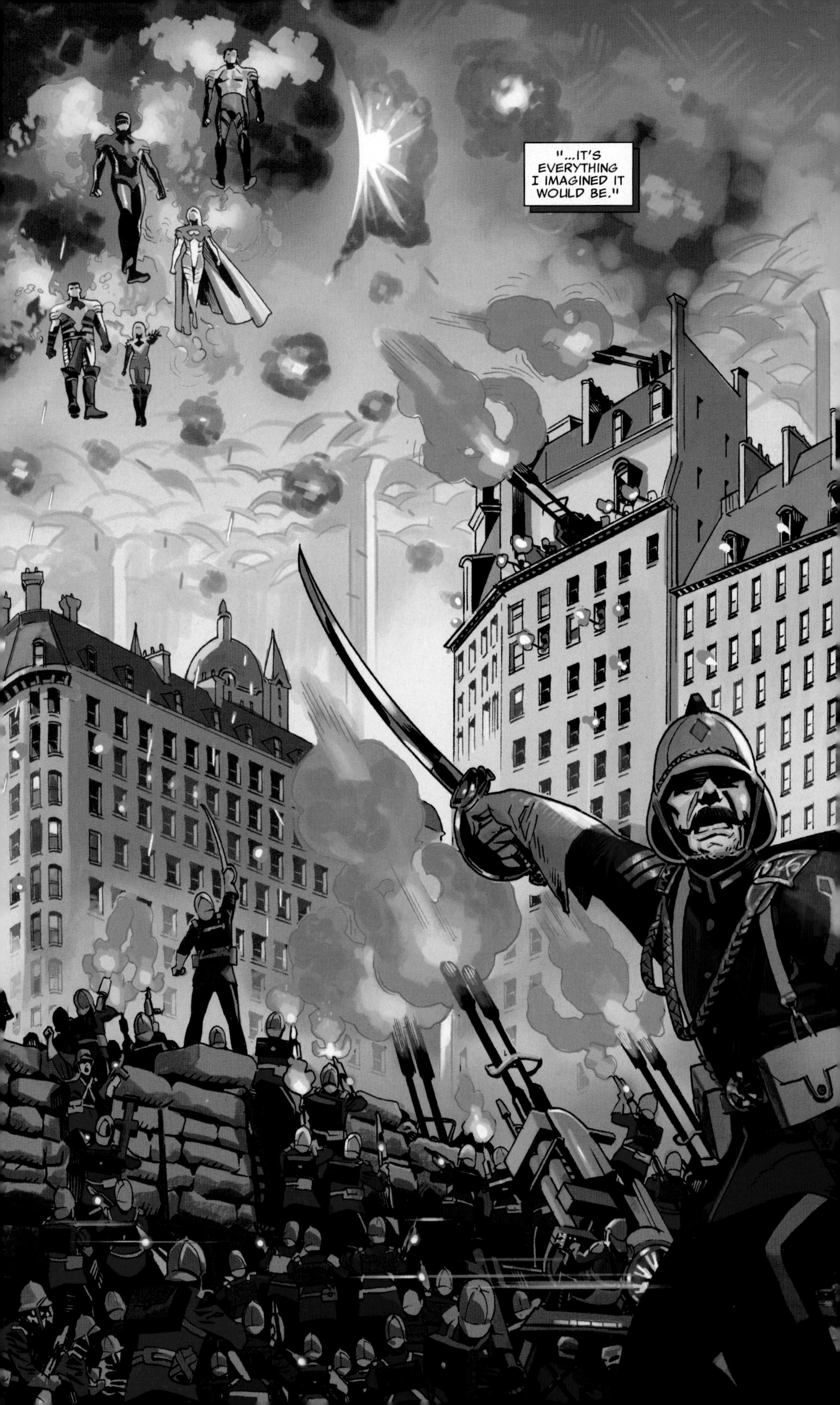
"...IT'S EVERYTHING I IMAGINED IT WOULD BE."

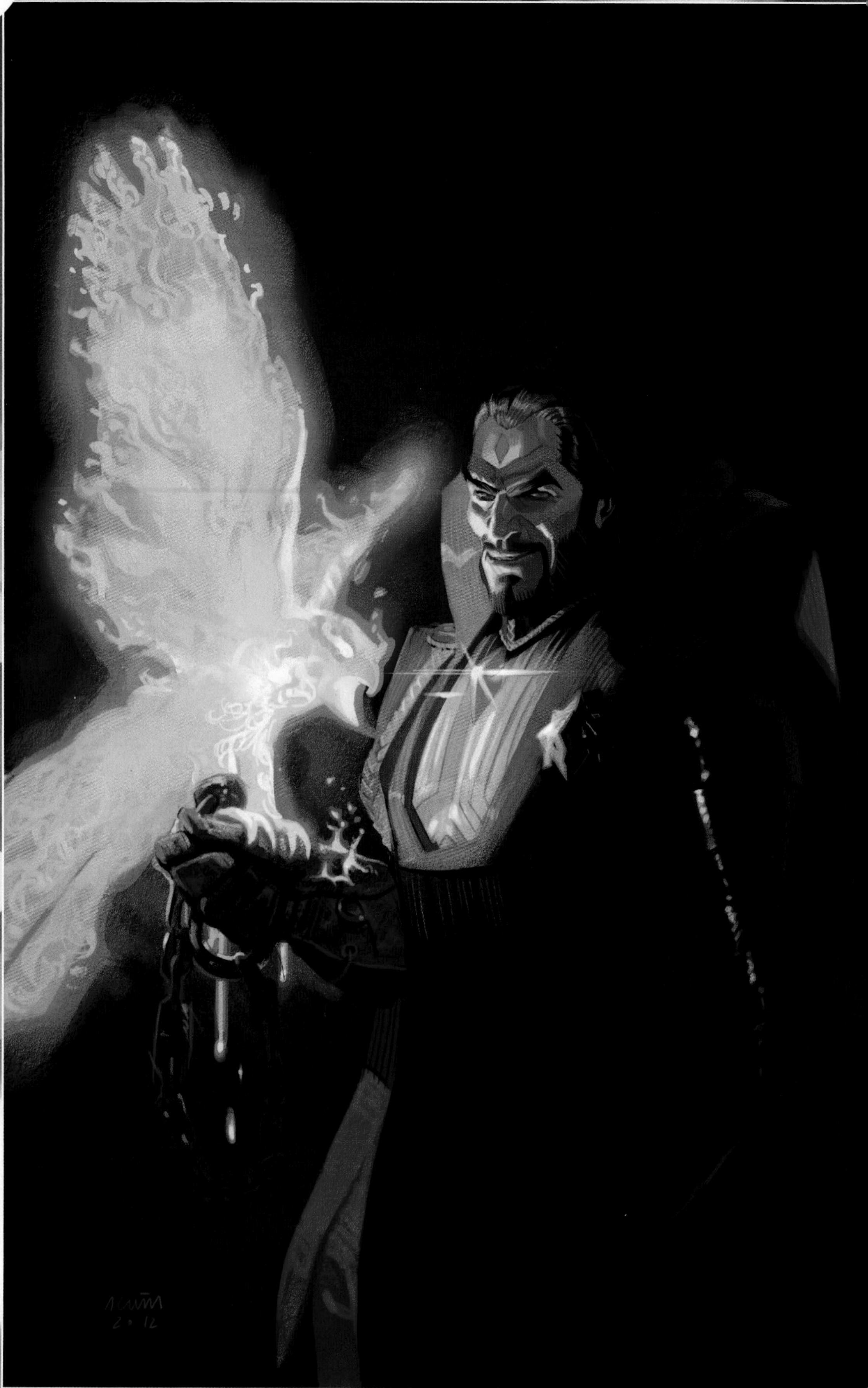

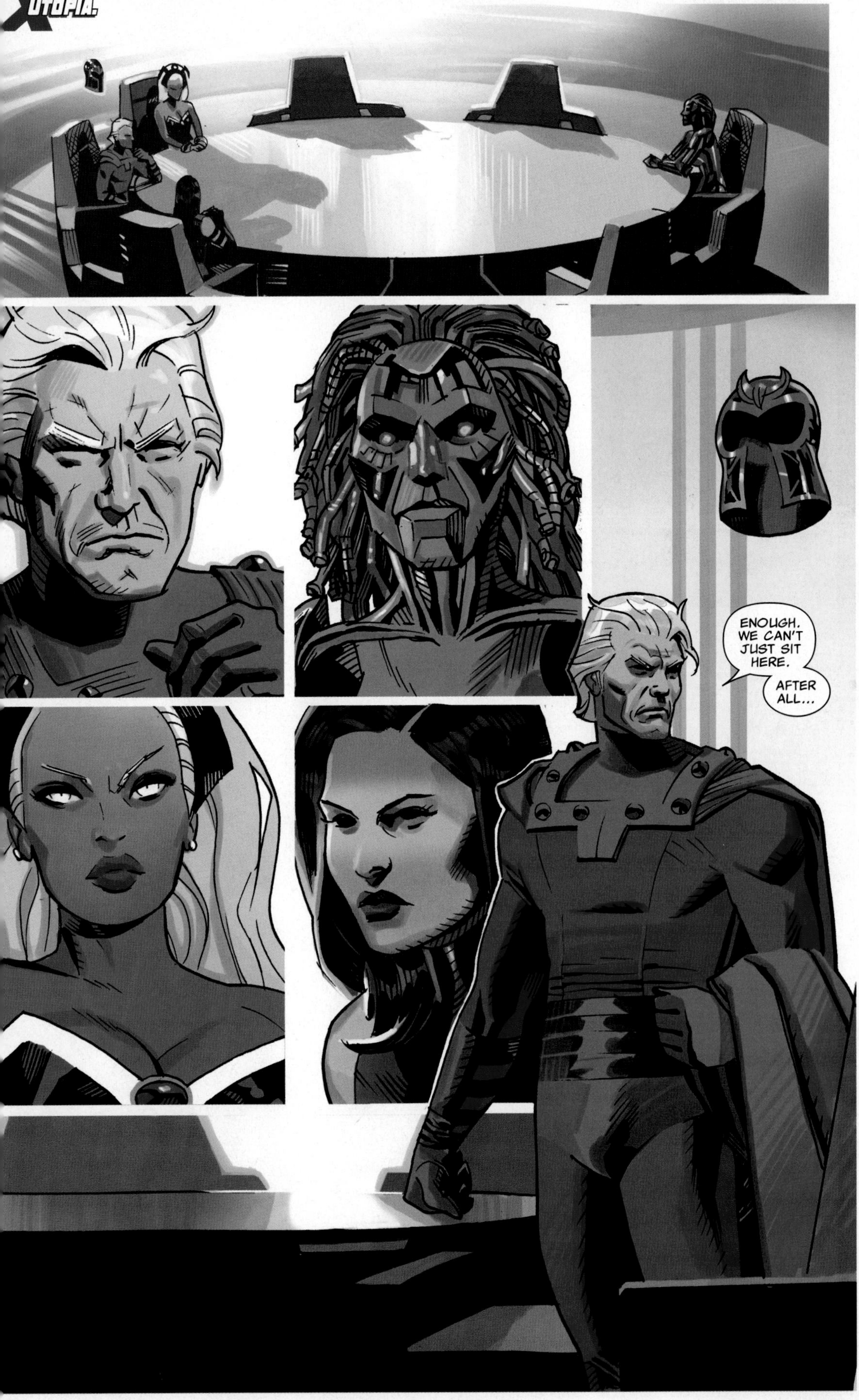
ENOUGH. WE CAN'T JUST SIT HERE.
AFTER ALL...

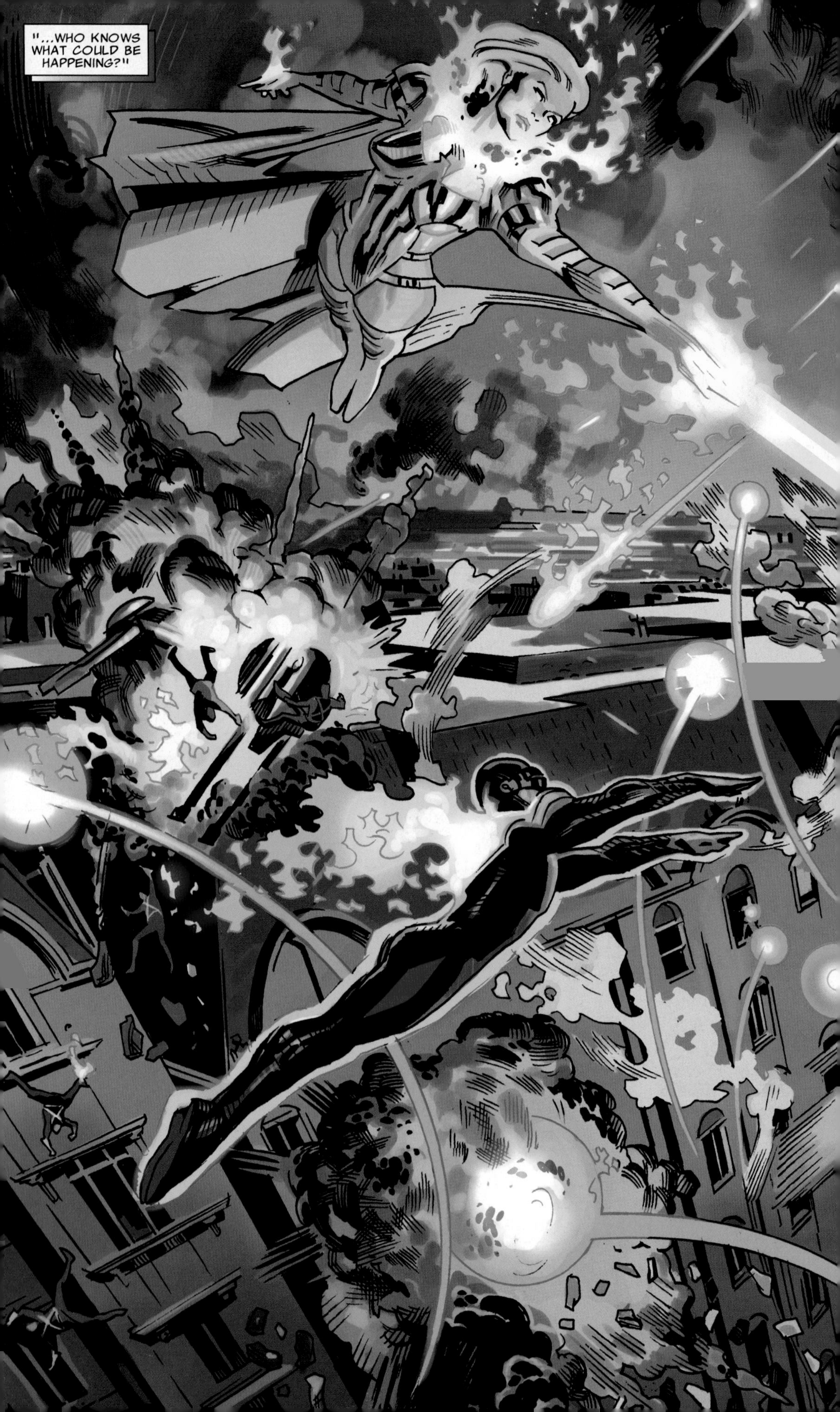
"...WHO KNOWS WHAT COULD BE HAPPENING?"

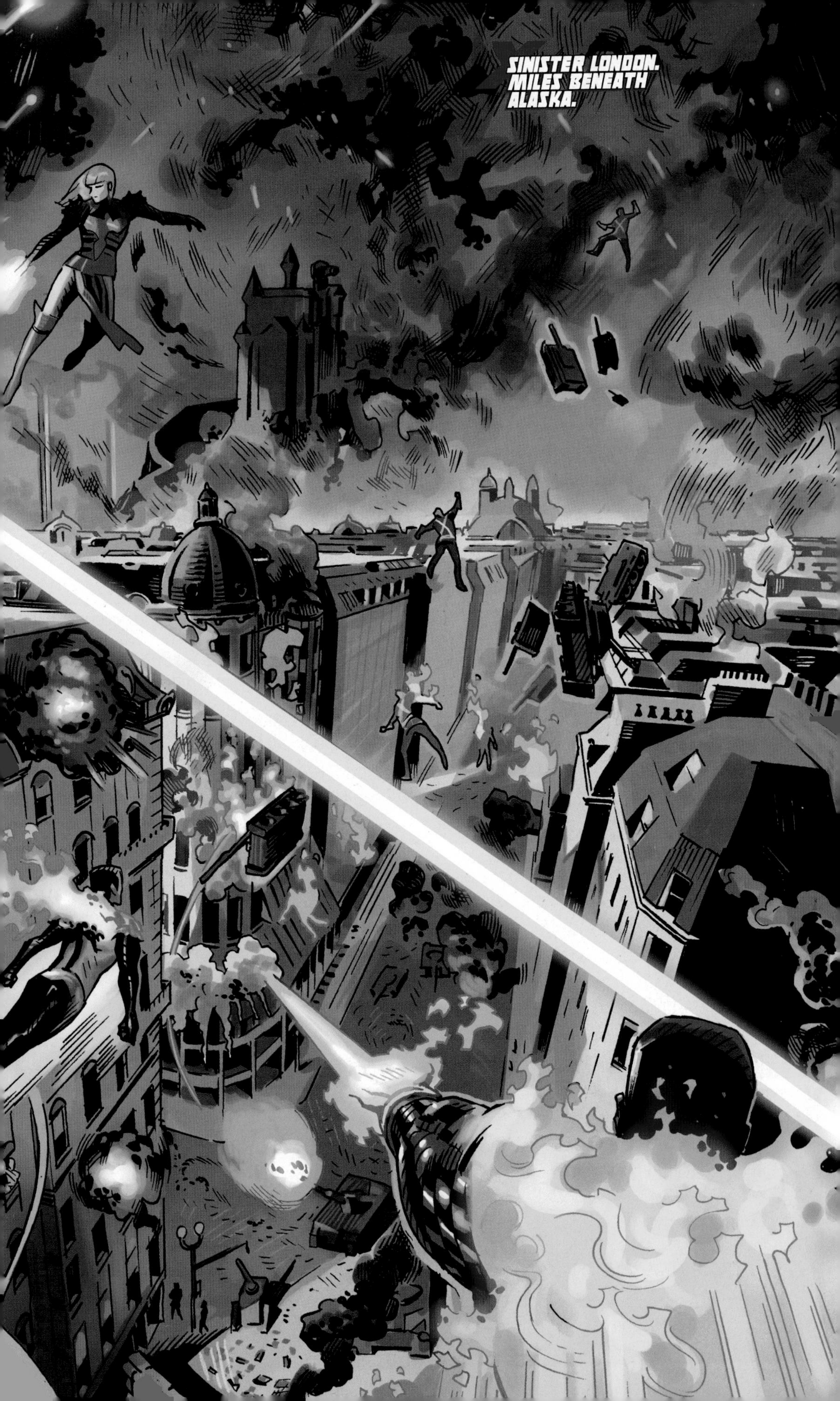
SINISTER LONDON.
MILES BENEATH
ALASKA.

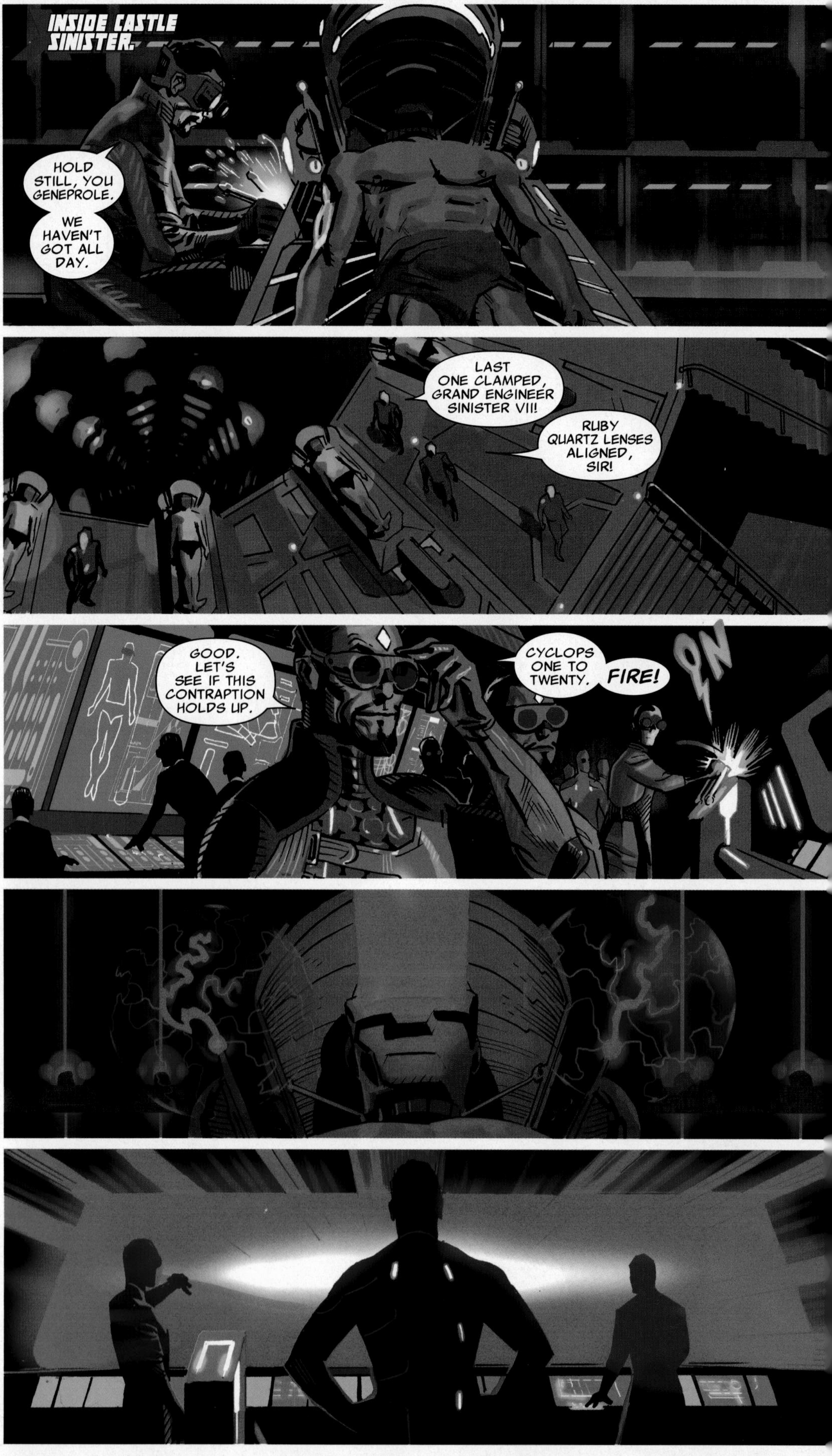
INSIDE CASTLE SINISTER.
HOLD STILL, YOU GENEPROLE.
WE HAVEN'T GOT ALL DAY.
LAST ONE CLAMPED, GRAND ENGINEER SINISTER VII!
RUBY QUARTZ LENSES ALIGNED, SIR!
GOOD. LET'S SEE IF THIS CONTRAPTION HOLDS UP.
CYCLOPS ONE TO TWENTY. FIRE!
ON

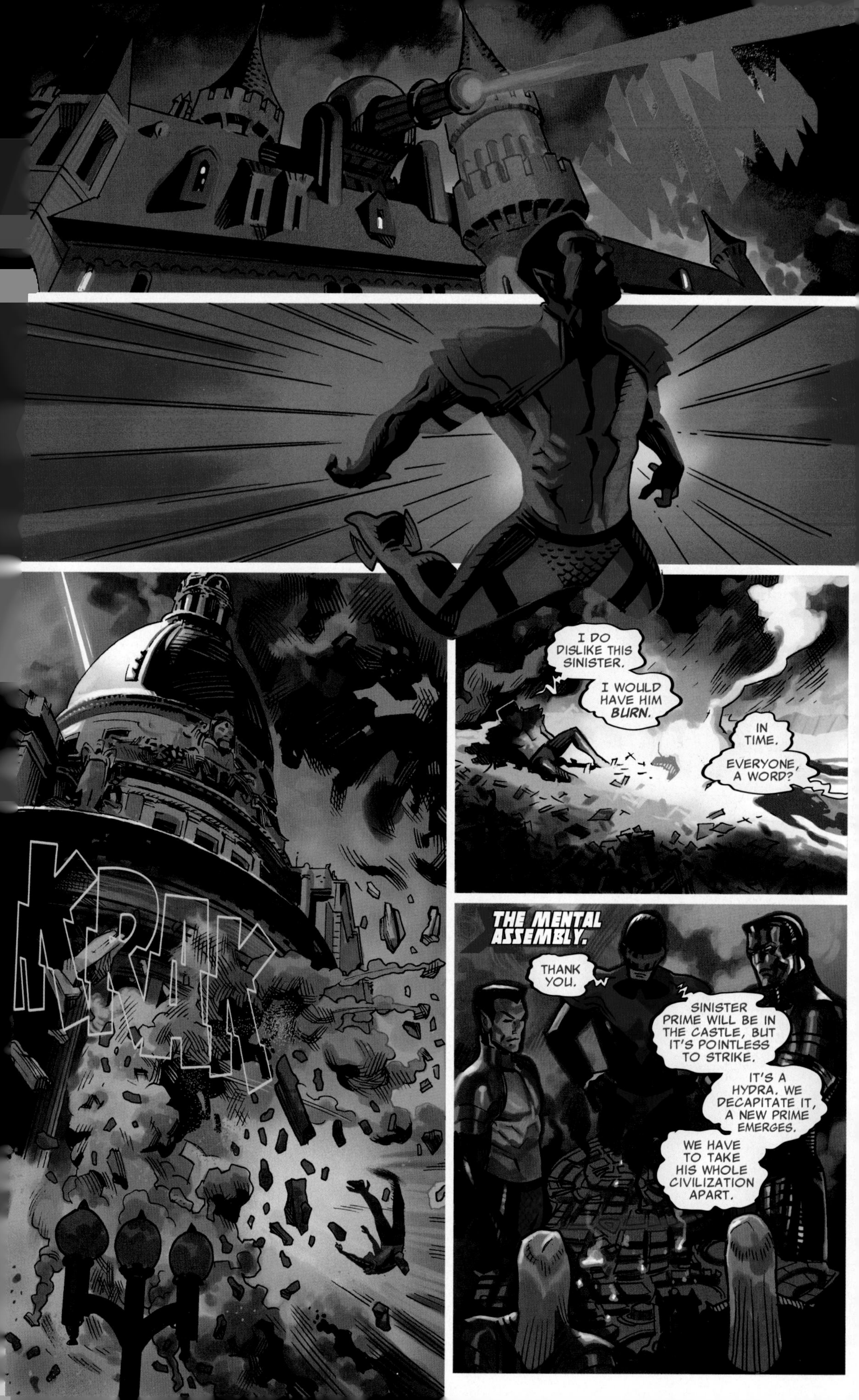
KRAK
I DO DISLIKE THIS SINISTER.
I WOULD HAVE HIM BURN.
IN TIME.
EVERYONE, A WORD?
THE MENTAL ASSEMBLY.
THANK YOU.
SINISTER PRIME WILL BE IN THE CASTLE, BUT IT'S POINTLESS TO STRIKE.
IT'S A HYDRA. WE DECAPITATE IT, A NEW PRIME EMERGES.
WE HAVE TO TAKE HIS WHOLE CIVILIZATION APART.

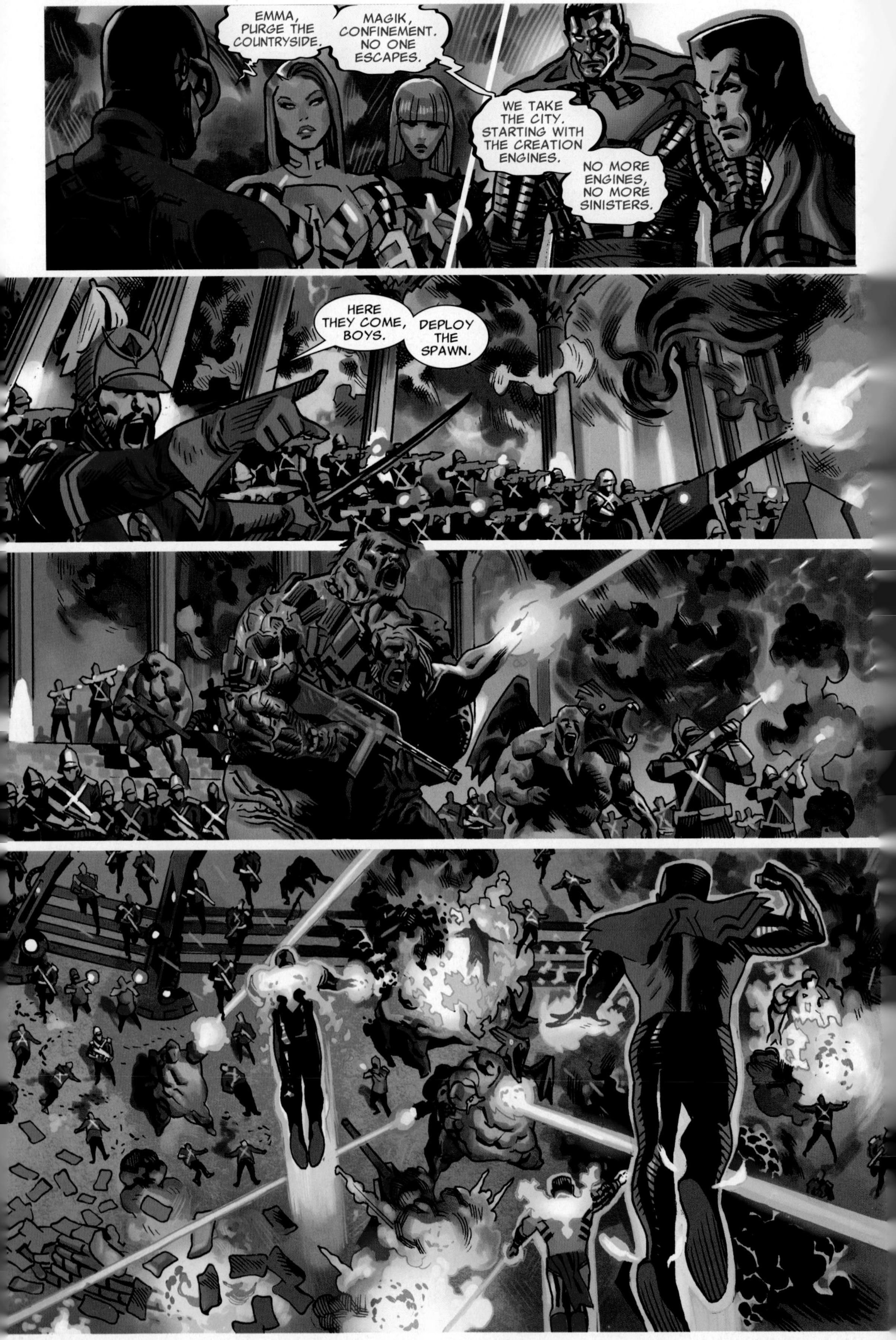
EMMA, PURGE THE COUNTRYSIDE.
MAGIK, CONFINEMENT. NO ONE ESCAPES.
WE TAKE THE CITY. STARTING WITH THE CREATION ENGINES.
NO MORE ENGINES, NO MORE SINISTERS.
HERE THEY COME, BOYS.
DEPLOY THE SPAWN.

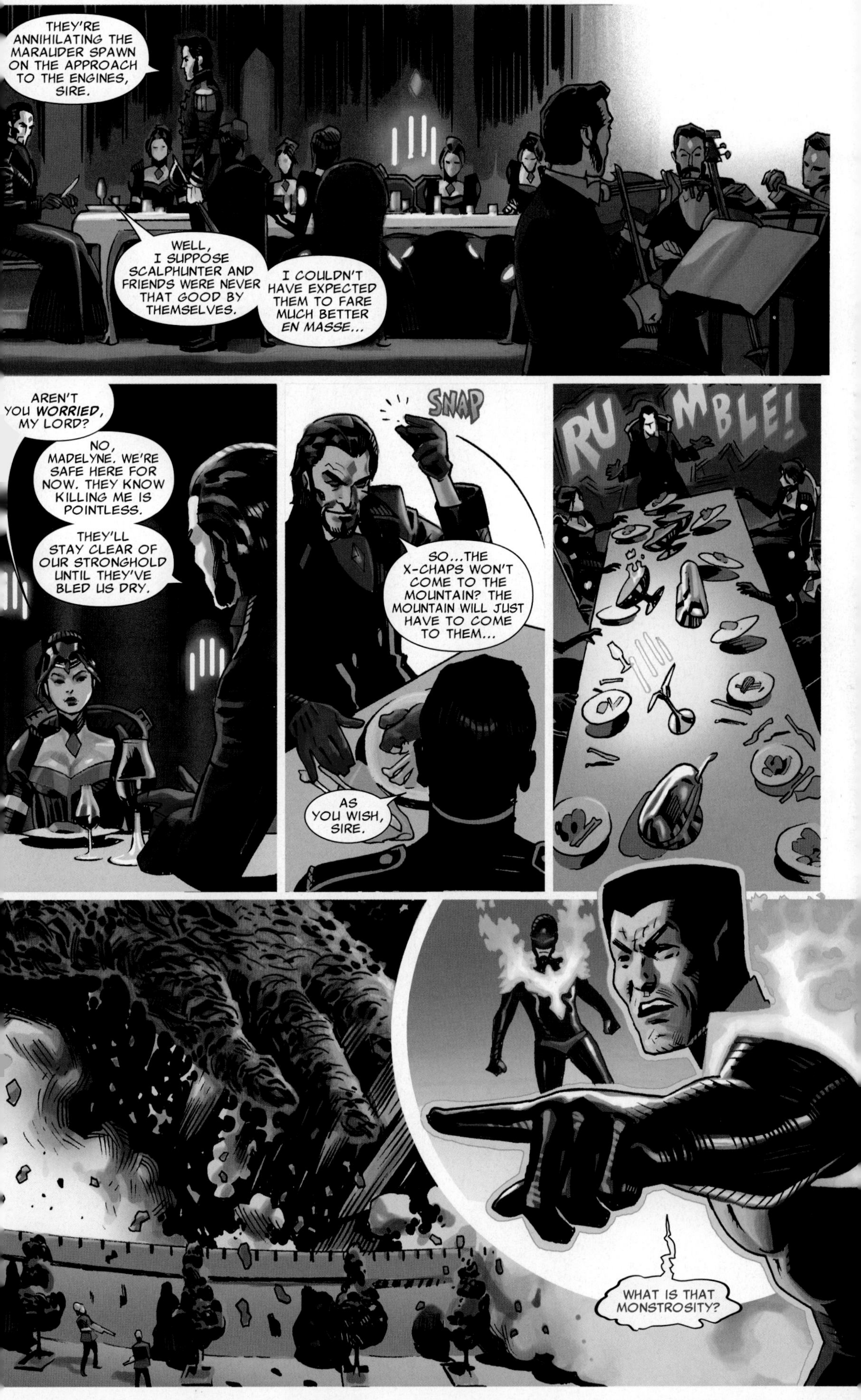
THEY'RE ANNIHILATING THE MARAUDER SPAWN ON THE APPROACH TO THE ENGINES, SIRE.
WELL, I SUPPOSE SCALPHUNTER AND FRIENDS WERE NEVER THAT GOOD BY THEMSELVES.
I COULDN'T HAVE EXPECTED THEM TO FARE MUCH BETTER EN MASSE...
AREN'T YOU WORRIED, MY LORD?
NO, MADELYNE. WE'RE SAFE HERE FOR NOW. THEY KNOW KILLING ME IS POINTLESS.
THEY'LL STAY CLEAR OF OUR STRONGHOLD UNTIL THEY'VE BLED US DRY.
SNAP
SO...THE X-CHAPS WON'T COME TO THE MOUNTAIN? THE MOUNTAIN WILL JUST HAVE TO COME TO THEM...
AS YOU WISH, SIRE.
RUMBLE!
WHAT IS THAT MONSTROSITY?

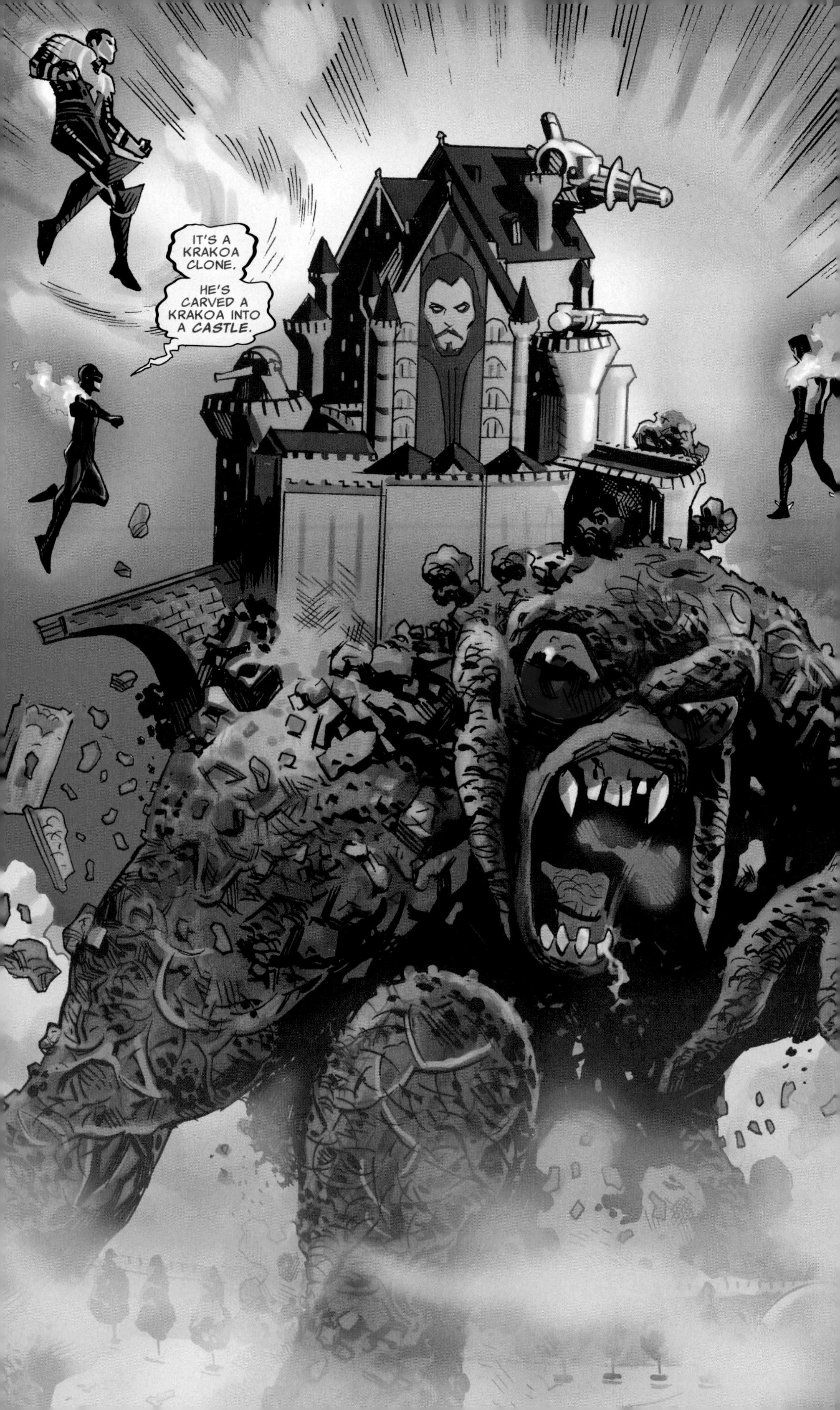
IT'S A KRAKOA CLONE.
HE'S CARVED A KRAKOA INTO A CASTLE.

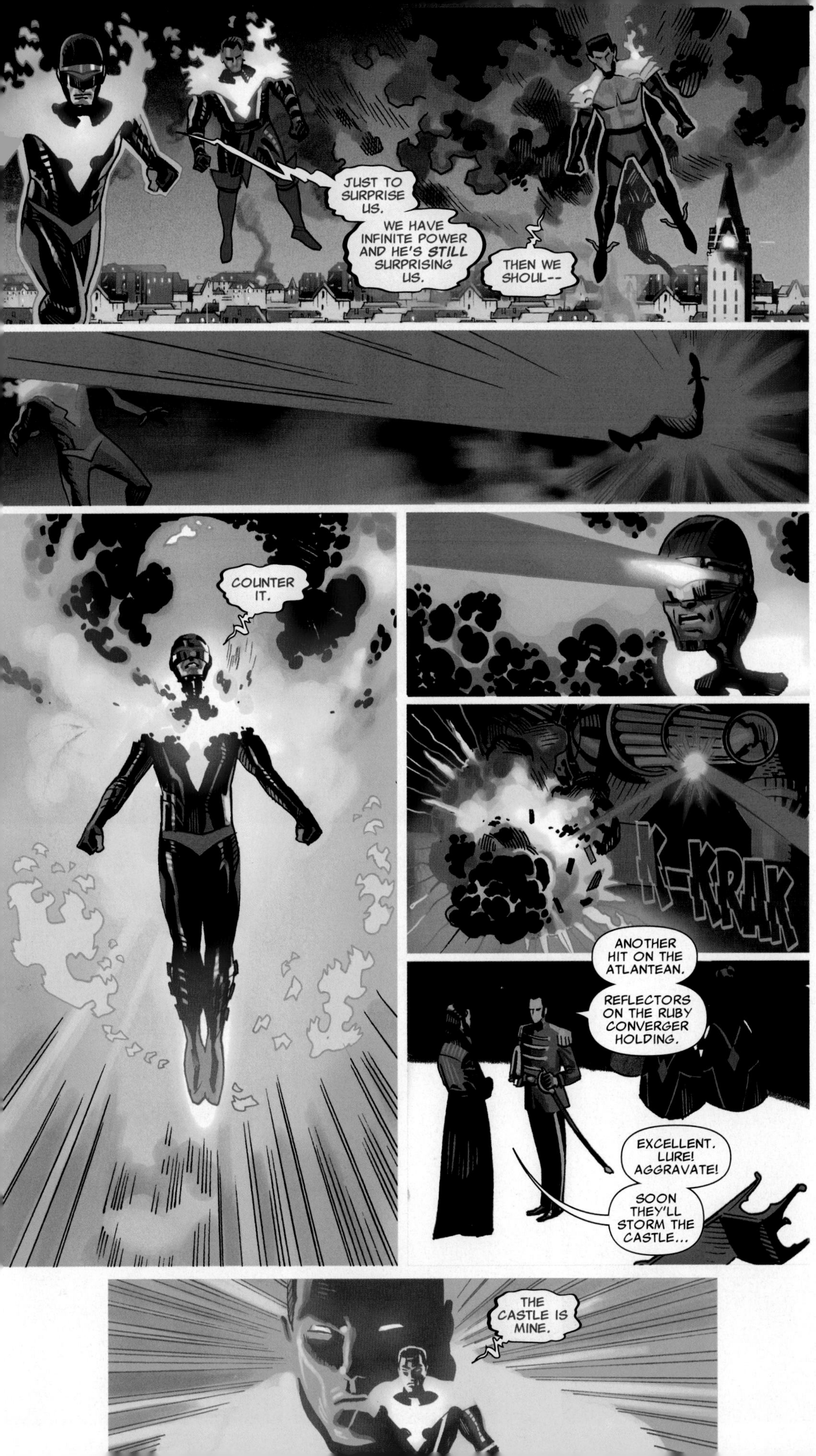
JUST TO SURPRISE US.
WE HAVE INFINITE POWER AND HE'S STILL SURPRISING US.
THEN WE SHOUL--
COUNTER IT.
K-KRAK
ANOTHER HIT ON THE ATLANTEAN.
REFLECTORS ON THE RUBY CONVERGER HOLDING.
EXCELLENT. LURE! AGGRAVATE!
SOON THEY'LL STORM THE CASTLE...
THE CASTLE IS MINE.

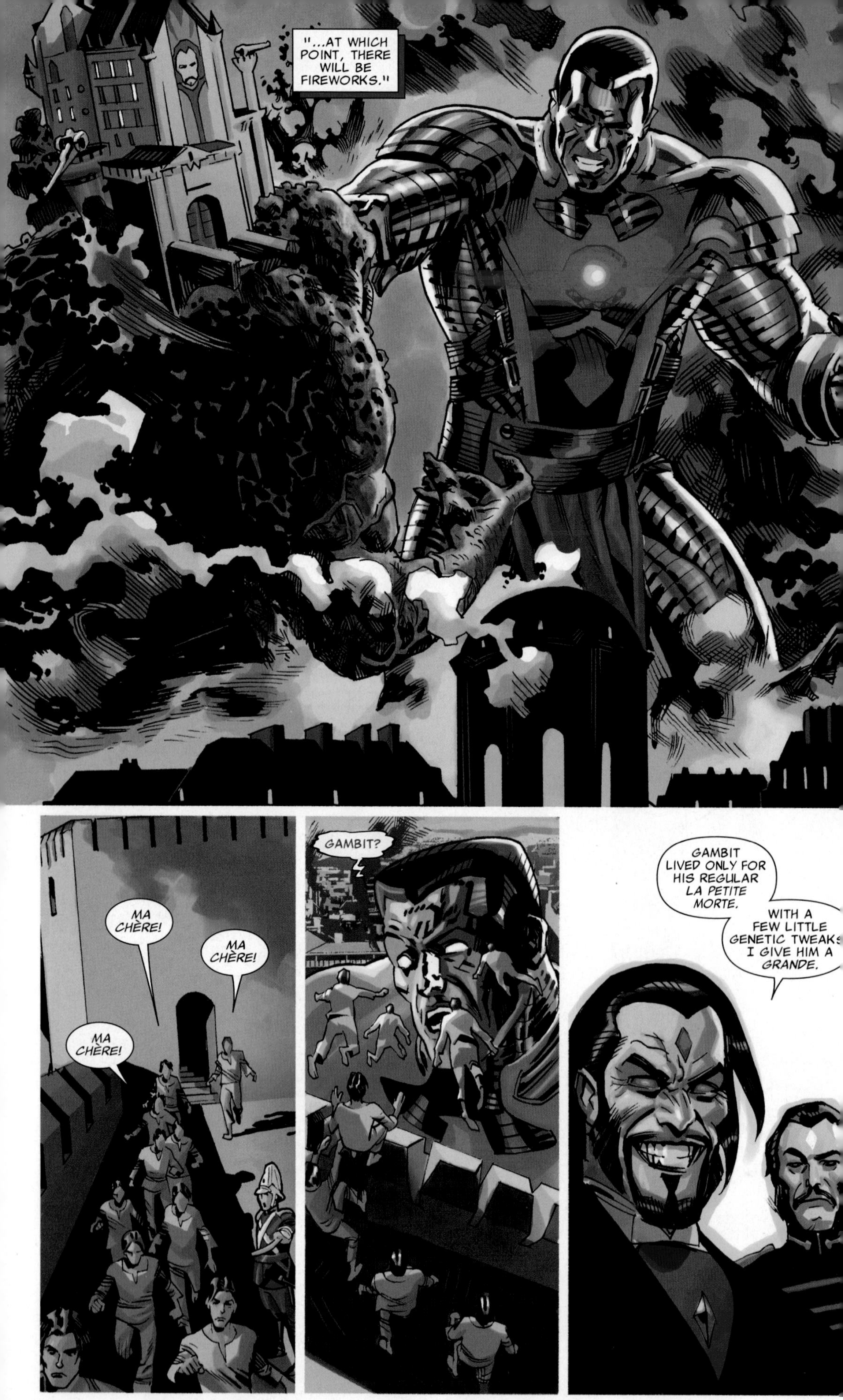
"...AT WHICH POINT, THERE WILL BE FIREWORKS."
MA CHÈRE!
MA CHÈRE!
MA CHÈRE!
GAMBIT?
GAMBIT LIVED ONLY FOR HIS REGULAR LA PETITE MORTE.
WITH A FEW LITTLE GENETIC TWEAKS I GIVE HIM A GRANDE.

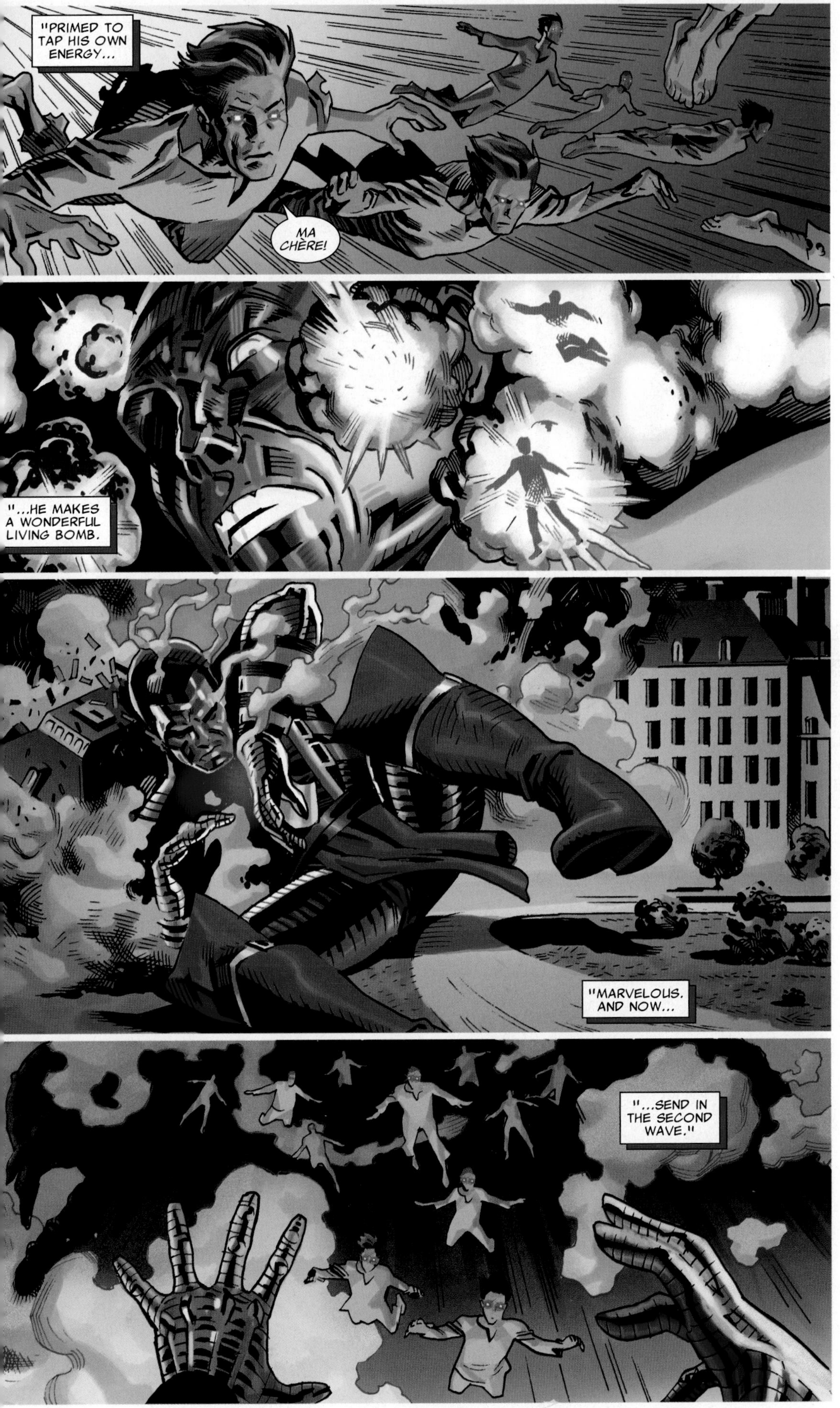
"PRIMED TO TAP HIS OWN ENERGY...
MA CHÈRE!
"...HE MAKES A WONDERFUL LIVING BOMB.
"MARVELOUS. AND NOW...
"...SEND IN THE SECOND WAVE."

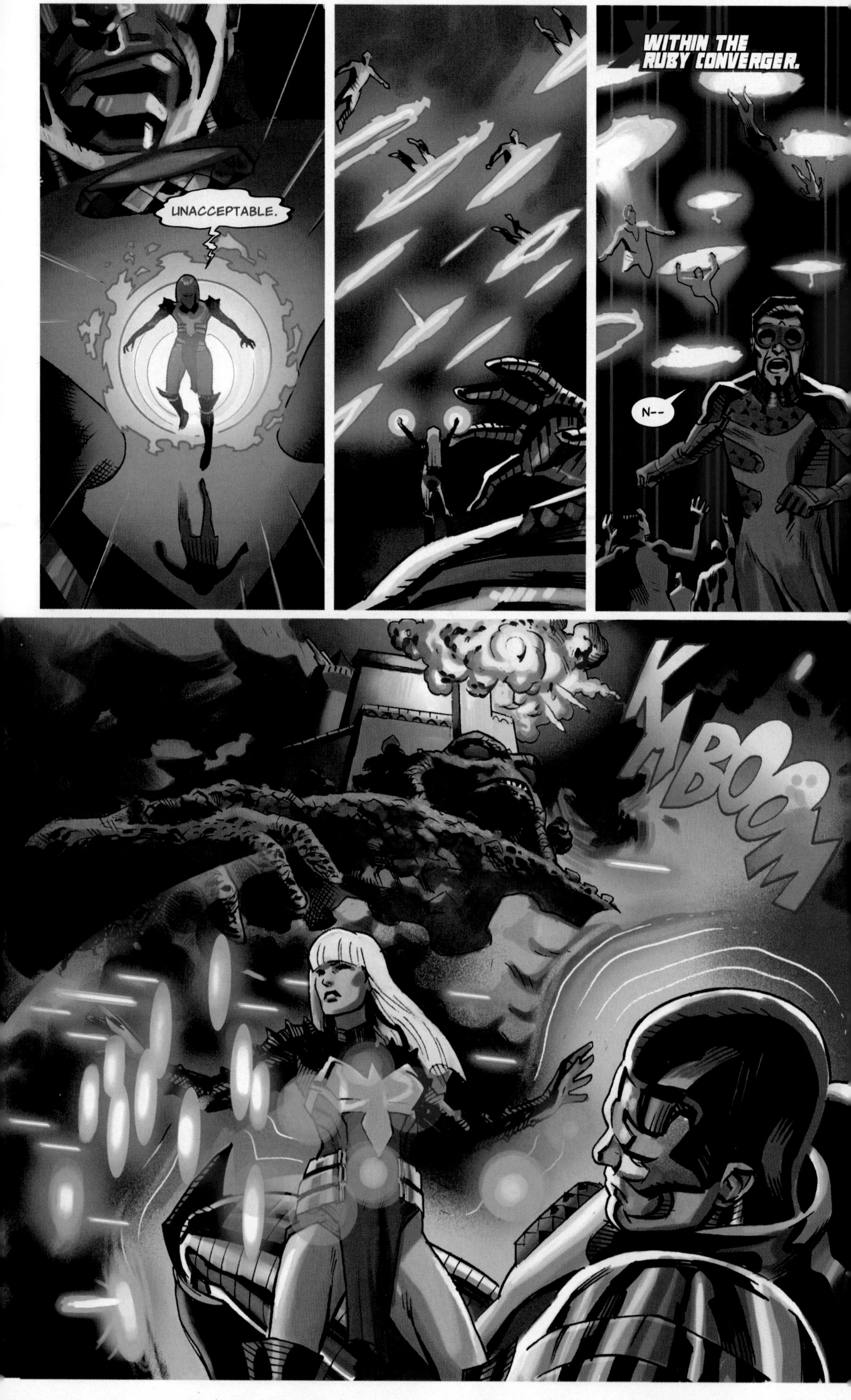
UNACCEPTABLE.
WITHIN THE RUBY CONVERGER.
N--
KABOOM

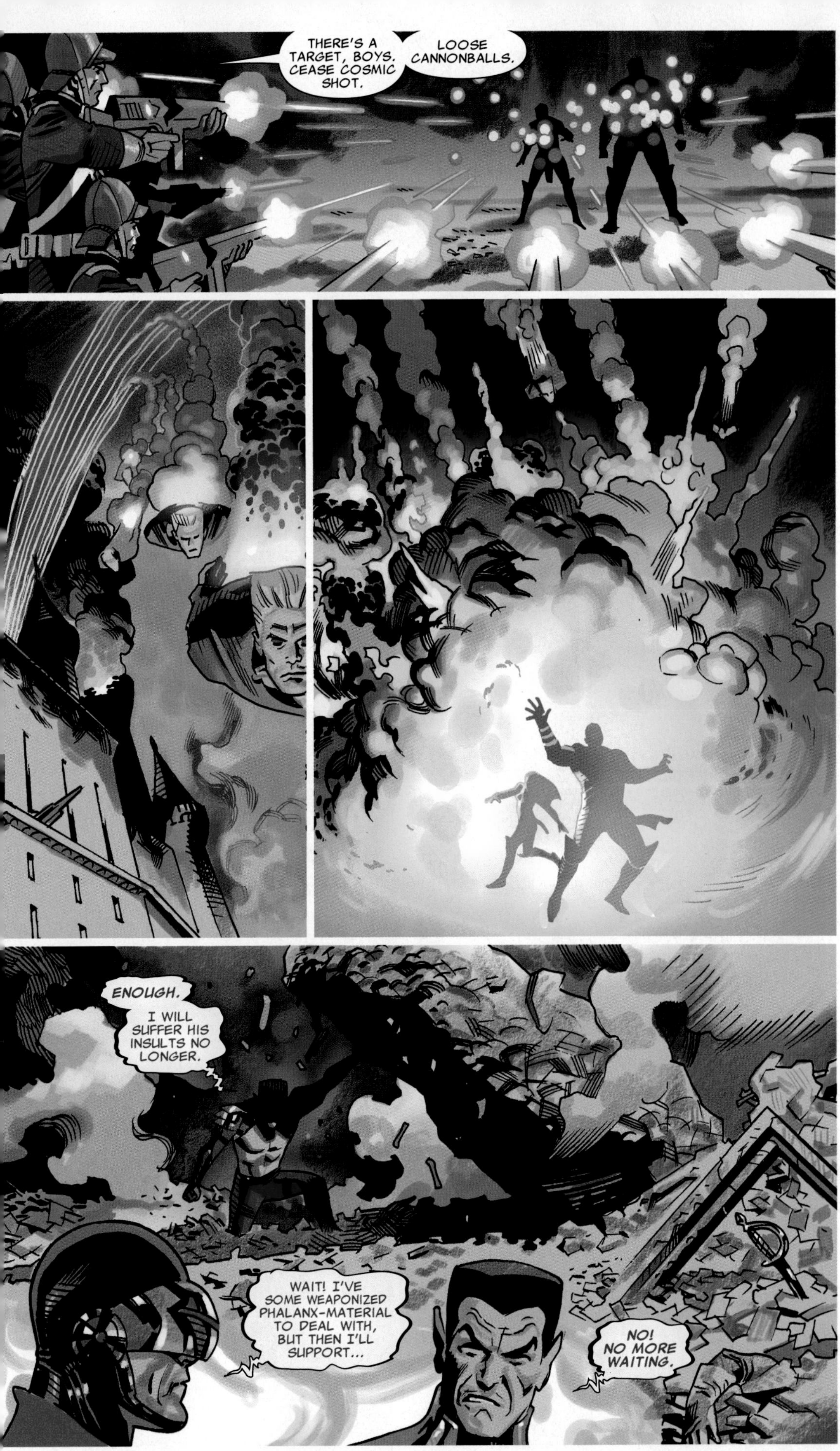
THERE'S A TARGET, BOYS. CEASE COSMIC SHOT.
LOOSE CANNONBALLS.
ENOUGH.
I WILL SUFFER HIS INSULTS NO LONGER.
WAIT! I'VE SOME WEAPONIZED PHALANX-MATERIAL TO DEAL WITH, BUT THEN I'LL SUPPORT...
NO! NO MORE WAITING.

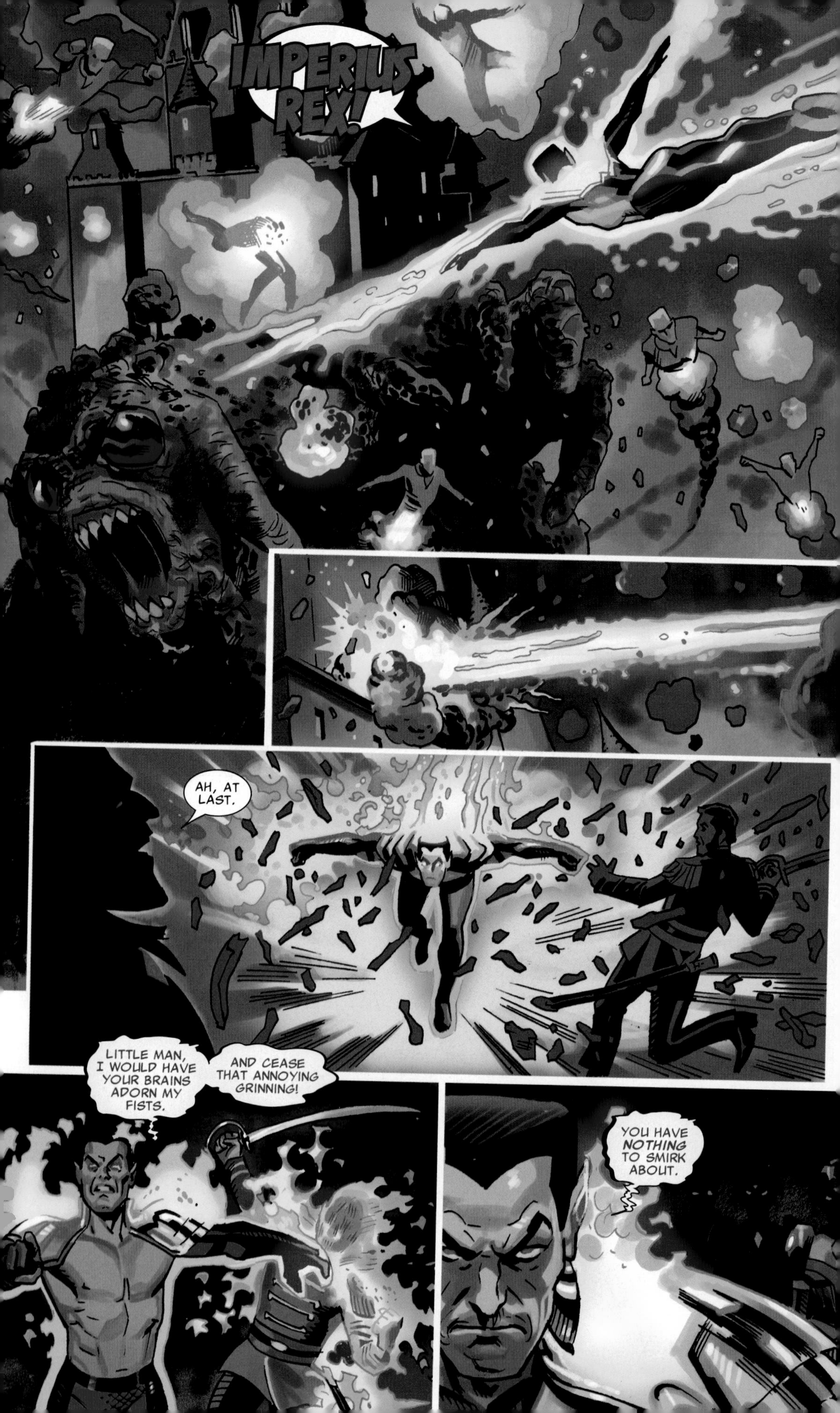
IMPERIUS REX!
AH, AT LAST.
LITTLE MAN, I WOULD HAVE YOUR BRAINS ADORN MY FISTS.
AND CEASE THAT ANNOYING GRINNING!
YOU HAVE NOTHING TO SMIRK ABOUT.

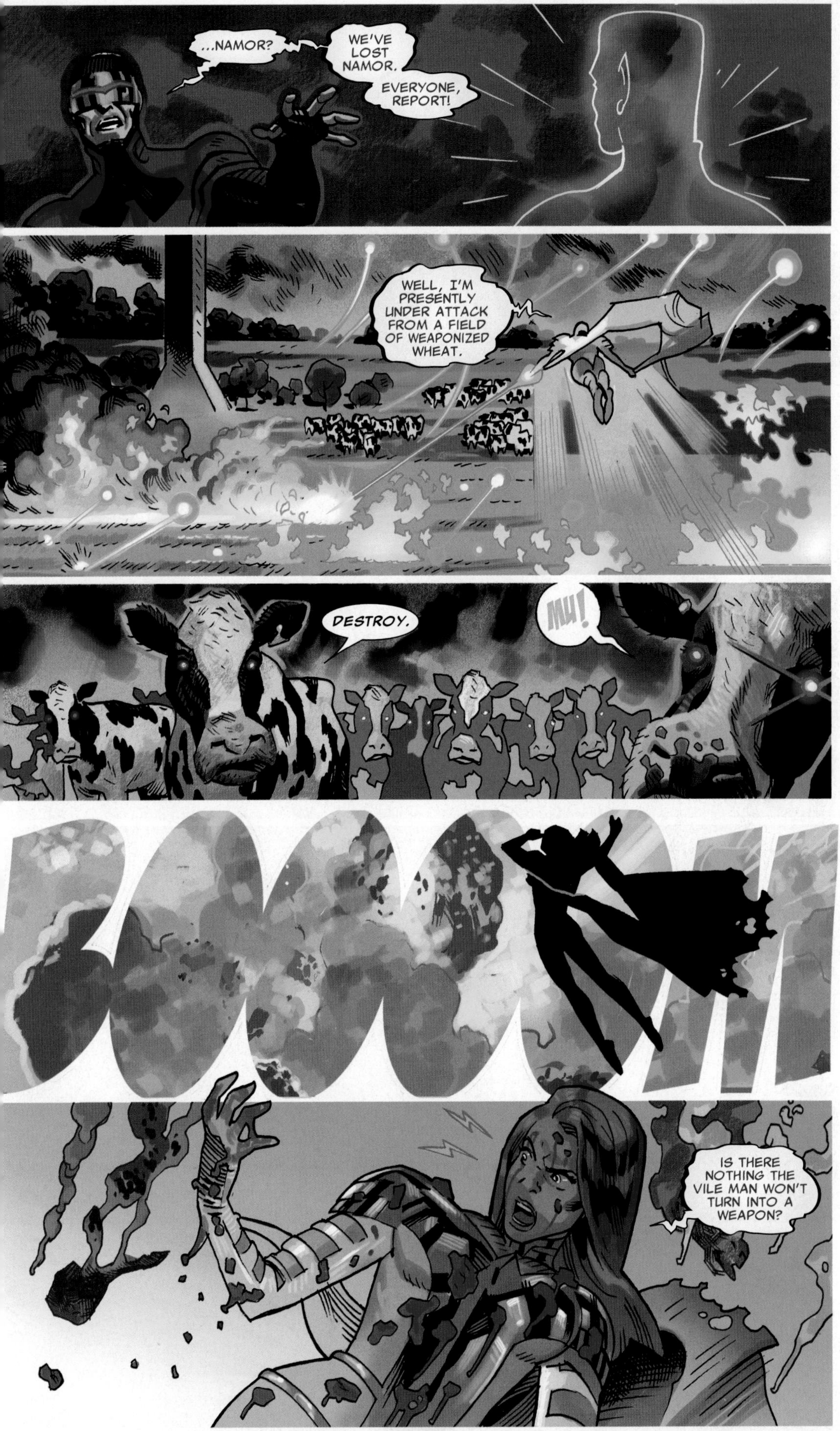
...NAMOR?
WE'VE LOST NAMOR.
EVERYONE, REPORT!
WELL, I'M PRESENTLY UNDER ATTACK FROM A FIELD OF WEAPONIZED WHEAT.
DESTROY.
MU!
IS THERE NOTHING THE VILE MAN WON'T TURN INTO A WEAPON?

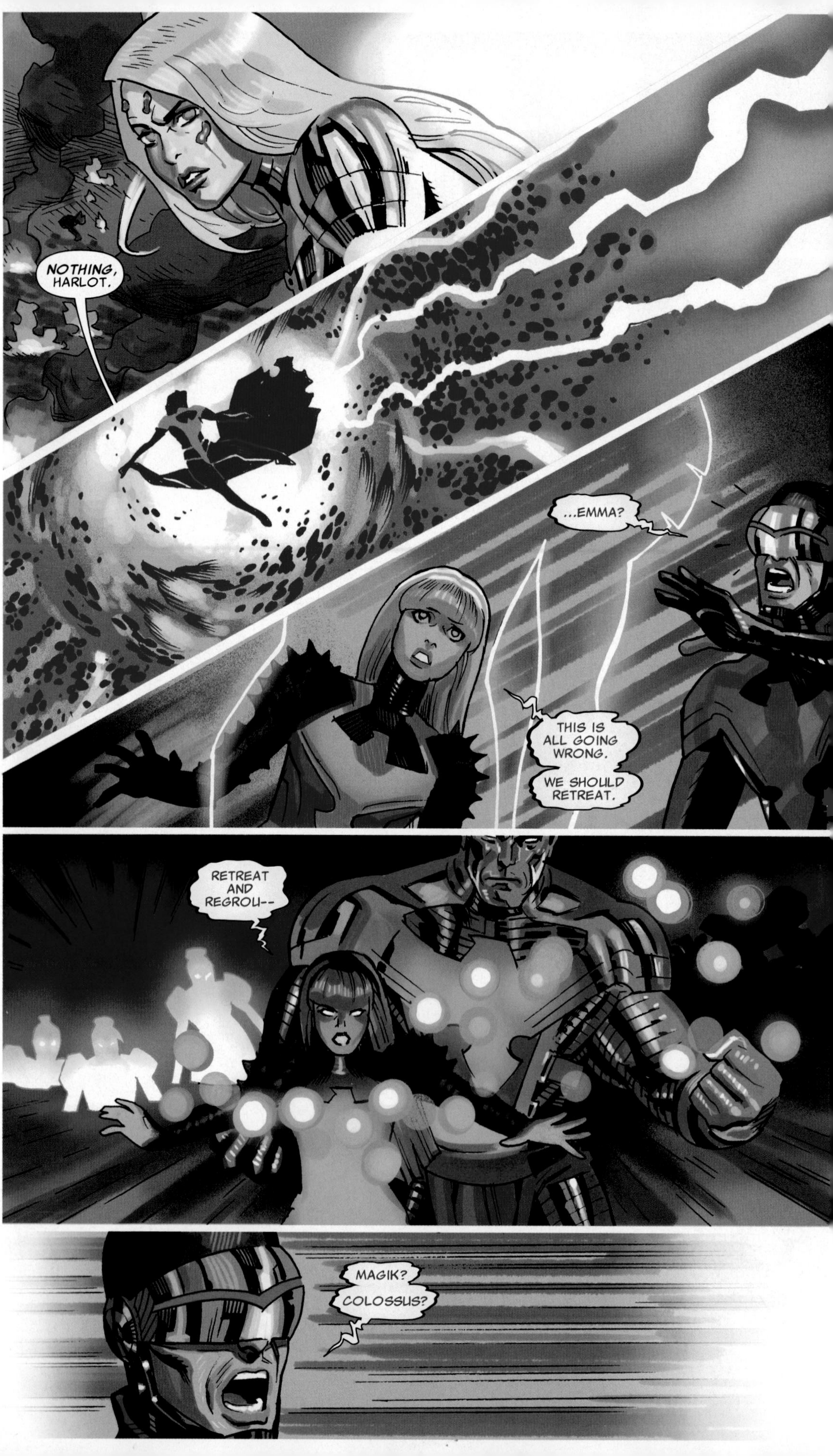
NOTHING, HARLOT.
...EMMA?
THIS IS ALL GOING WRONG.
WE SHOULD RETREAT.
RETREAT AND REGROU--
MAGIK?
COLOSSUS?

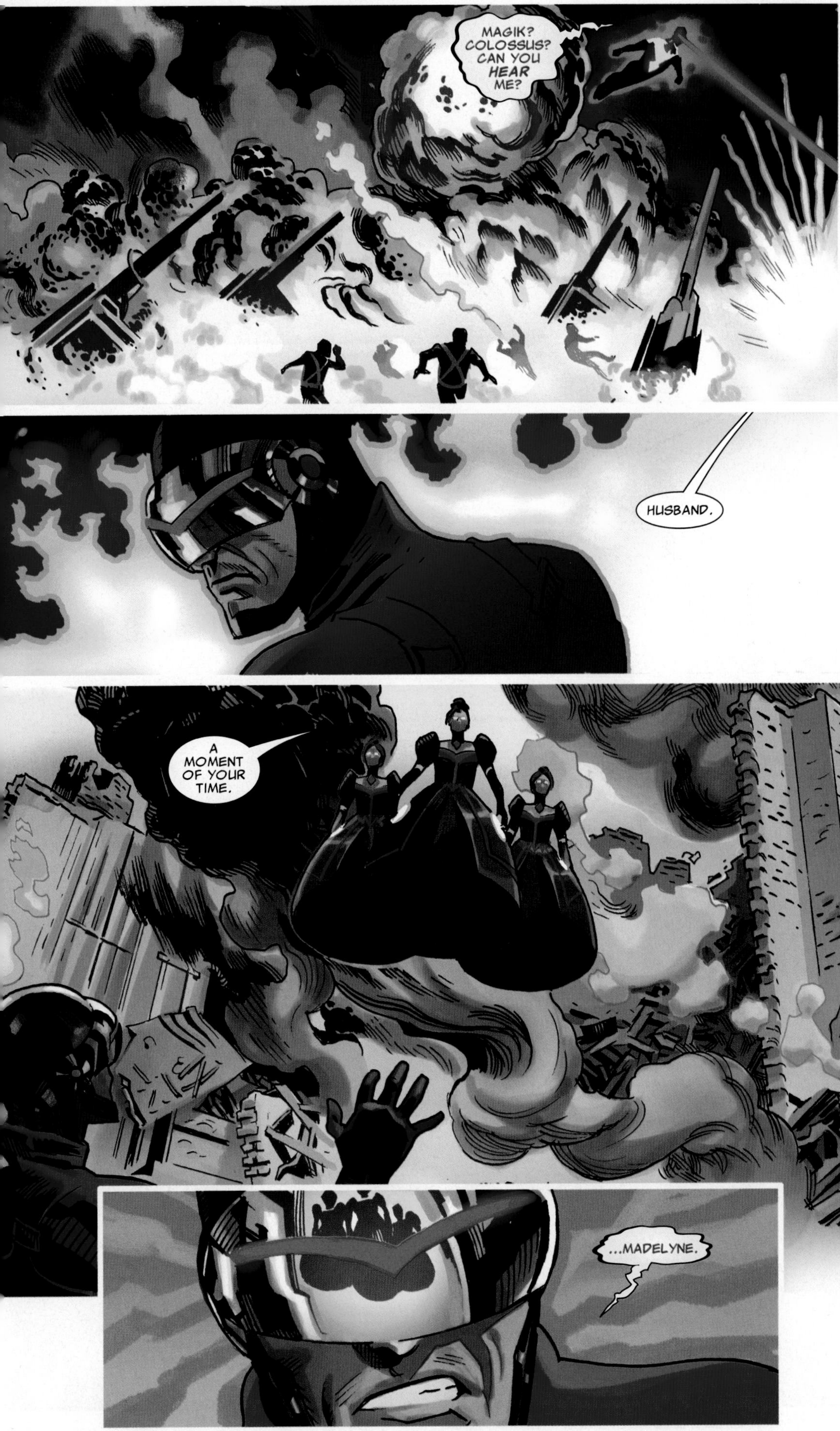
MAGIK? COLOSSUS? CAN YOU HEAR ME?
HUSBAND.
A MOMENT OF YOUR TIME.
...MADELYNE.

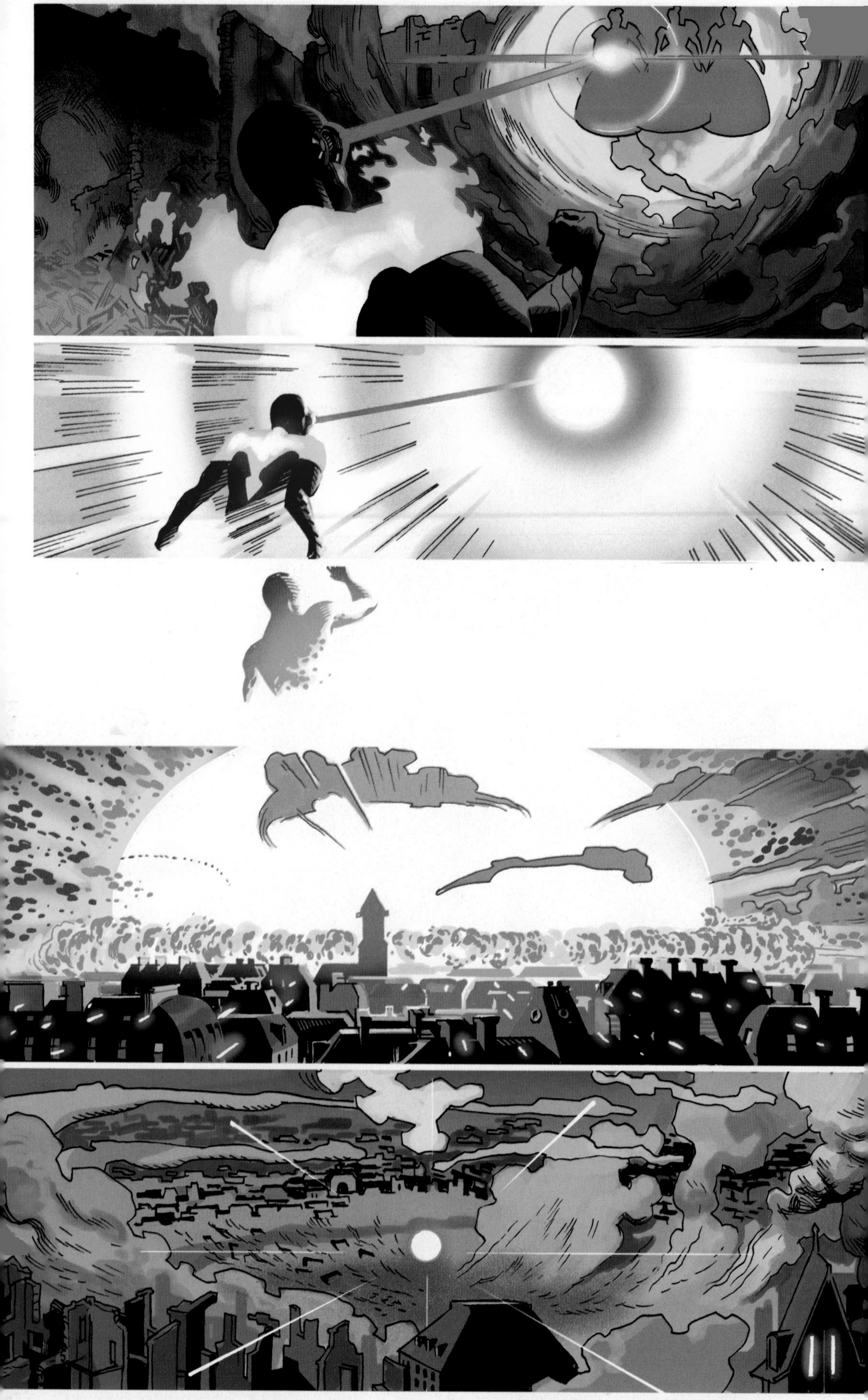

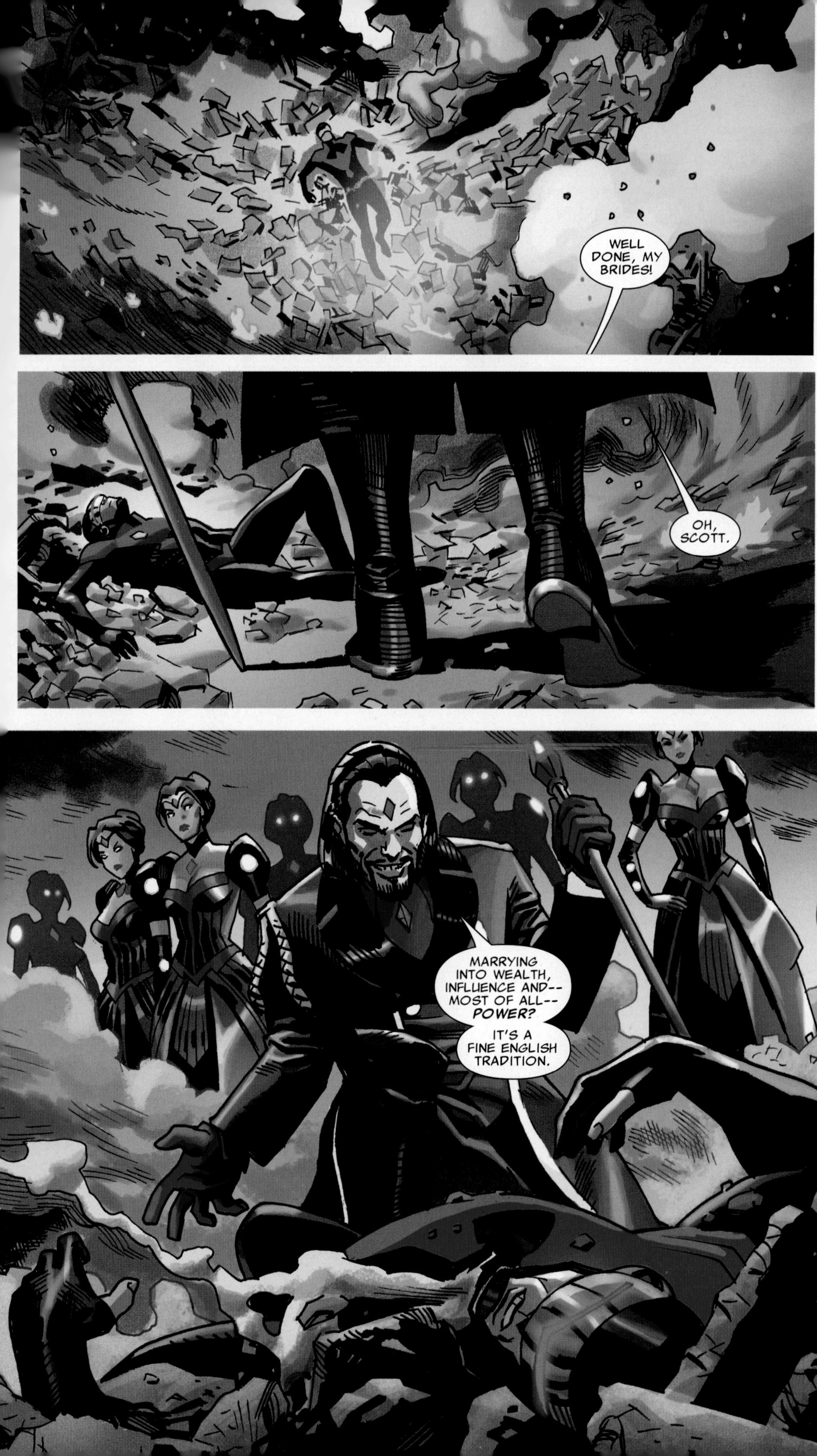
WELL DONE, MY BRIDES!
OH, SCOTT.
MARRYING INTO WEALTH, INFLUENCE AND-- MOST OF ALL-- POWER?
IT'S A FINE ENGLISH TRADITION.

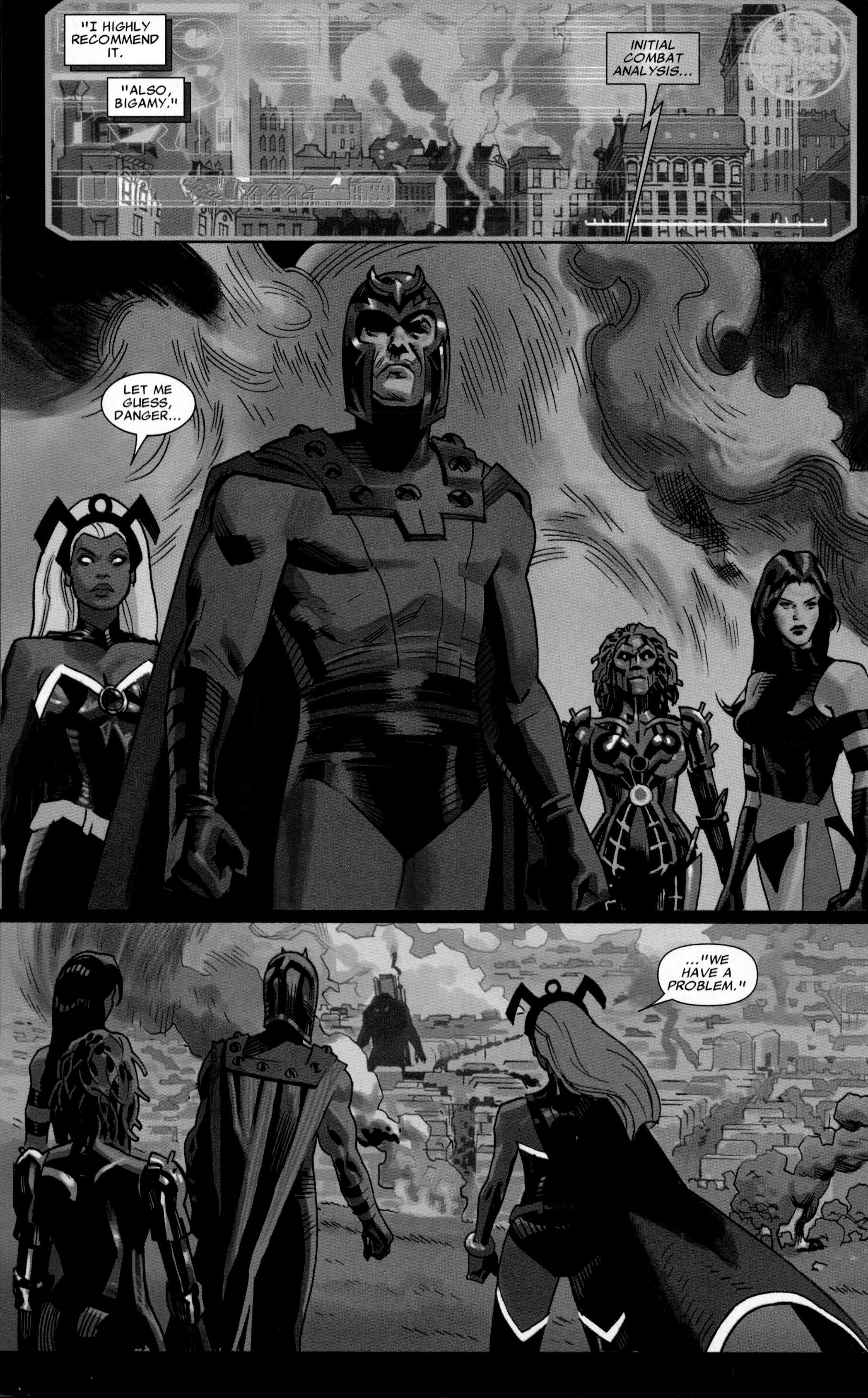
"I HIGHLY RECOMMEND IT.
"ALSO, BIGAMY."
INITIAL COMBAT ANALYSIS...
LET ME GUESS, DANGER...
..."WE HAVE A PROBLEM."

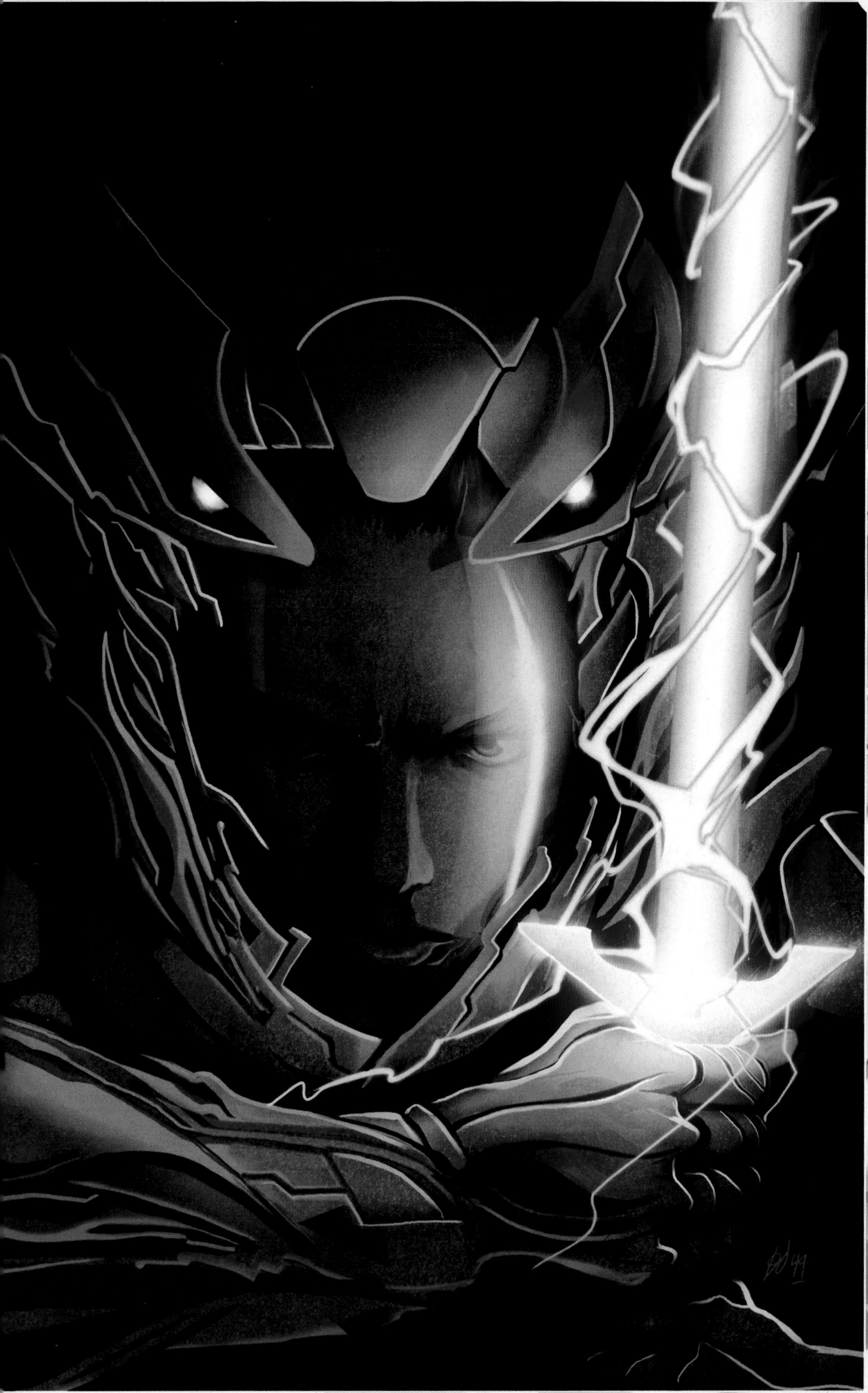

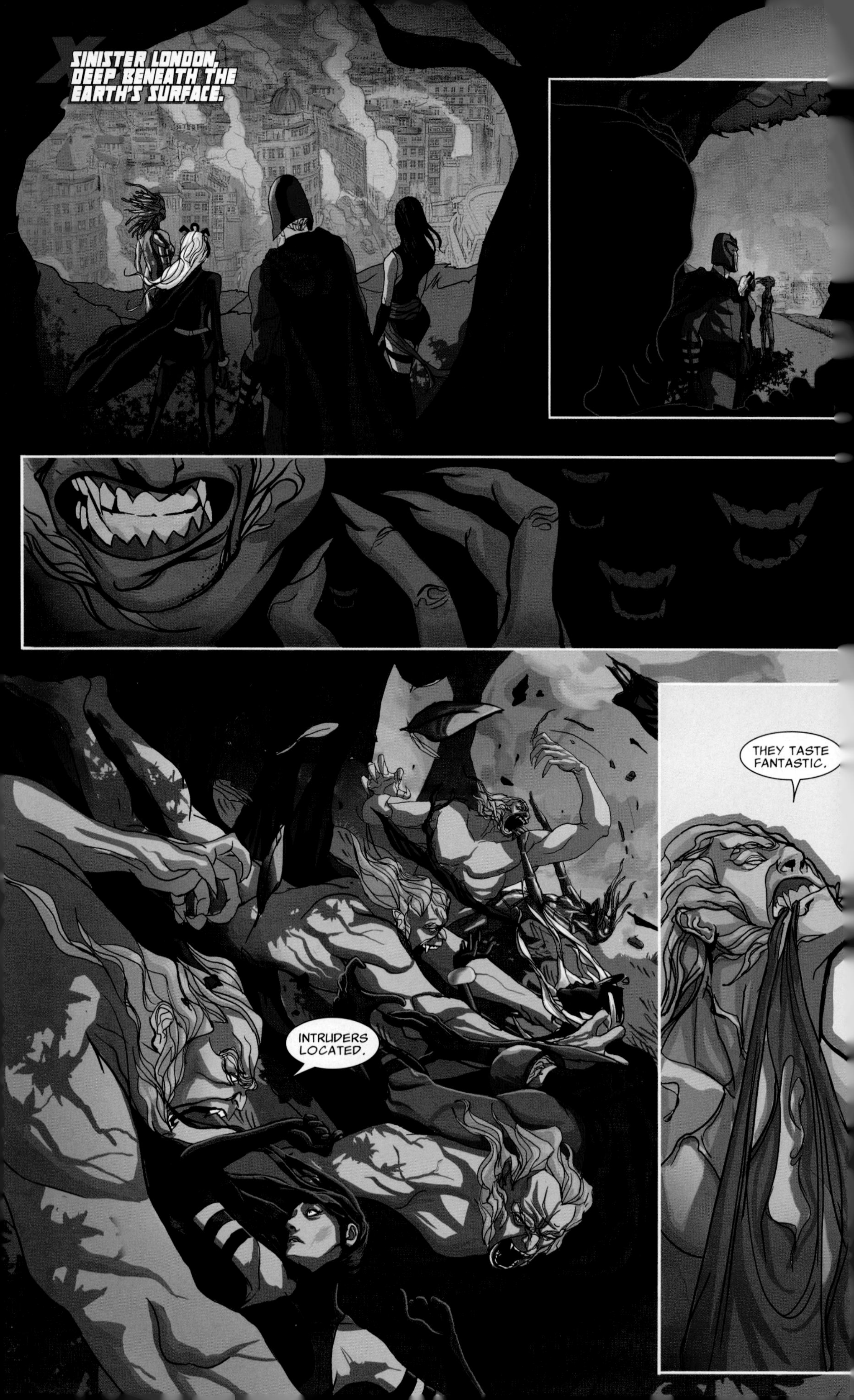
SINISTER LONDON, DEEP BENEATH THE EARTH'S SURFACE.
INTRUDERS LOCATED.
THEY TASTE FANTASTIC.

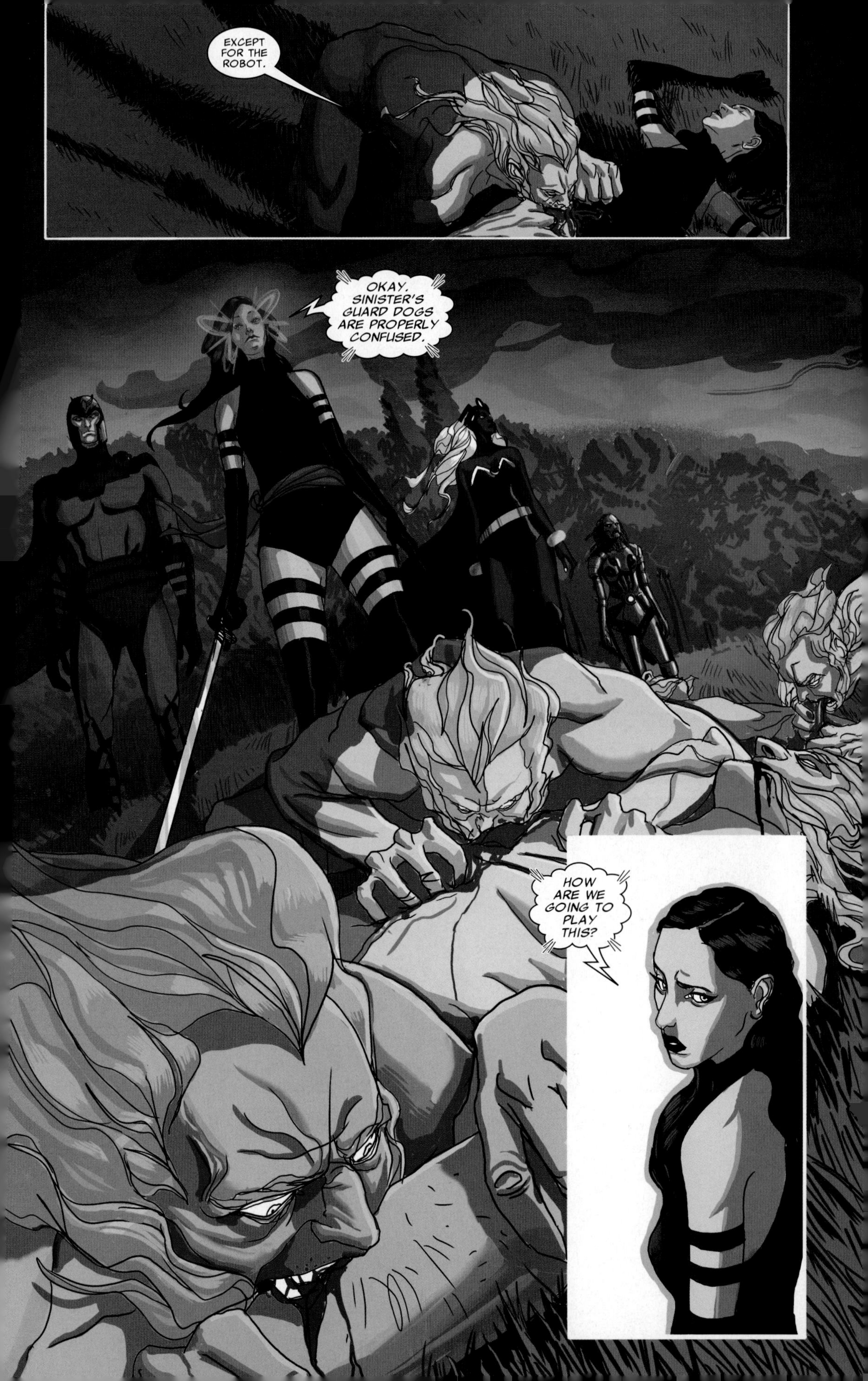
EXCEPT FOR THE ROBOT.
OKAY. SINISTER'S GUARD DOGS ARE PROPERLY CONFUSED.
HOW ARE WE GOING TO PLAY THIS?

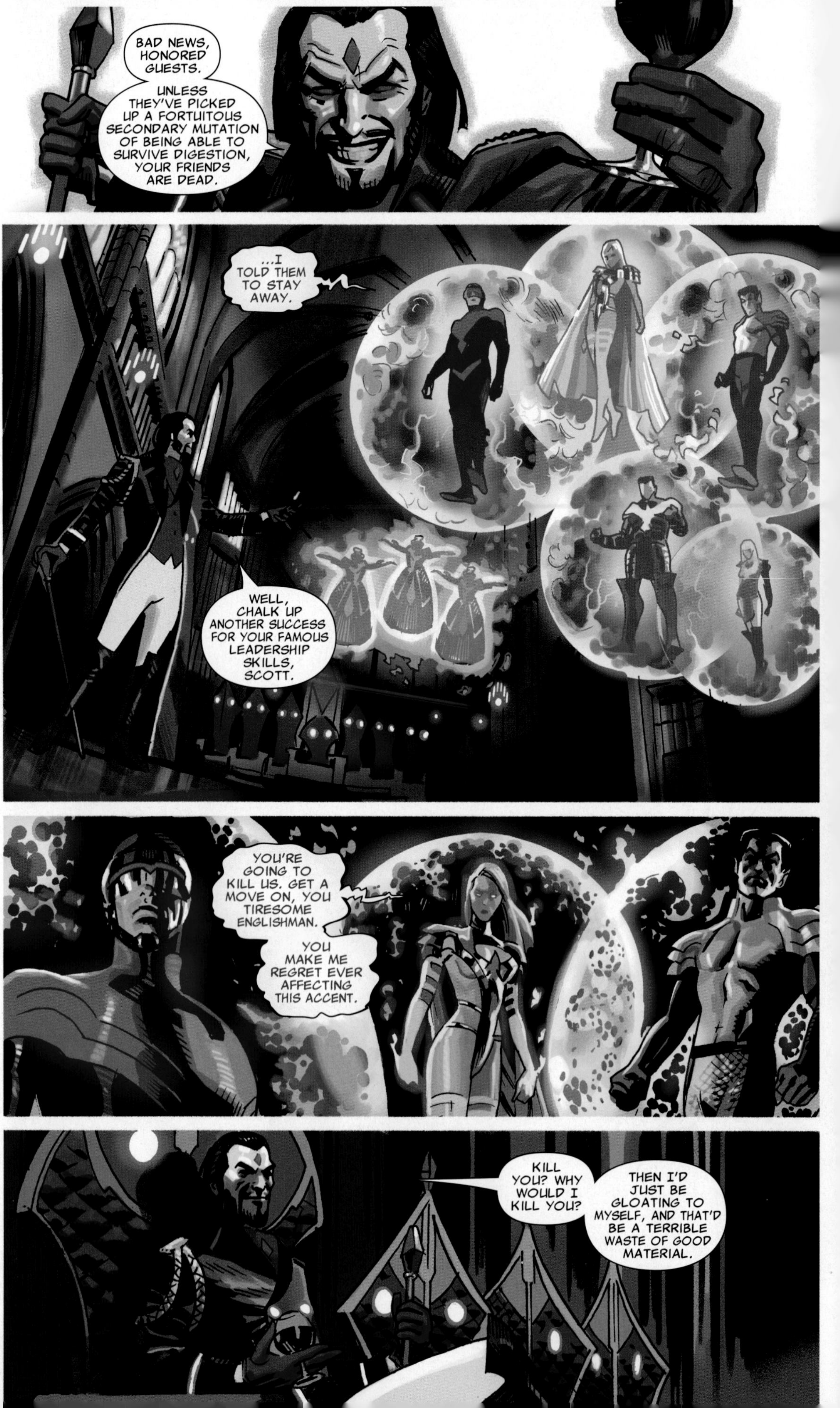
BAD NEWS, HONORED GUESTS.
UNLESS THEY'VE PICKED UP A FORTUITOUS SECONDARY MUTATION OF BEING ABLE TO SURVIVE DIGESTION, YOUR FRIENDS ARE DEAD.
...I TOLD THEM TO STAY AWAY.
WELL, CHALK UP ANOTHER SUCCESS FOR YOUR FAMOUS LEADERSHIP SKILLS, SCOTT.
YOU'RE GOING TO KILL US. GET A MOVE ON, YOU TIRESOME ENGLISHMAN.
YOU MAKE ME REGRET EVER AFFECTING THIS ACCENT.
KILL YOU? WHY WOULD I KILL YOU?
THEN I'D JUST BE GLOATING TO MYSELF, AND THAT'D BE A TERRIBLE WASTE OF GOOD MATERIAL.

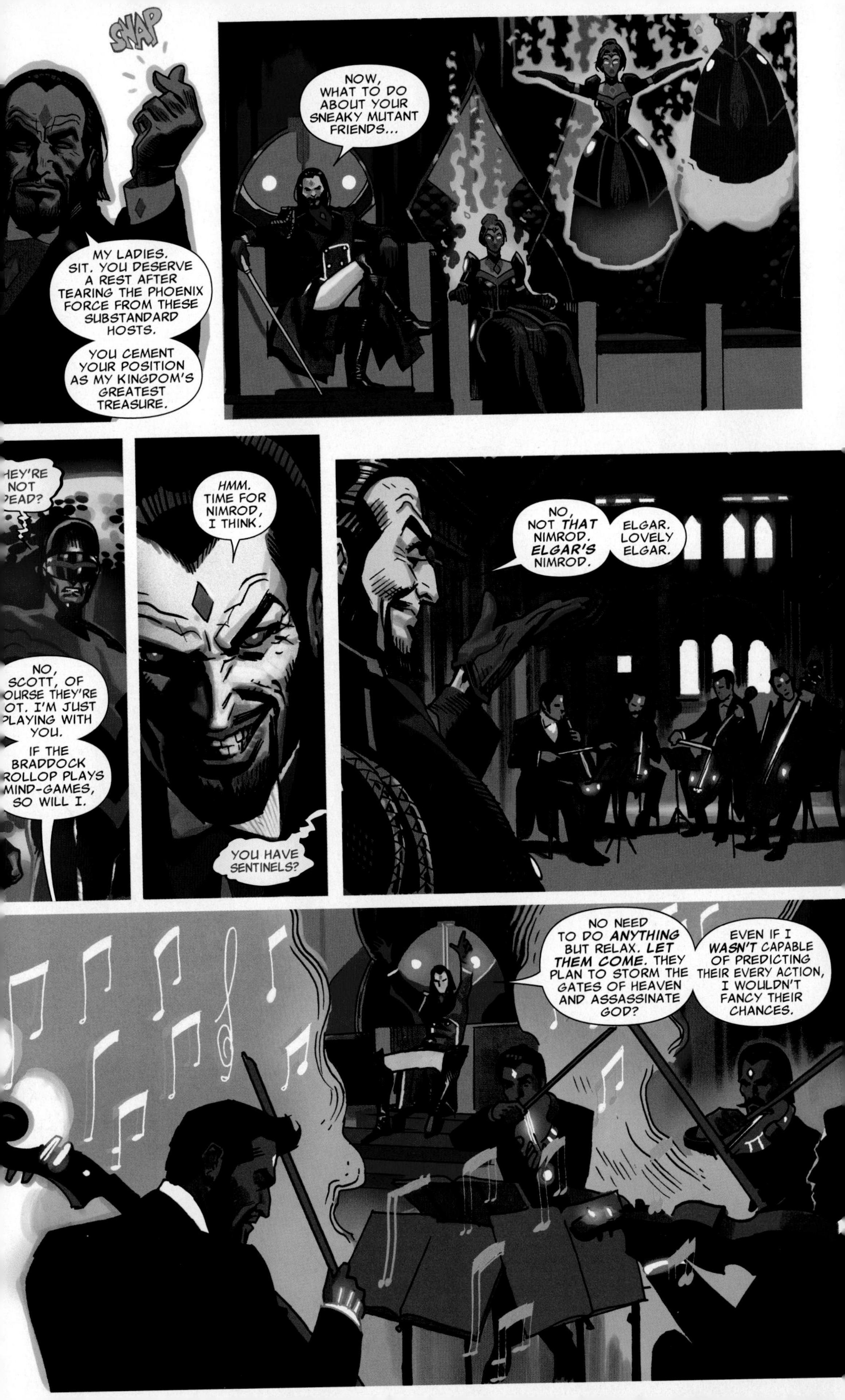
SNAP
MY LADIES. SIT. YOU DESERVE A REST AFTER TEARING THE PHOENIX FORCE FROM THESE SUBSTANDARD HOSTS.
YOU CEMENT YOUR POSITION AS MY KINGDOM'S GREATEST TREASURE.
NOW, WHAT TO DO ABOUT YOUR SNEAKY MUTANT FRIENDS...
HEY'RE NOT DEAD?
NO, SCOTT, OF OURSE THEY'RE OT. I'M JUST PLAYING WITH YOU.
IF THE BRADDOCK ROLLOP PLAYS MIND-GAMES, SO WILL I.
HMM. TIME FOR NIMROD, I THINK.
YOU HAVE SENTINELS?
NO, NOT THAT NIMROD. ELGAR'S NIMROD.
ELGAR. LOVELY ELGAR.
NO NEED TO DO ANYTHING BUT RELAX. LET THEM COME. THEY PLAN TO STORM THE GATES OF HEAVEN AND ASSASSINATE GOD?
EVEN IF I WASN'T CAPABLE OF PREDICTING THEIR EVERY ACTION, I WOULDN'T FANCY THEIR CHANCES.

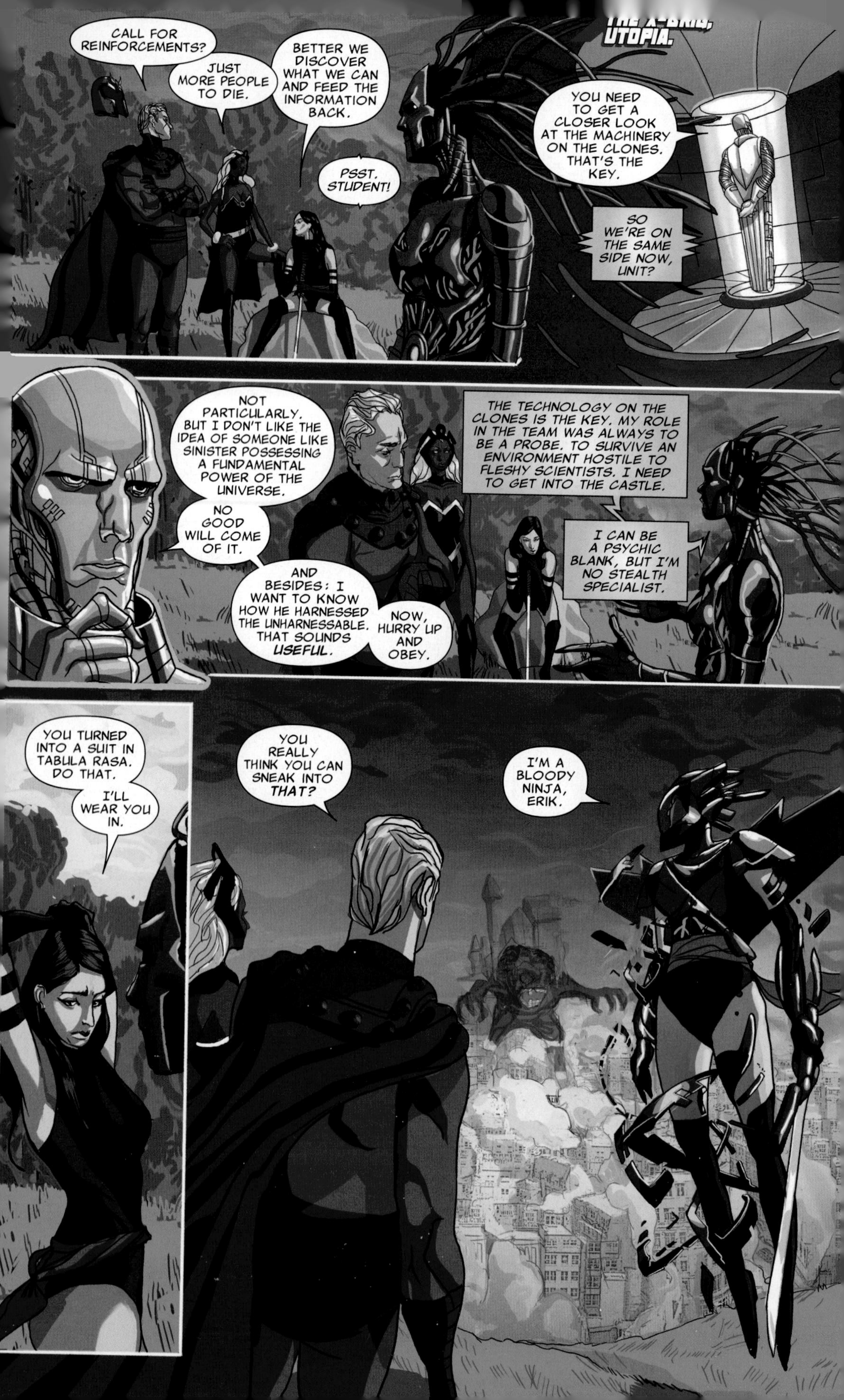
CALL FOR REINFORCEMENTS?
JUST MORE PEOPLE TO DIE.
BETTER WE DISCOVER WHAT WE CAN AND FEED THE INFORMATION BACK.
PSST. STUDENT!
UTOPIA.
YOU NEED TO GET A CLOSER LOOK AT THE MACHINERY ON THE CLONES. THAT'S THE KEY.
SO WE'RE ON THE SAME SIDE NOW, UNIT?
NOT PARTICULARLY. BUT I DON'T LIKE THE IDEA OF SOMEONE LIKE SINISTER POSSESSING A FUNDAMENTAL POWER OF THE UNIVERSE.
NO GOOD WILL COME OF IT.
AND BESIDES: I WANT TO KNOW HOW HE HARNESSED THE UNHARNESSABLE. THAT SOUNDS USEFUL.
NOW, HURRY UP AND OBEY.
THE TECHNOLOGY ON THE CLONES IS THE KEY. MY ROLE IN THE TEAM WAS ALWAYS TO BE A PROBE. TO SURVIVE AN ENVIRONMENT HOSTILE TO FLESHY SCIENTISTS. I NEED TO GET INTO THE CASTLE.
I CAN BE A PSYCHIC BLANK, BUT I'M NO STEALTH SPECIALIST.
YOU TURNED INTO A SUIT IN TABULA RASA. DO THAT.
I'LL WEAR YOU IN.
YOU REALLY THINK YOU CAN SNEAK INTO THAT?
I'M A BLOODY NINJA, ERIK.

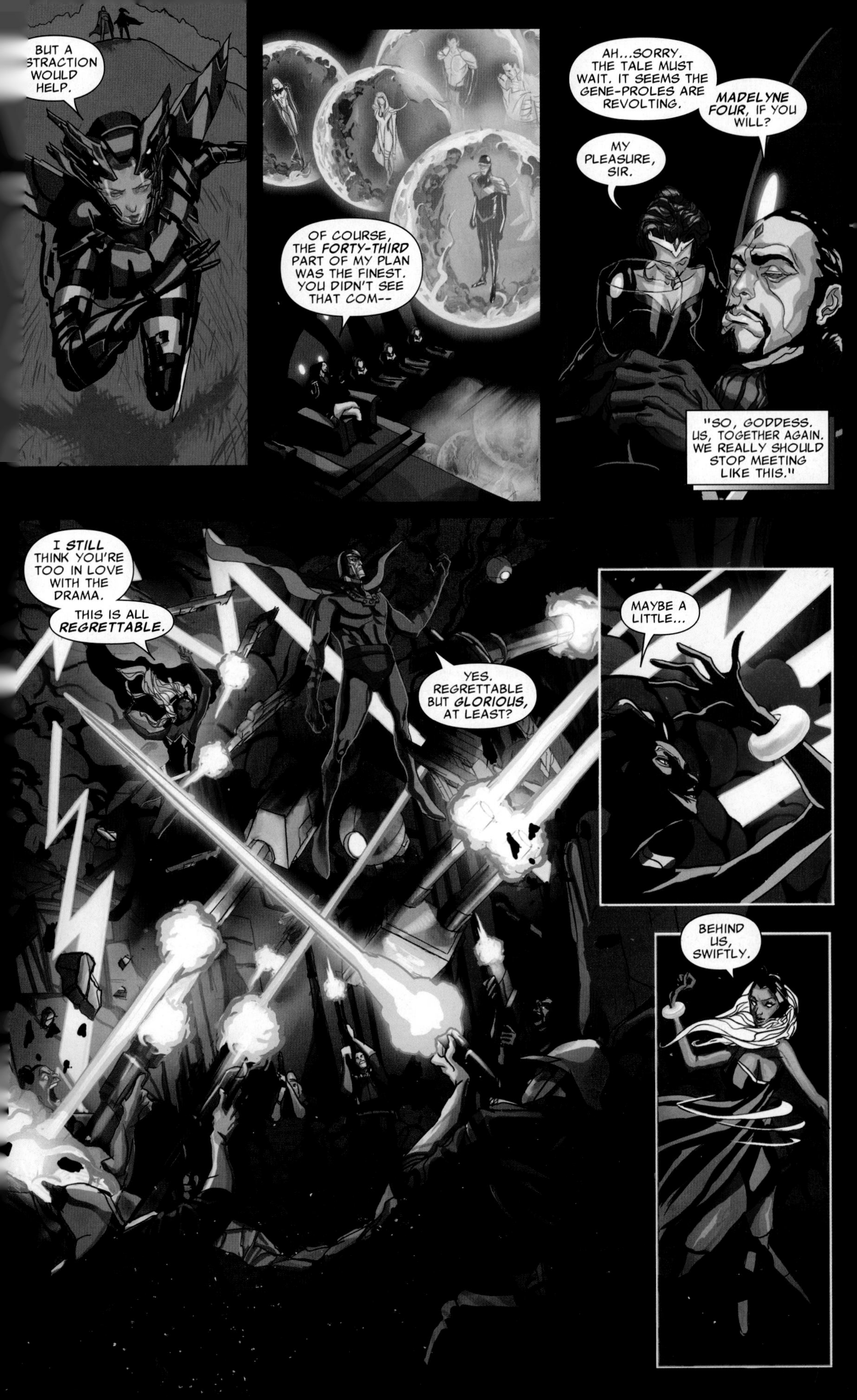
BUT A
STRACTION
WOULD
HELP.
OF COURSE, THE FORTY-THIRD PART OF MY PLAN WAS THE FINEST. YOU DIDN'T SEE THAT COM--
AH...SORRY. THE TALE MUST WAIT. IT SEEMS THE GENE-PROLES ARE REVOLTING.
MADELYNE FOUR, IF YOU WILL?
MY PLEASURE, SIR.
"SO, GODDESS. US, TOGETHER AGAIN. WE REALLY SHOULD STOP MEETING LIKE THIS."
I STILL THINK YOU'RE TOO IN LOVE WITH THE DRAMA.
THIS IS ALL REGRETTABLE.
YES. REGRETTABLE BUT GLORIOUS, AT LEAST?
MAYBE A LITTLE...
BEHIND US, SWIFTLY.

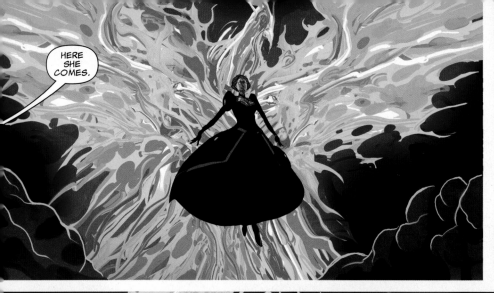

HERE SHE COMES.

GODDESS GIVE M STRENGT

KRAKA-THOOM

HOW TROUBLE-SOME!

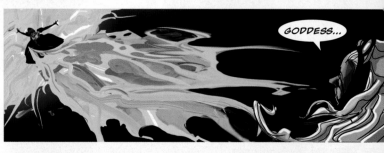

GODDESS...

...SAVE ME.

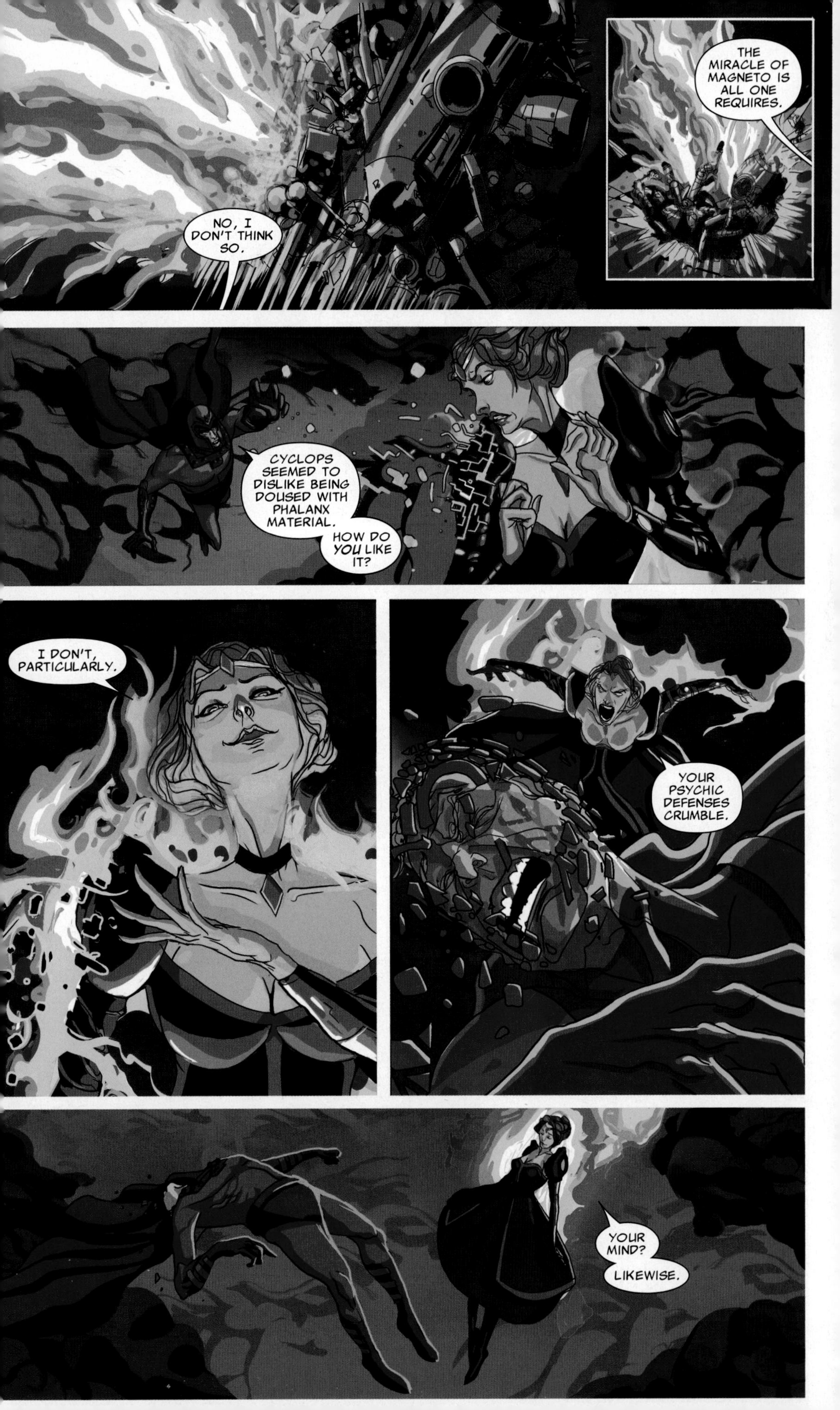

THE MIRACLE OF MAGNETO IS ALL ONE REQUIRES.
NO, I DON'T THINK SO.
CYCLOPS SEEMED TO DISLIKE BEING DOUSED WITH PHALANX MATERIAL.
HOW DO YOU LIKE IT?
I DON'T, PARTICULARLY.
YOUR PSYCHIC DEFENSES CRUMBLE.
YOUR MIND?
LIKEWISE.

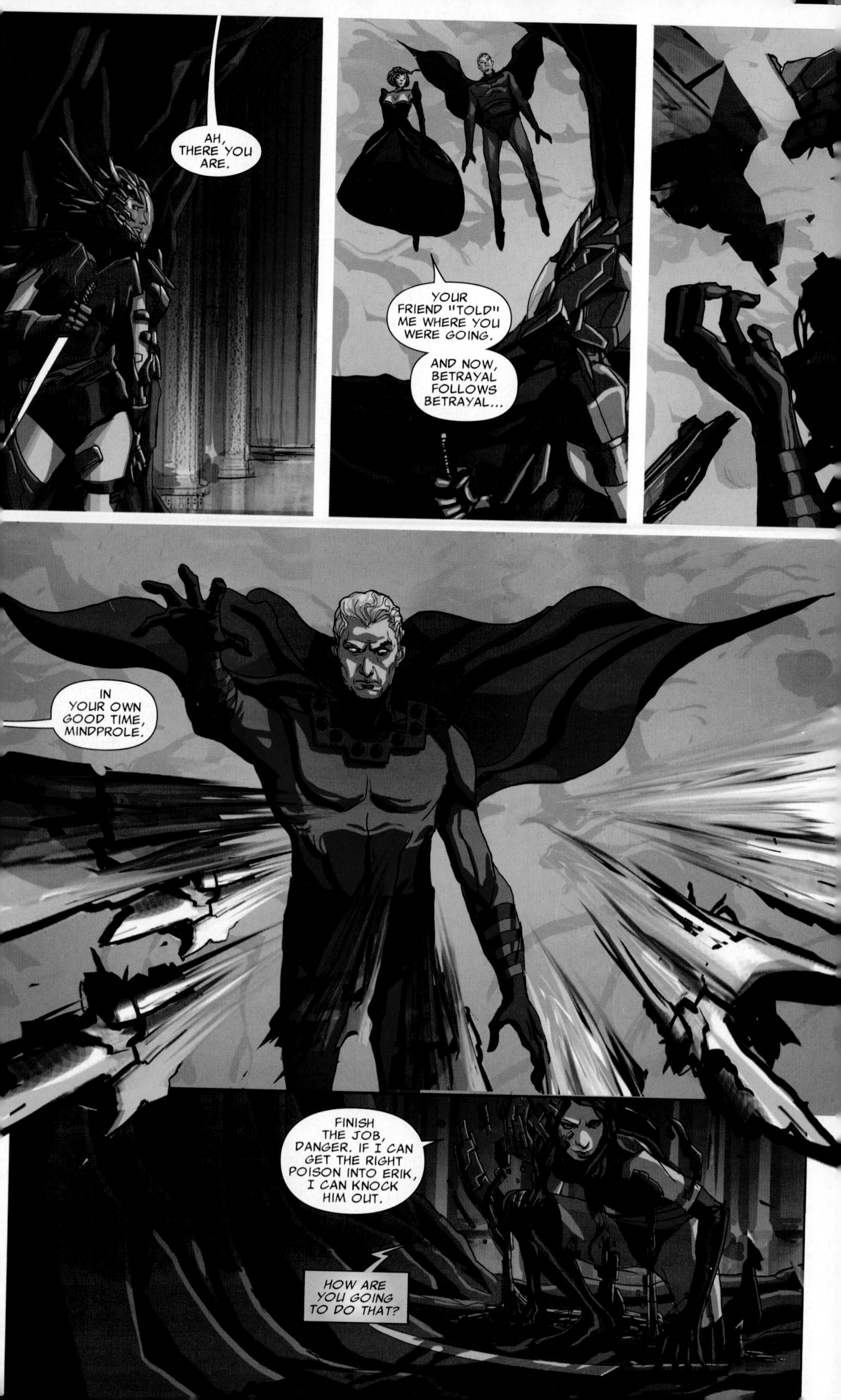
AH, THERE YOU ARE.
YOUR FRIEND "TOLD" ME WHERE YOU WERE GOING.
AND NOW, BETRAYAL FOLLOWS BETRAYAL...
IN YOUR OWN GOOD TIME, MINDPROLE.
FINISH THE JOB, DANGER. IF I CAN GET THE RIGHT POISON INTO ERIK, I CAN KNOCK HIM OUT.
HOW ARE YOU GOING TO DO THAT?

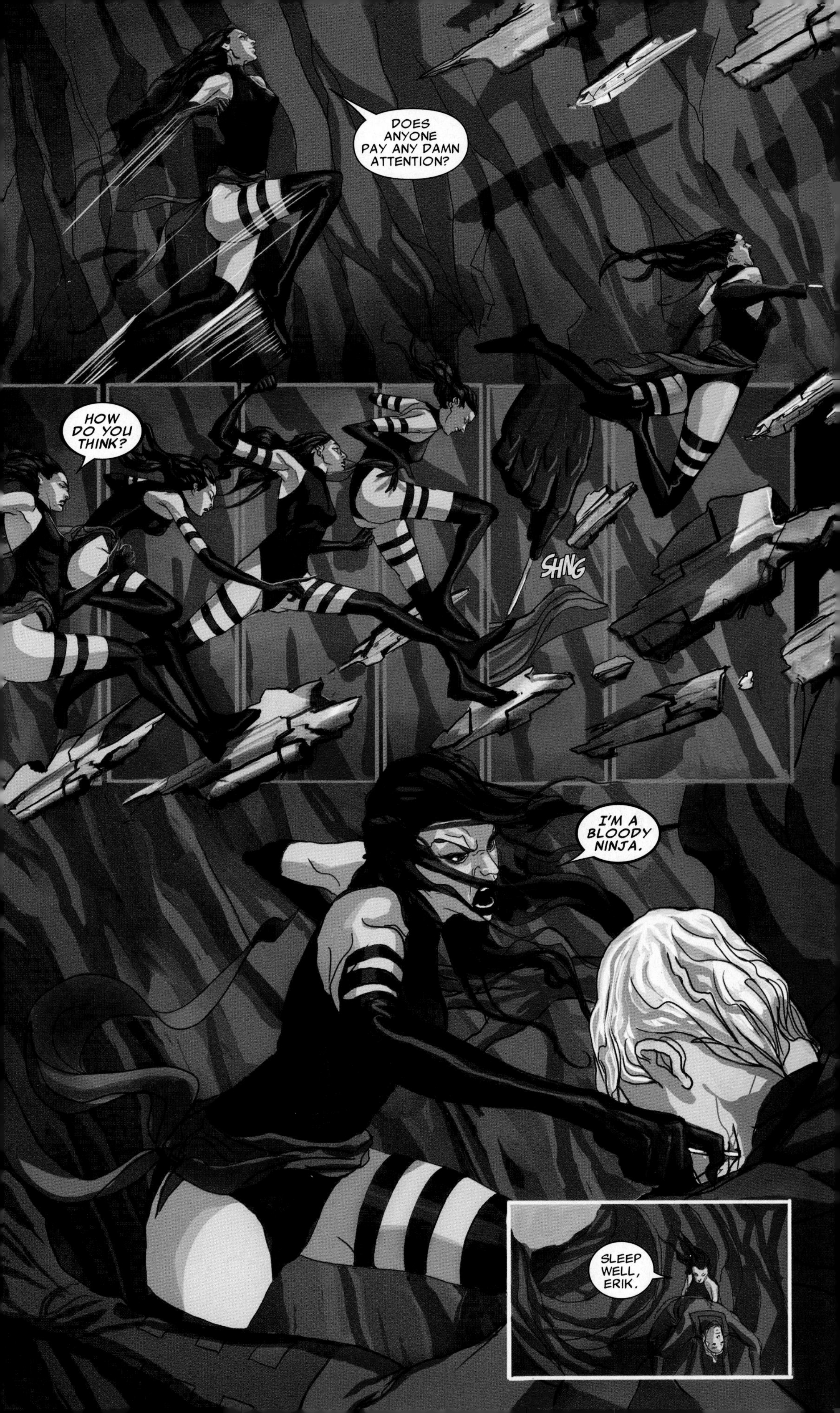
DOES ANYONE PAY ANY DAMN ATTENTION?
HOW DO YOU THINK?
SHNG
I'M A BLOODY NINJA.
SLEEP WELL, ERIK.

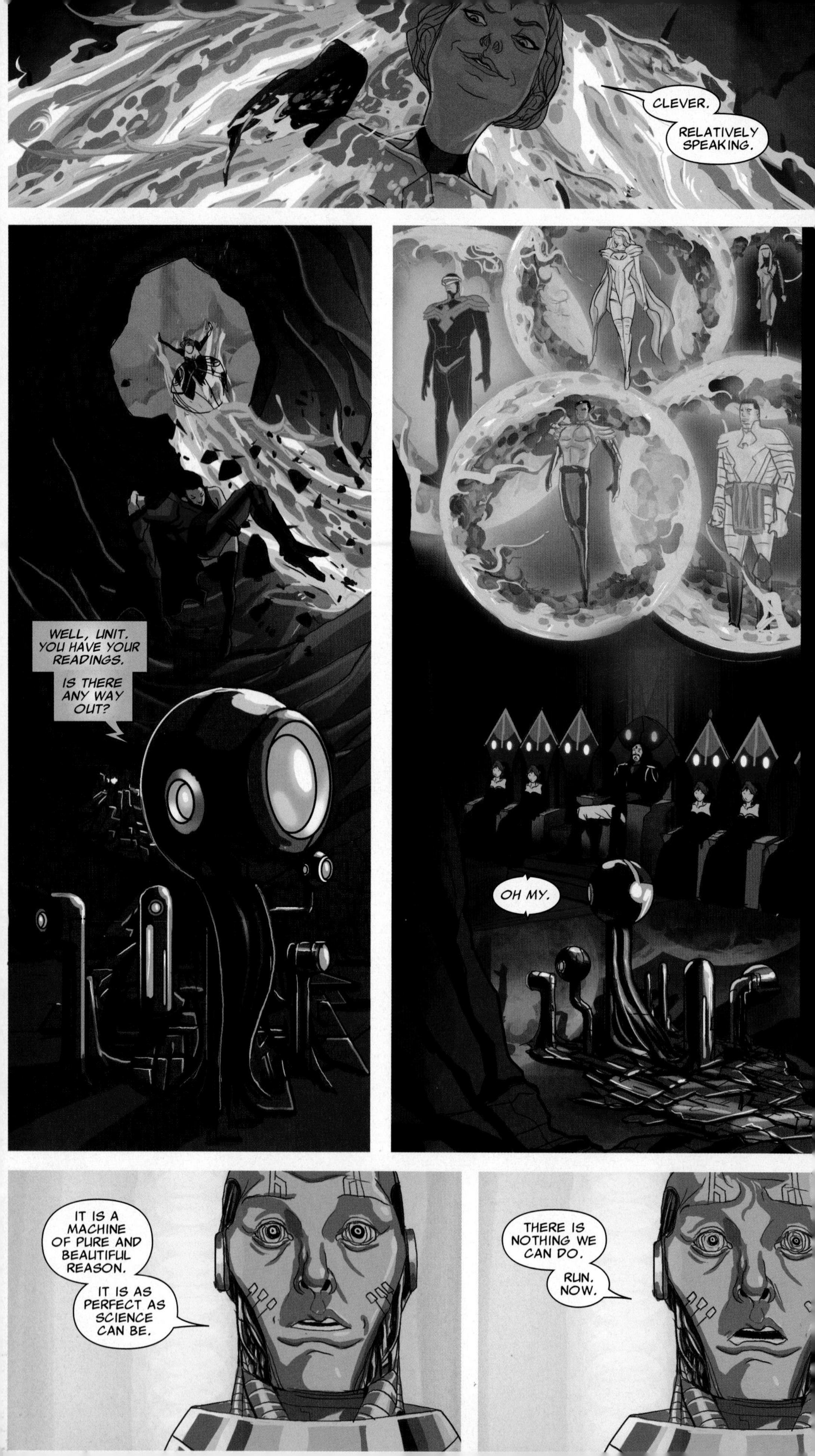
CLEVER.
RELATIVELY SPEAKING.
WELL, UNIT. YOU HAVE YOUR READINGS.
IS THERE ANY WAY OUT?
OH MY.
IT IS A MACHINE OF PURE AND BEAUTIFUL REASON.
IT IS AS PERFECT AS SCIENCE CAN BE.
THERE IS NOTHING WE CAN DO.
RUN. NOW.

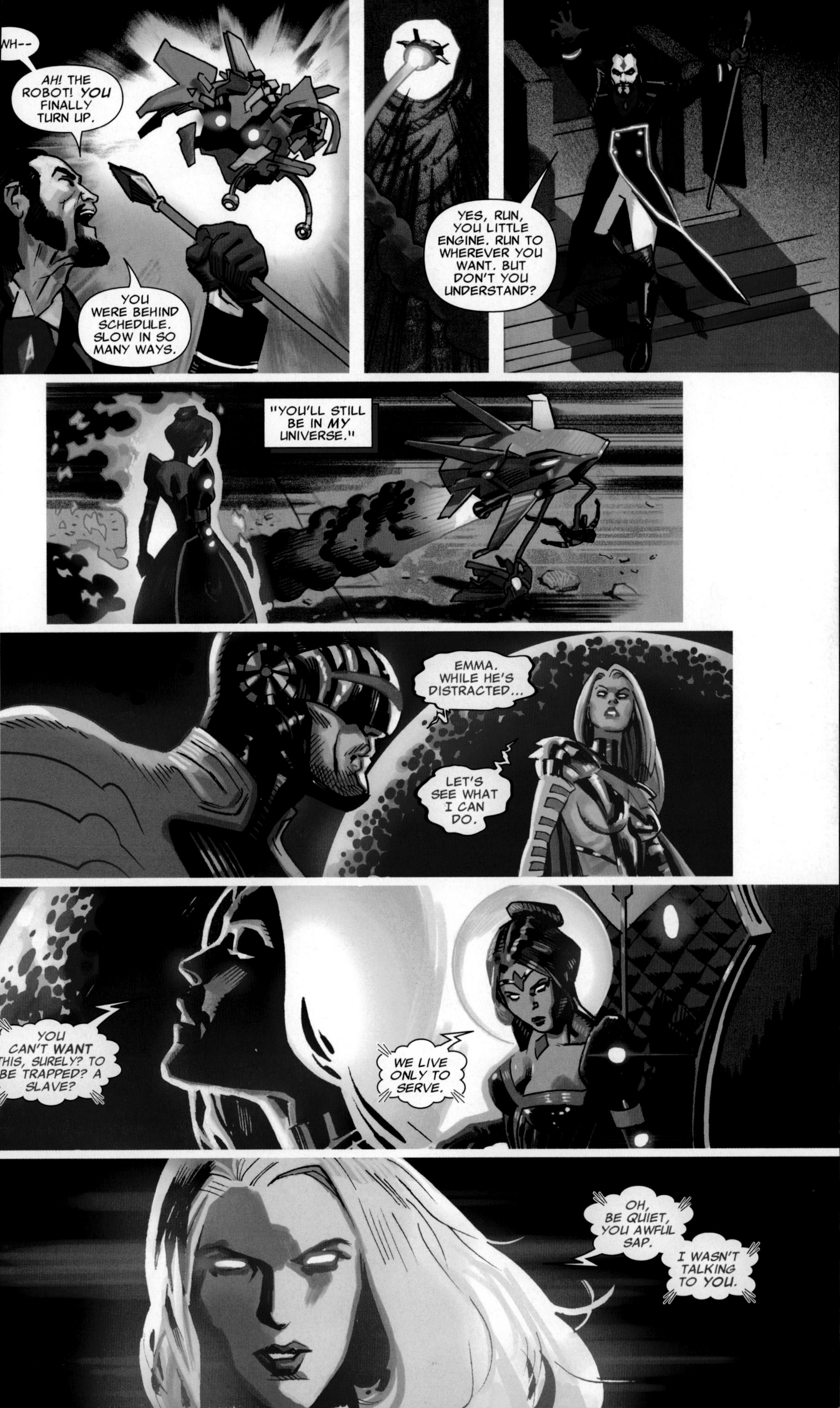
WH--
AH! THE ROBOT! YOU FINALLY TURN UP.
YOU WERE BEHIND SCHEDULE. SLOW IN SO MANY WAYS.
YES, RUN, YOU LITTLE ENGINE. RUN TO WHEREVER YOU WANT. BUT DON'T YOU UNDERSTAND?
"YOU'LL STILL BE IN MY UNIVERSE."
EMMA. WHILE HE'S DISTRACTED...
LET'S SEE WHAT I CAN DO.
YOU CAN'T WANT THIS, SURELY? TO BE TRAPPED? A SLAVE?
WE LIVE ONLY TO SERVE.
OH, BE QUIET, YOU AWFUL SAP.
I WASN'T TALKING TO YOU.

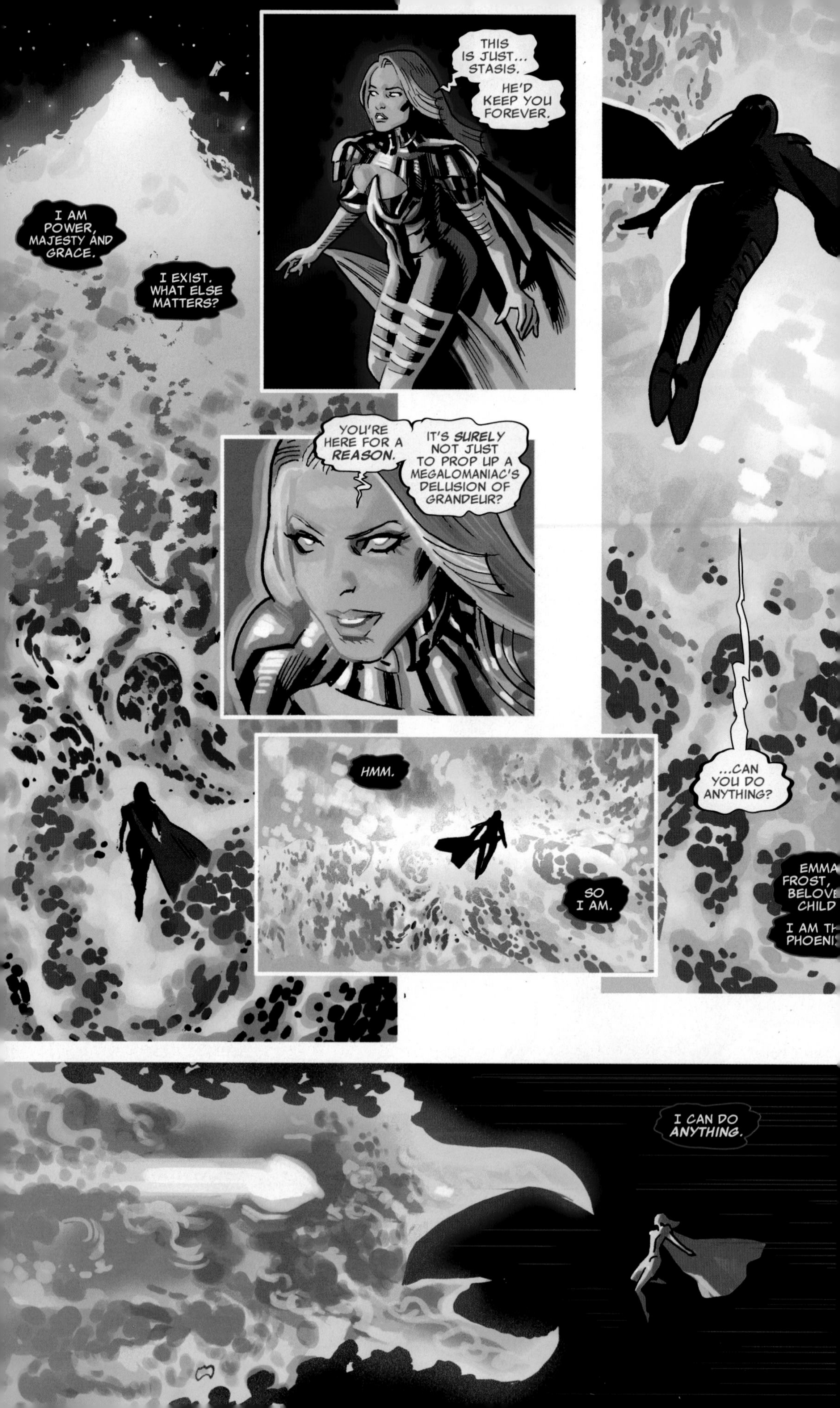
I AM POWER, MAJESTY AND GRACE.
I EXIST. WHAT ELSE MATTERS?
THIS IS JUST... STASIS.
HE'D KEEP YOU FOREVER.
YOU'RE HERE FOR A REASON.
IT'S SURELY NOT JUST TO PROP UP A MEGALOMANIAC'S DELUSION OF GRANDEUR?
HMM.
SO I AM.
...CAN YOU DO ANYTHING?
I CAN DO ANYTHING.

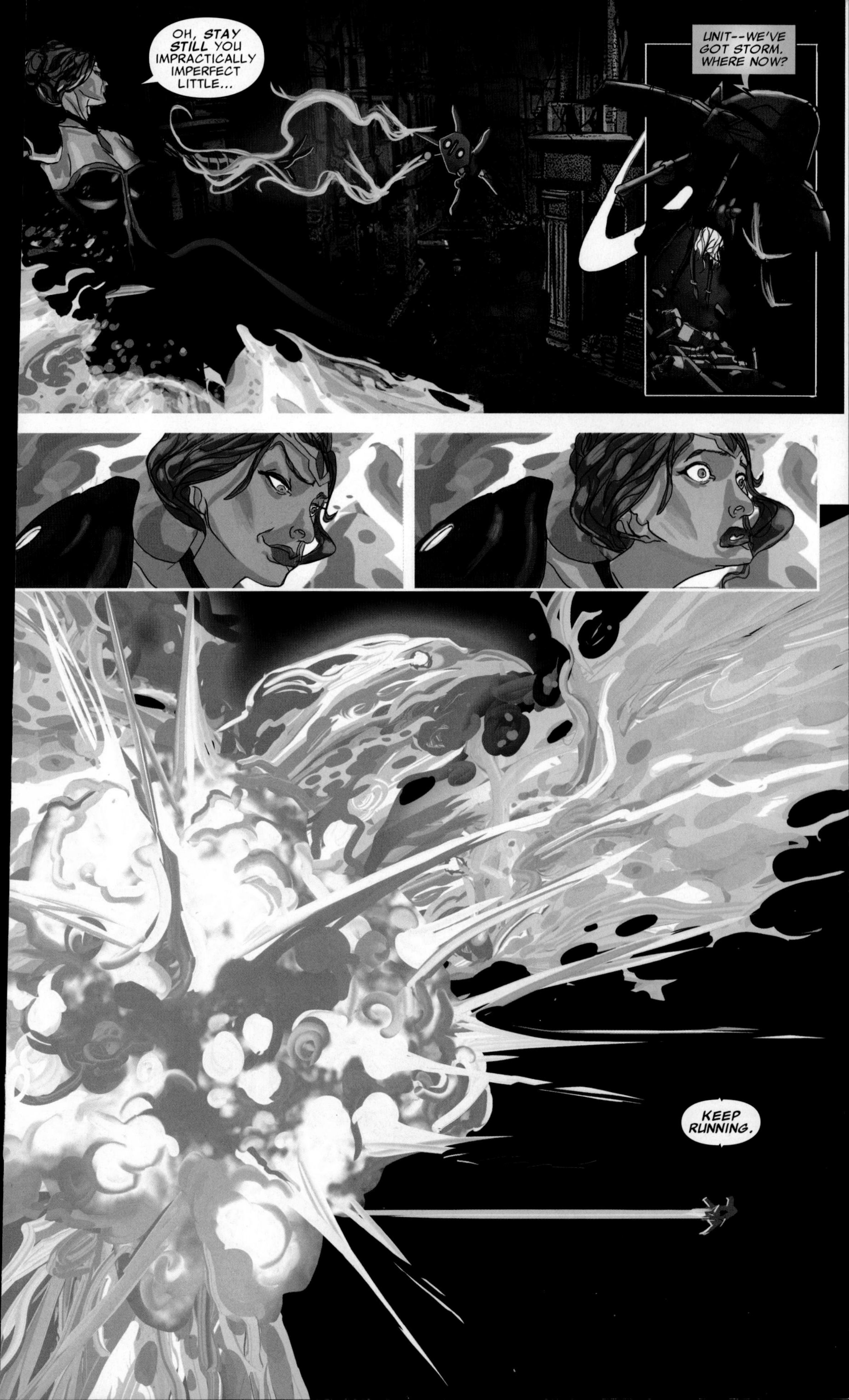
OH, STAY STILL YOU IMPRACTICALLY IMPERFECT LITTLE...
UNIT--WE'VE GOT STORM. WHERE NOW?
KEEP RUNNING.

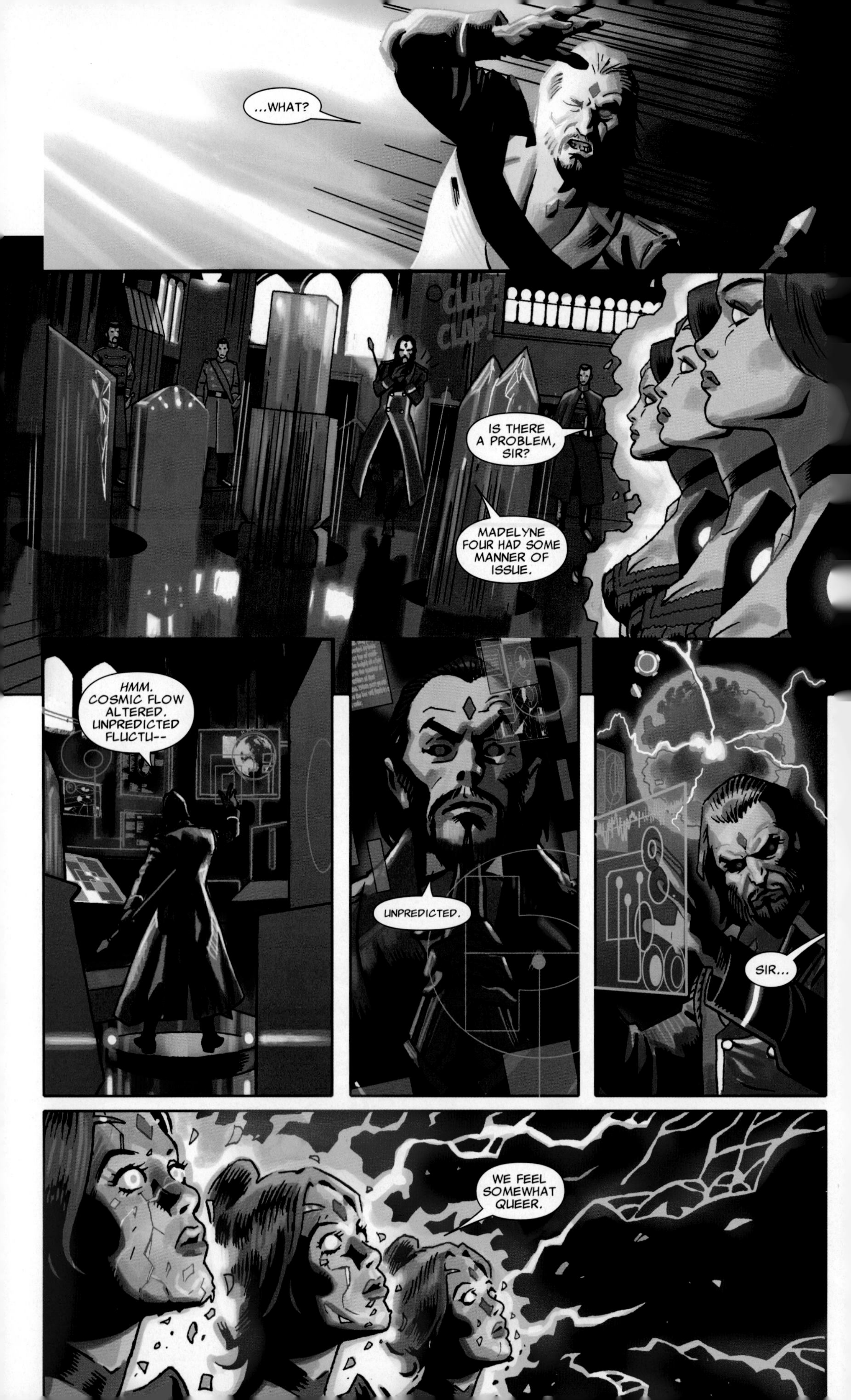
...WHAT?
CLAP! CLAP!
IS THERE A PROBLEM, SIR?
MADELYNE FOUR HAD SOME MANNER OF ISSUE.
HMM. COSMIC FLOW ALTERED. UNPREDICTED FLUCTU--
UNPREDICTED.
SIR...
WE FEEL SOMEWHAT QUEER.

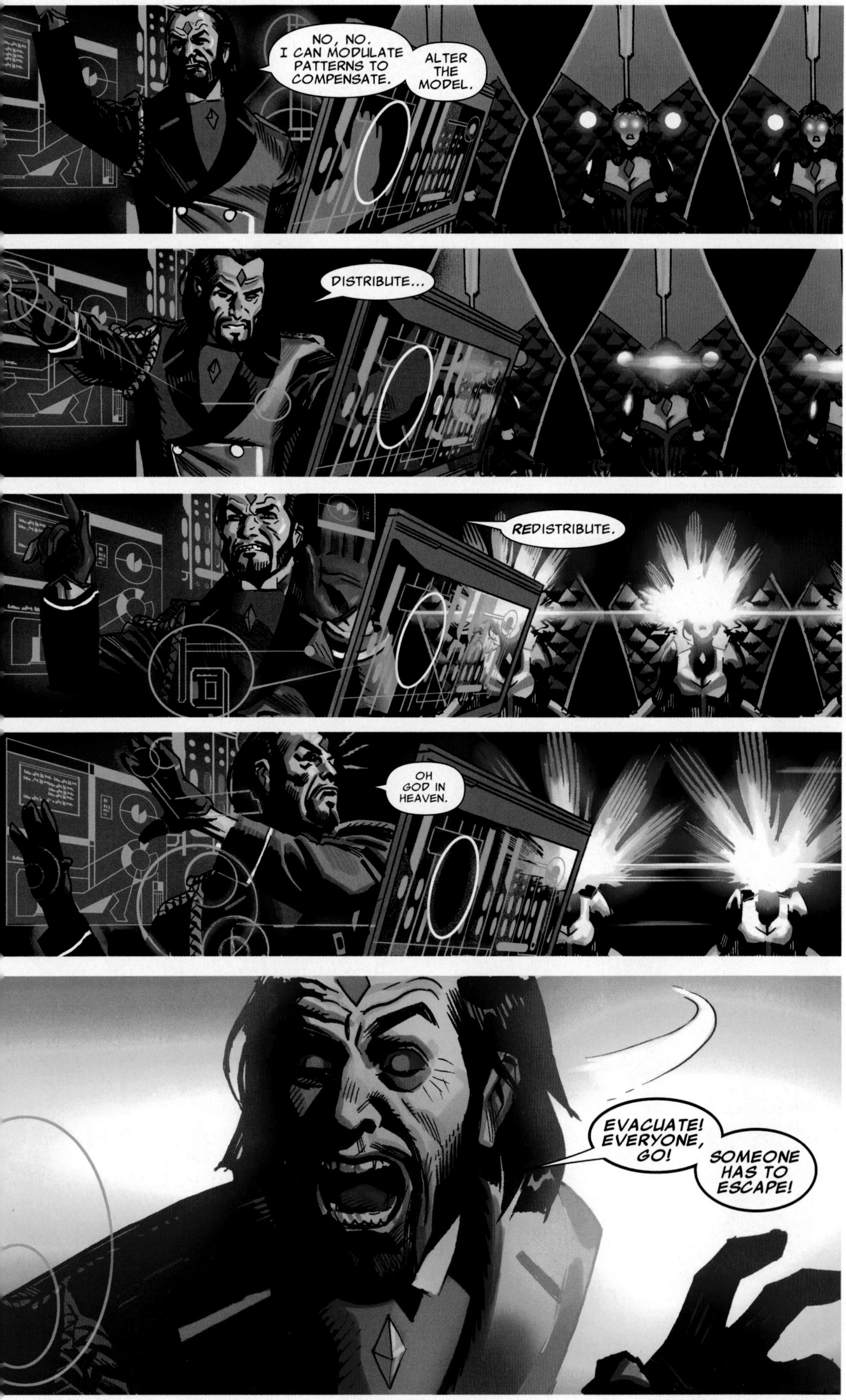
NO, NO. I CAN MODULATE PATTERNS TO COMPENSATE.
ALTER THE MODEL.
DISTRIBUTE...
REDISTRIBUTE.
OH GOD IN HEAVEN.
EVACUATE! EVERYONE, GO!
SOMEONE HAS TO ESCAPE!

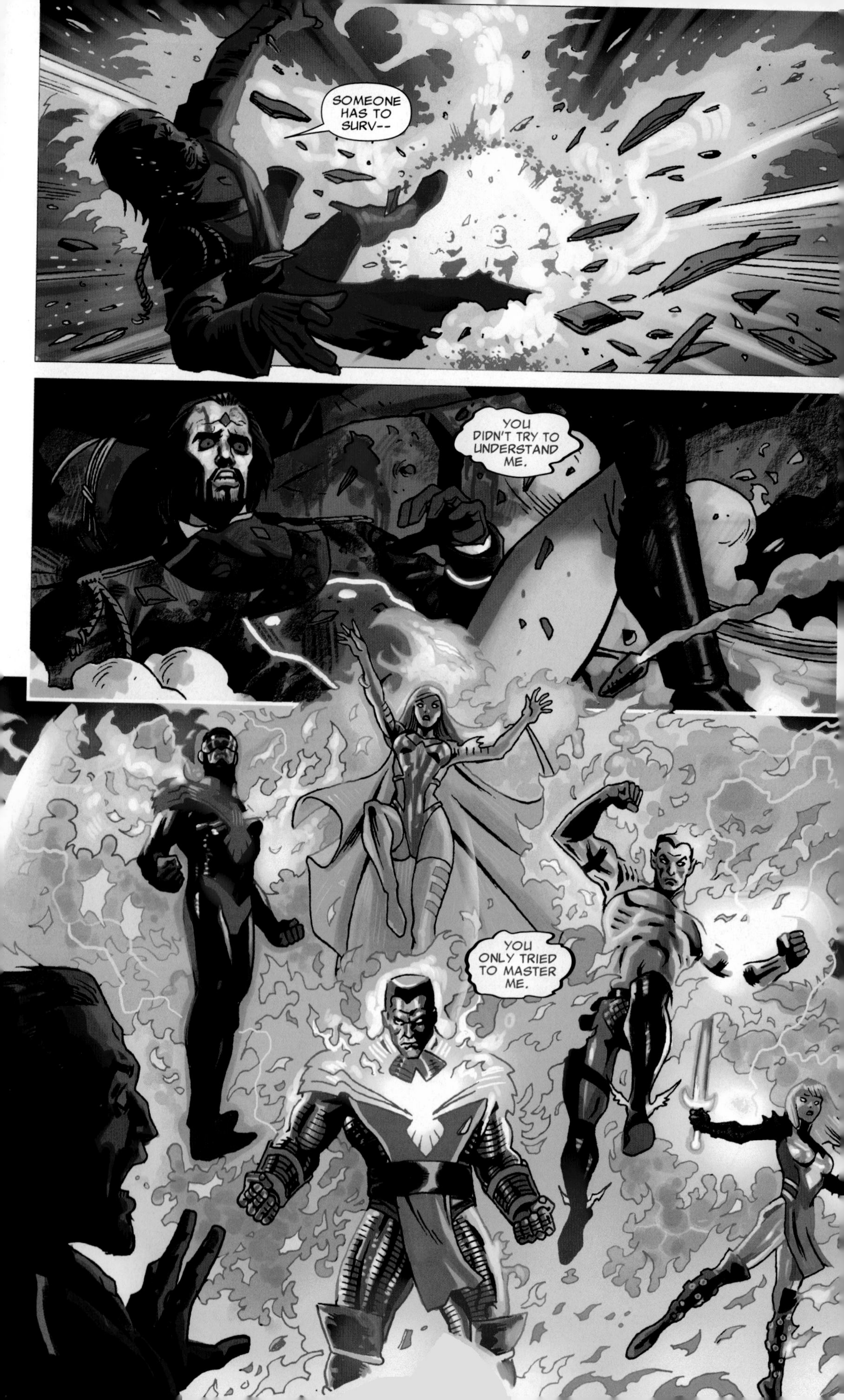
SOMEONE HAS TO SURV--
YOU DIDN'T TRY TO UNDERSTAND ME.
YOU ONLY TRIED TO MASTER ME.

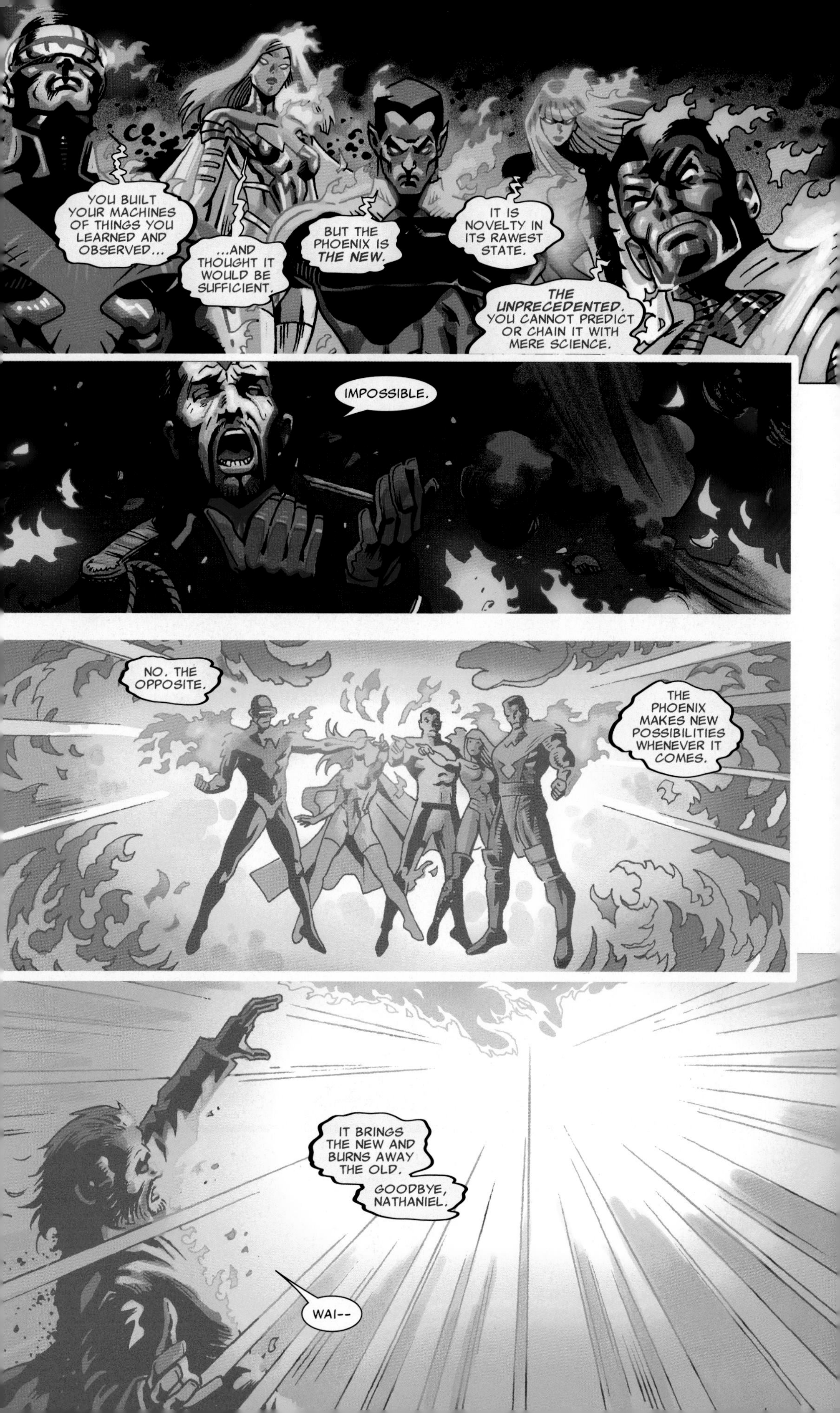
YOU BUILT YOUR MACHINES OF THINGS YOU LEARNED AND OBSERVED...
...AND THOUGHT IT WOULD BE SUFFICIENT.
BUT THE PHOENIX IS THE NEW.
IT IS NOVELTY IN ITS RAWEST STATE.
THE UNPRECEDENTED. YOU CANNOT PREDICT OR CHAIN IT WITH MERE SCIENCE.
IMPOSSIBLE.
NO. THE OPPOSITE.
THE PHOENIX MAKES NEW POSSIBILITIES WHENEVER IT COMES.
IT BRINGS THE NEW AND BURNS AWAY THE OLD.
GOODBYE, NATHANIEL.
WAI--

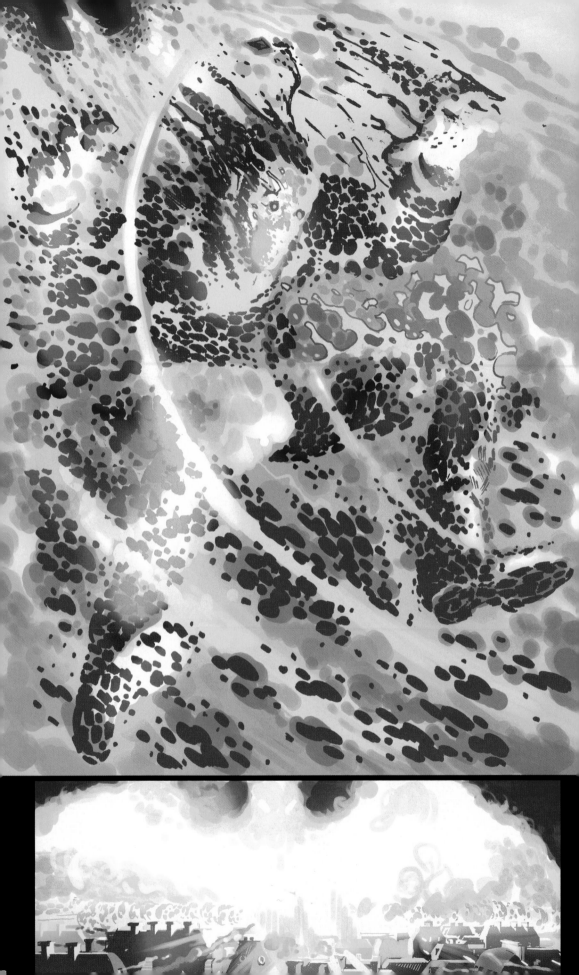

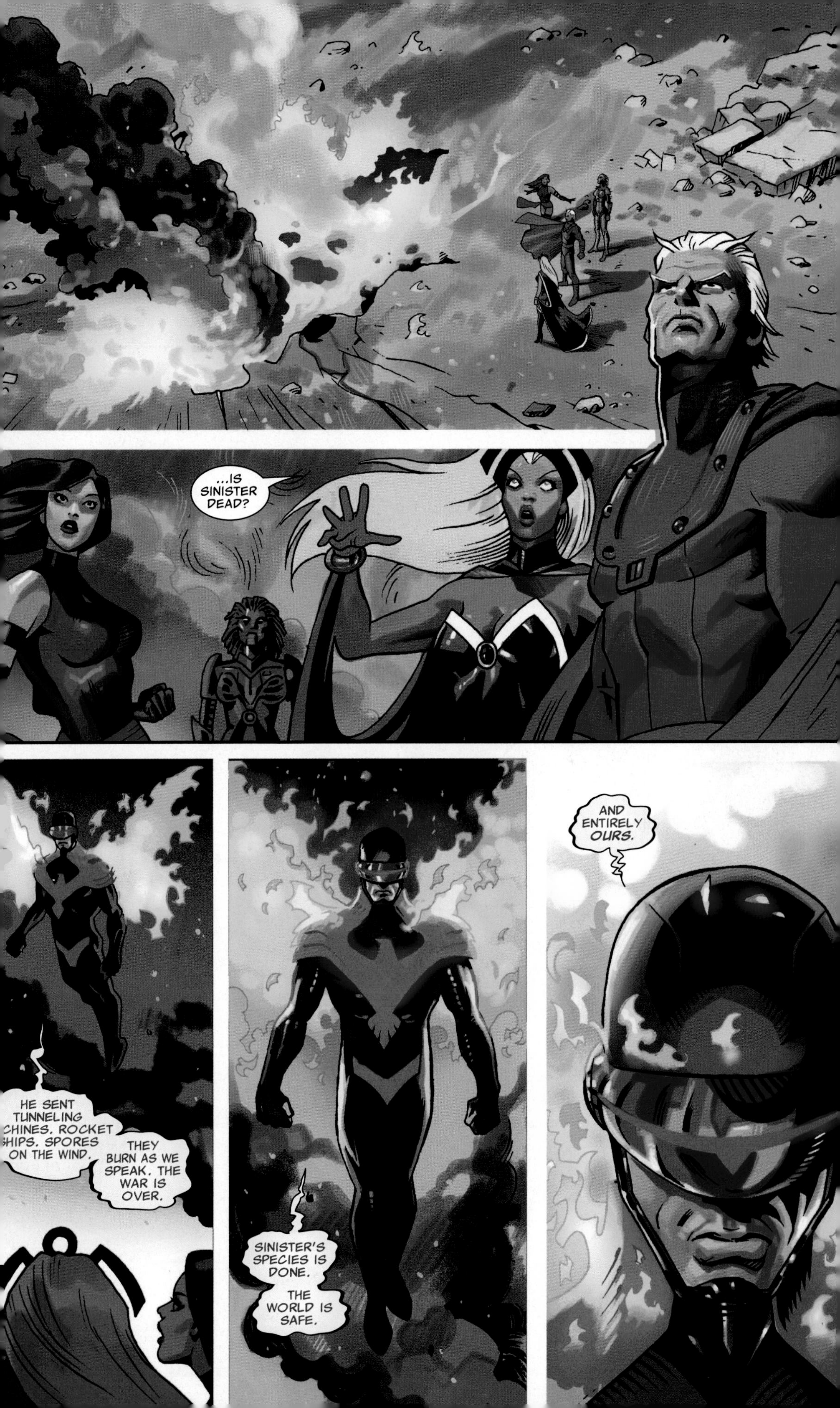
...IS SINISTER DEAD?
HE SENT TUNNELING CHINES. ROCKET SHIPS. SPORES ON THE WIND.
THEY BURN AS WE SPEAK. THE WAR IS OVER.
SINISTER'S SPECIES IS DONE.
THE WORLD IS SAFE.
AND ENTIRELY OURS.

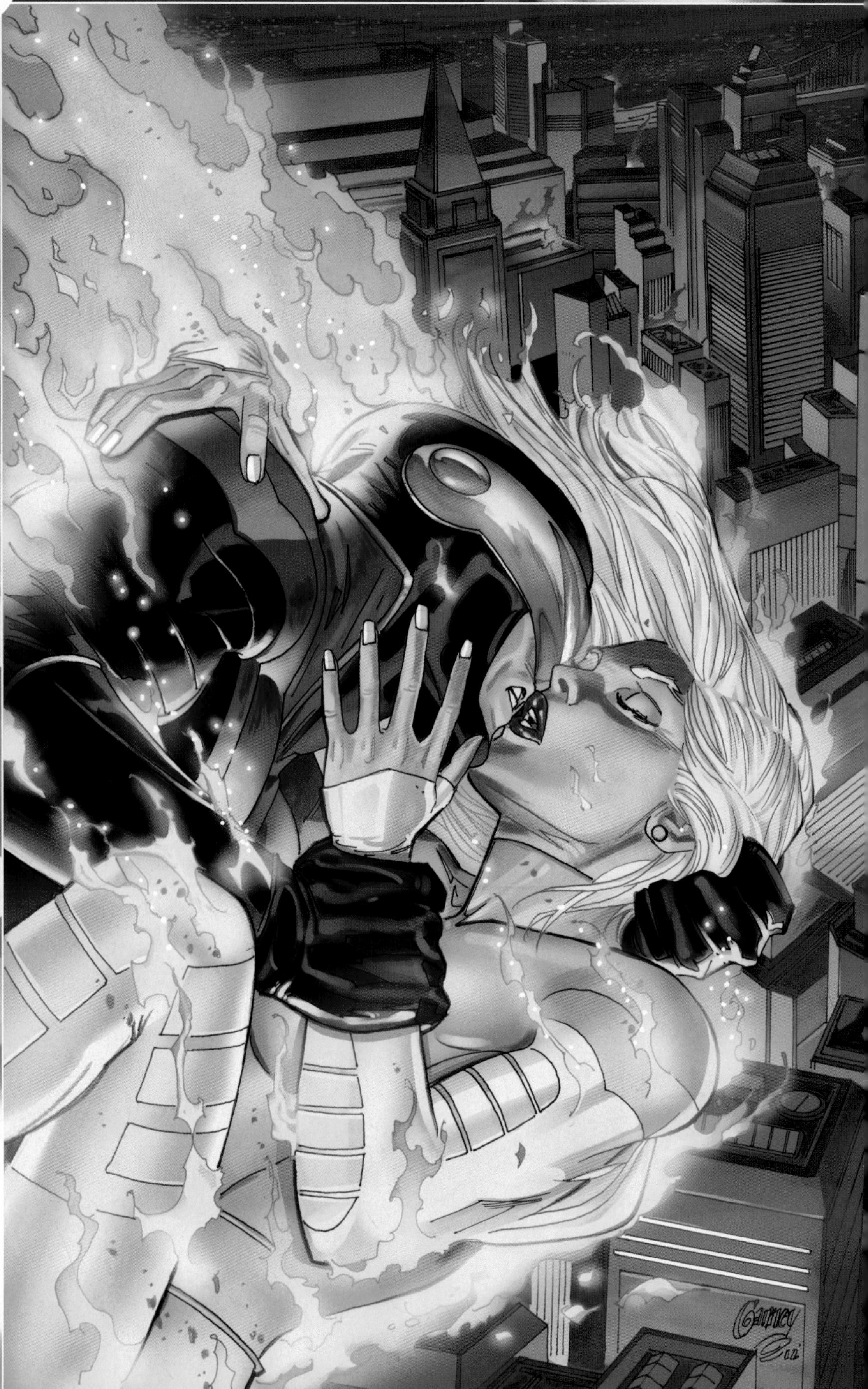

rn with powers and
ilities beyond those of
rmal humans, mutantkind
s long been hated and
ared by those they sought
protect. Now, from their
and nation of Utopia, Cyclops
ads the most powerful group
mutants ever assembled
protect what is left of
s dwindling species.
ated and feared? When
u are as powerful as
e Uncanny X-Men,
es it matter?

UNCANNY X-MEN

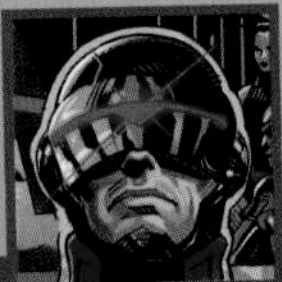

CYCLOPS
ye-blasting leader

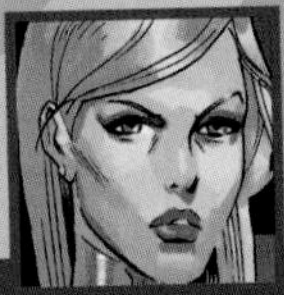

EMMA FROST
telepath with diamond form

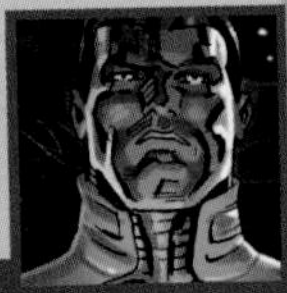

COLOSSUS
steel-skinned juggernaut

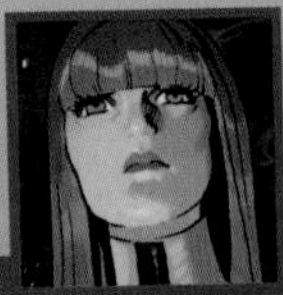

MAGIK
magic-using teleporter

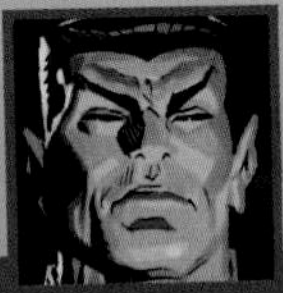

NAMOR
king of Atlantis

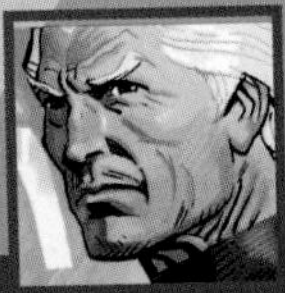

MAGNETO
master of magnetism

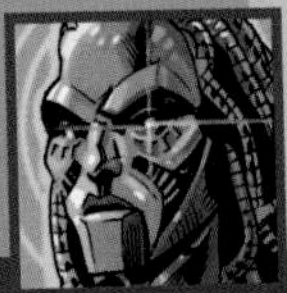

DANGER
light-shaping AI

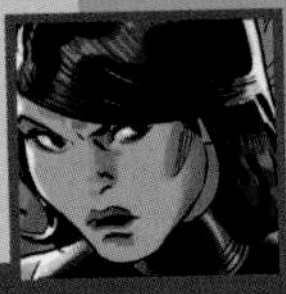

PSYLOCKE
telepathic ninja

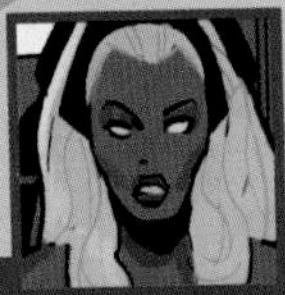

STORM
weather witch

PREVIOUSLY

hen the Phoenix Force returned to Earth it split into five parts, spreading its power to yclops, Emma Frost, Namor, Colossus, and Magik, now coined the Phoenix Five. Even with the tention to use their abilities for the good of mankind their opponents suspect the consuming ower of the Phoenix Force may corrupt them. The Five oppose anyone who stands in their ay, and subsequently set the Avengers on the run, hunting them down like prey.

amor launched an all-out assault on the Avengers' hideout in Wakanda but was ultimately efeated by the Avengers. In his defeat, the Phoenix fled Namor, dividing its power among the emaining Phoenix Five, increasing their power. Not long after, Magik and Colossus also lost eir portions of the Phoenix Force when a brutal clash with Spider-Man tricked the siblings to taking each other out while attempting to steal the power from one another. The only emaining possessors of the Phoenix Force are Cyclops and Emma Frost, who may be beyond edemption...

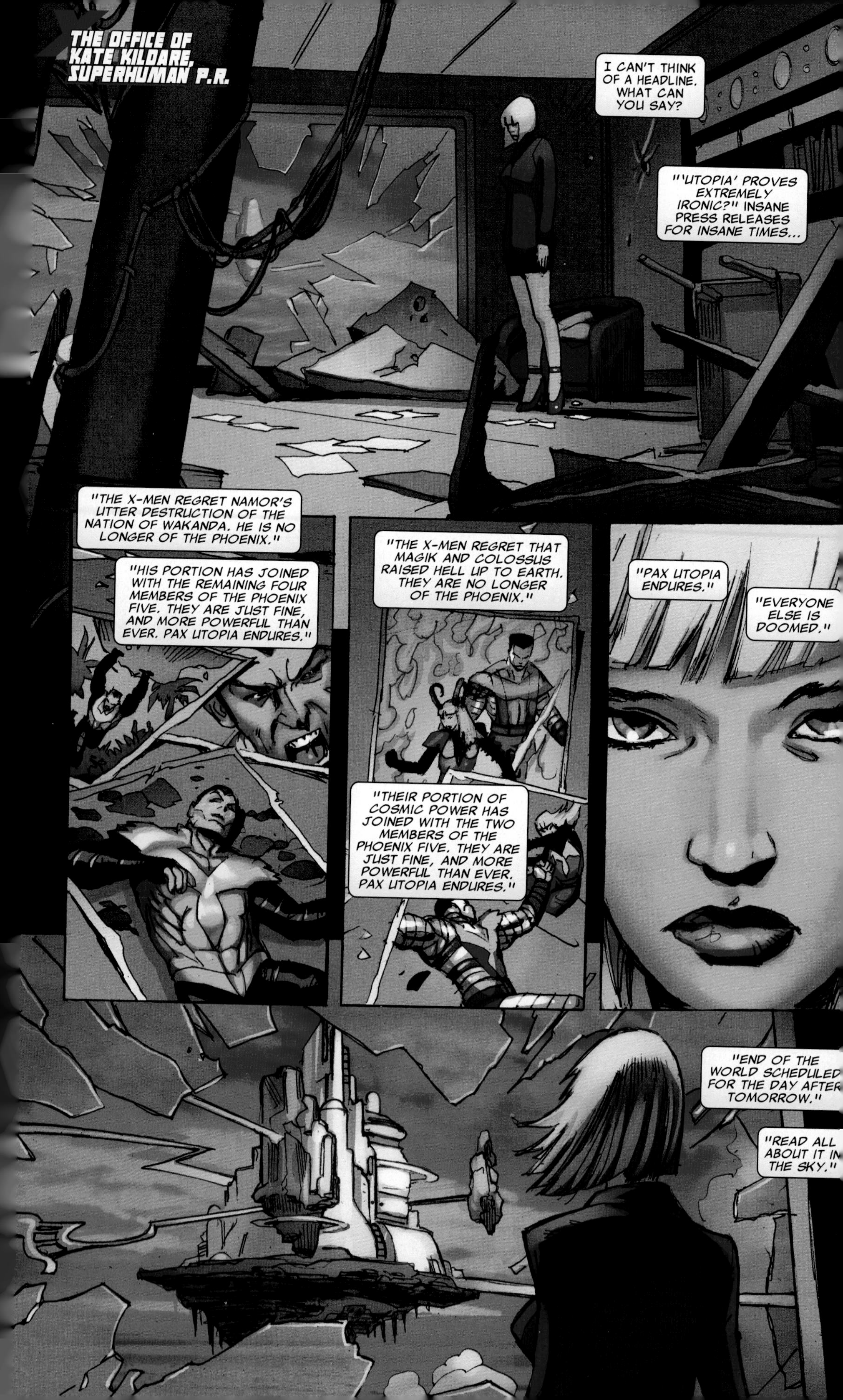
THE OFFICE OF KATE KILDARE, SUPERHUMAN P.R.
I CAN'T THINK OF A HEADLINE. WHAT CAN YOU SAY?
"'UTOPIA' PROVES EXTREMELY IRONIC?" INSANE PRESS RELEASES FOR INSANE TIMES...
"THE X-MEN REGRET NAMOR'S UTTER DESTRUCTION OF THE NATION OF WAKANDA. HE IS NO LONGER OF THE PHOENIX."
"HIS PORTION HAS JOINED WITH THE REMAINING FOUR MEMBERS OF THE PHOENIX FIVE. THEY ARE JUST FINE, AND MORE POWERFUL THAN EVER. PAX UTOPIA ENDURES."
"THE X-MEN REGRET THAT MAGIK AND COLOSSUS RAISED HELL UP TO EARTH. THEY ARE NO LONGER OF THE PHOENIX."
"THEIR PORTION OF COSMIC POWER HAS JOINED WITH THE TWO MEMBERS OF THE PHOENIX FIVE. THEY ARE JUST FINE, AND MORE POWERFUL THAN EVER. PAX UTOPIA ENDURES."
"PAX UTOPIA ENDURES."
"EVERYONE ELSE IS DOOMED."
"END OF THE WORLD SCHEDULED FOR THE DAY AFTER TOMORROW."
"READ ALL ABOUT IT IN THE SKY."

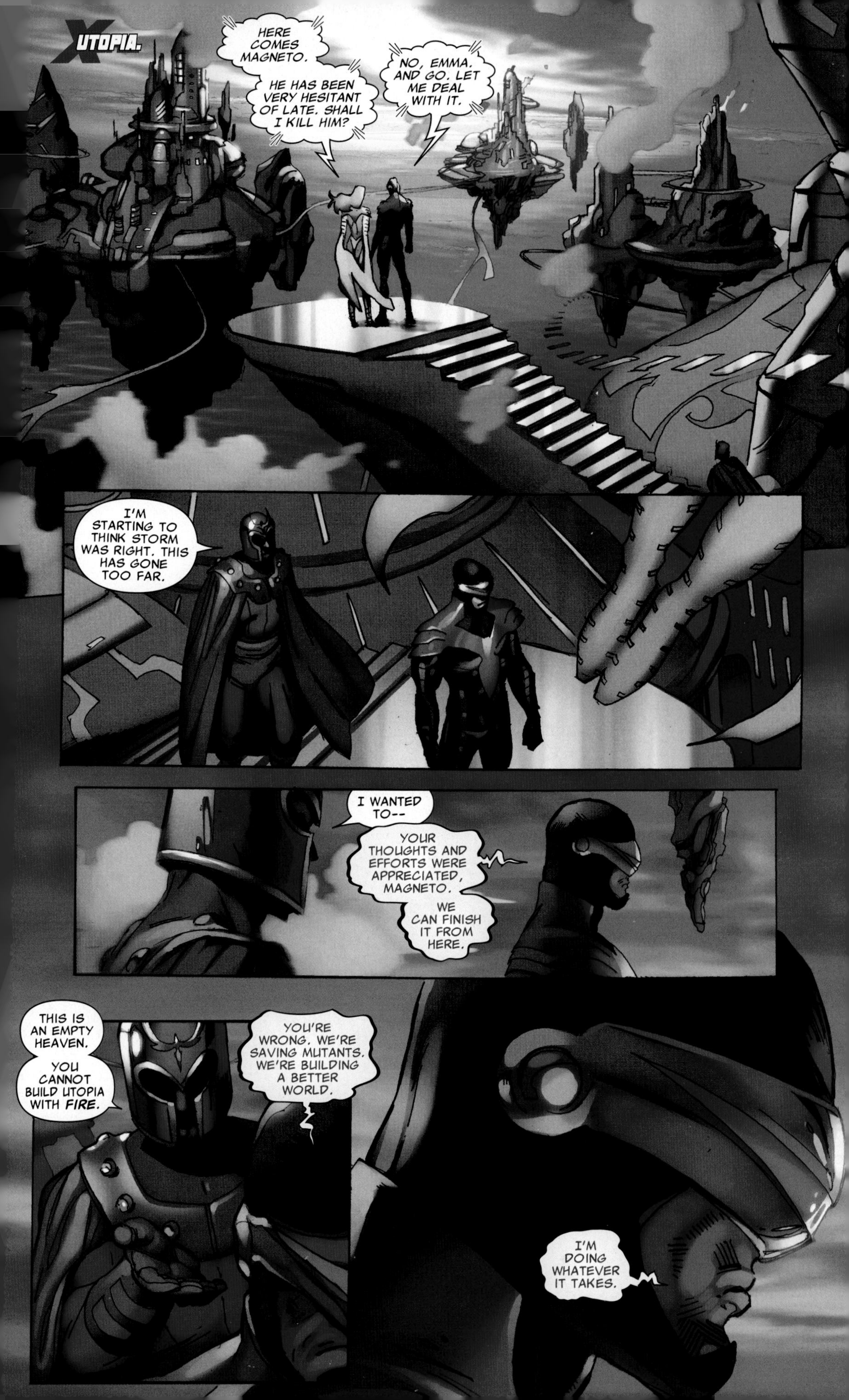
X UTOPIA.
HERE COMES MAGNETO.
HE HAS BEEN VERY HESITANT OF LATE. SHALL I KILL HIM?
NO, EMMA. AND GO. LET ME DEAL WITH IT.
I'M STARTING TO THINK STORM WAS RIGHT. THIS HAS GONE TOO FAR.
I WANTED TO--
YOUR THOUGHTS AND EFFORTS WERE APPRECIATED, MAGNETO.
WE CAN FINISH IT FROM HERE.
THIS IS AN EMPTY HEAVEN.
YOU CANNOT BUILD UTOPIA WITH FIRE.
YOU'RE WRONG. WE'RE SAVING MUTANTS. WE'RE BUILDING A BETTER WORLD.
I'M DOING WHATEVER IT TAKES.

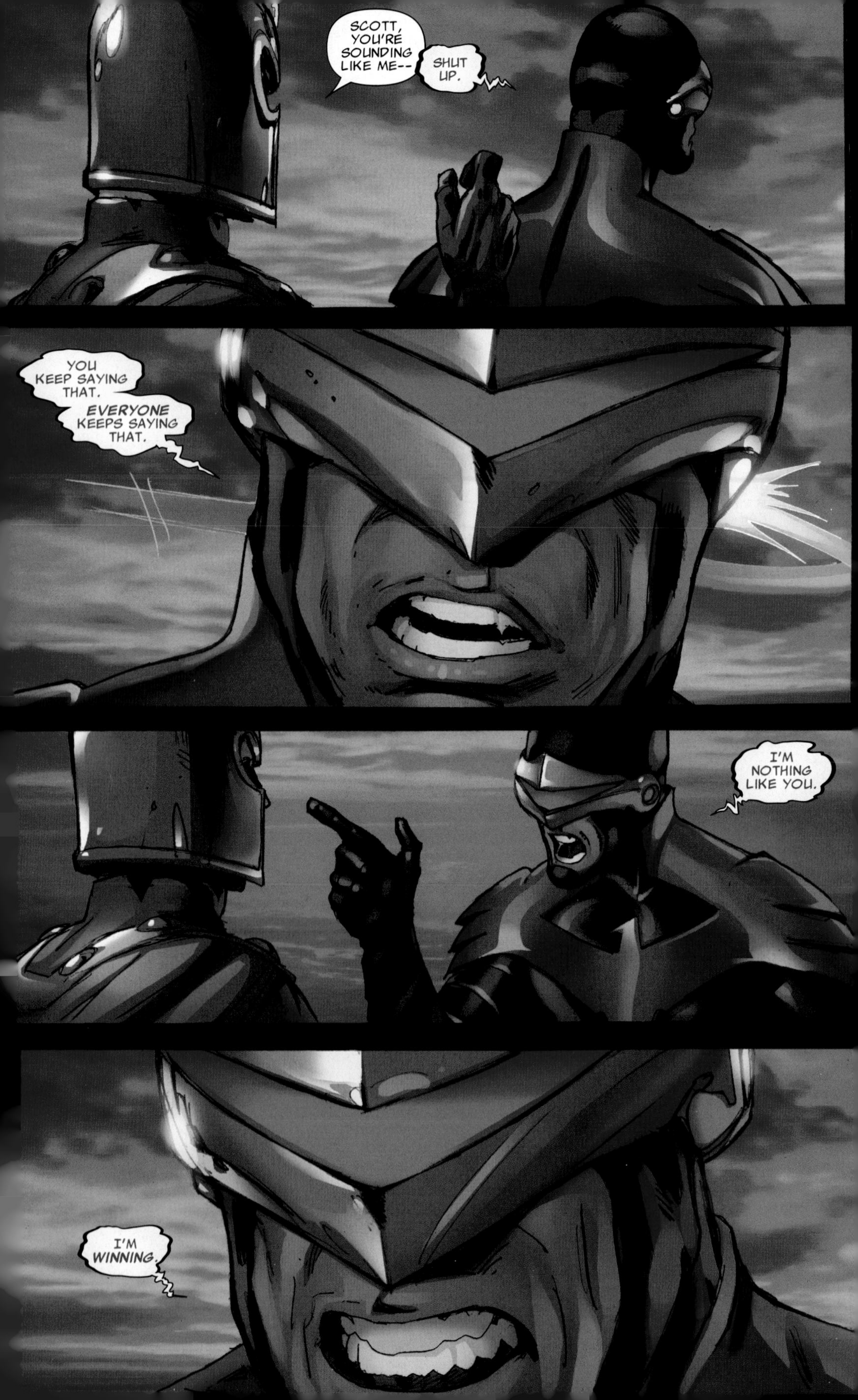
SCOTT, YOU'RE SOUNDING LIKE ME--
SHUT UP.
YOU KEEP SAYING THAT.
EVERYONE KEEPS SAYING THAT.
I'M NOTHING LIKE YOU.
I'M *WINNING.*

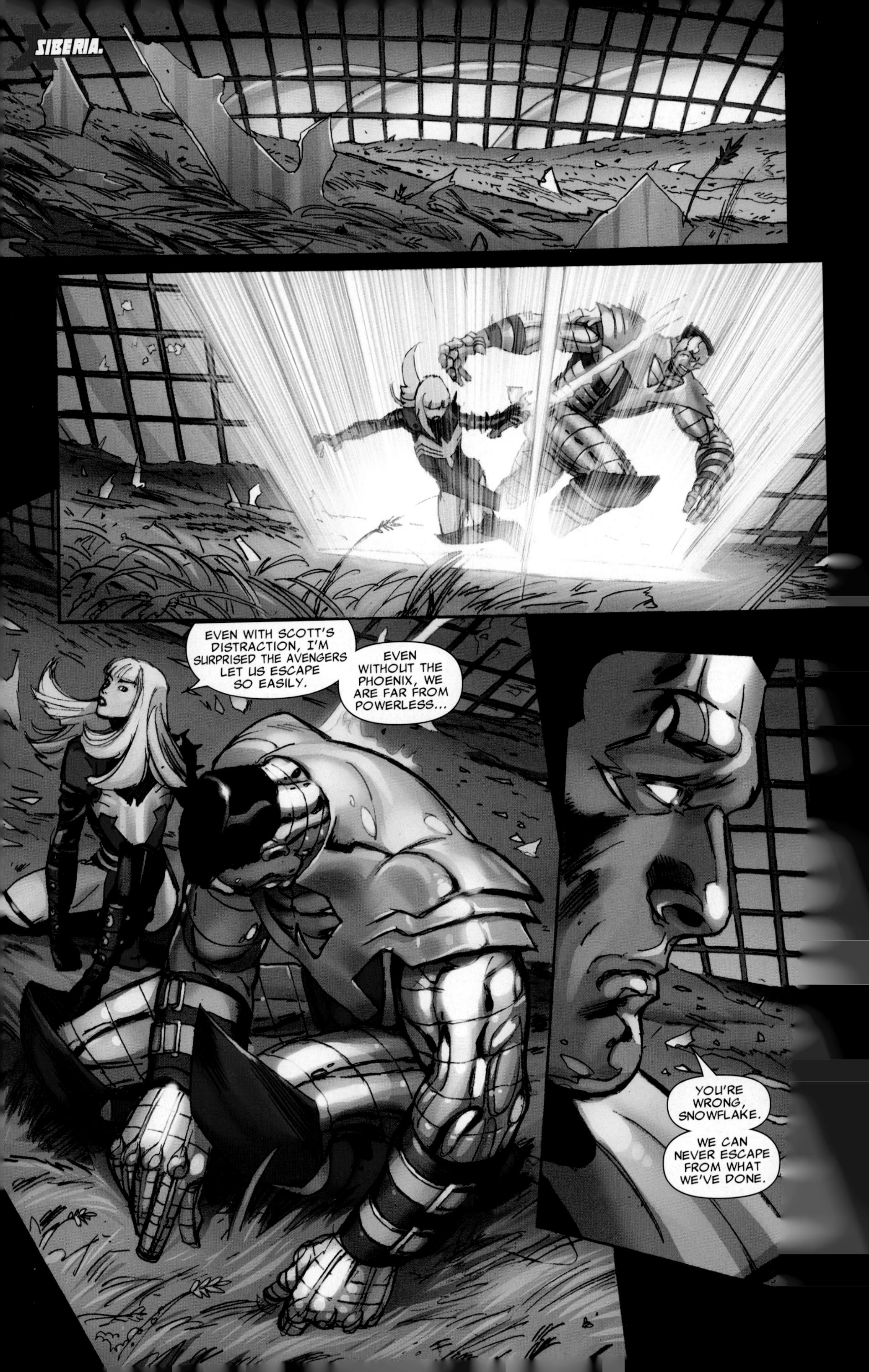
SIBERIA.
EVEN WITH SCOTT'S DISTRACTION, I'M SURPRISED THE AVENGERS LET US ESCAPE SO EASILY.
EVEN WITHOUT THE PHOENIX, WE ARE FAR FROM POWERLESS...
YOU'RE WRONG, SNOWFLAKE.
WE CAN NEVER ESCAPE FROM WHAT WE'VE DONE.

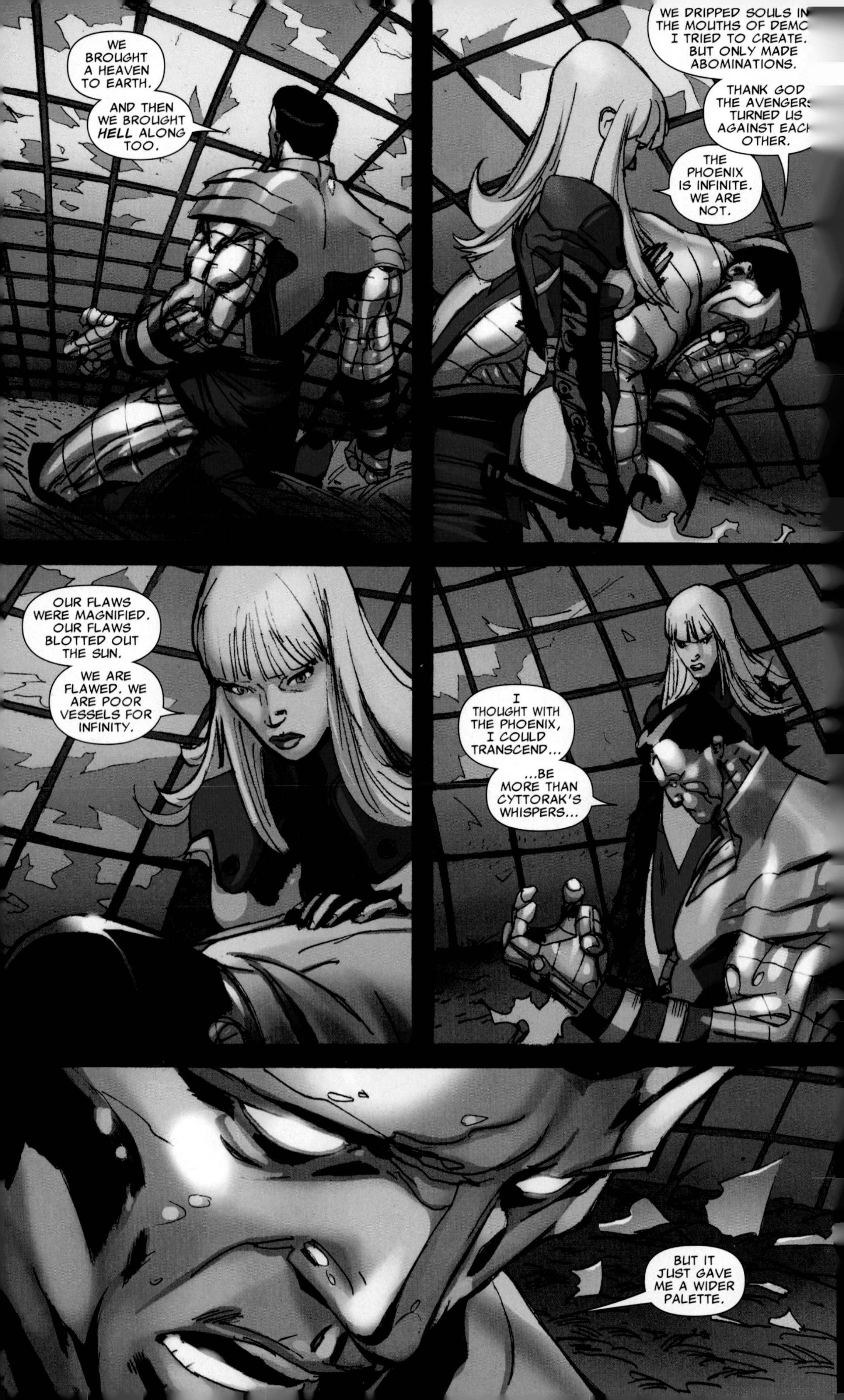

WE BROUGHT A HEAVEN TO EARTH.
AND THEN WE BROUGHT HELL ALONG TOO.
WE DRIPPED SOULS IN THE MOUTHS OF DEMO I TRIED TO CREATE. BUT ONLY MADE ABOMINATIONS.
THANK GOD THE AVENGERS TURNED US AGAINST EACH OTHER.
THE PHOENIX IS INFINITE. WE ARE NOT.
OUR FLAWS WERE MAGNIFIED. OUR FLAWS BLOTTED OUT THE SUN.
WE ARE FLAWED. WE ARE POOR VESSELS FOR INFINITY.
I THOUGHT WITH THE PHOENIX, I COULD TRANSCEND...
...BE MORE THAN CYTTORAK'S WHISPERS...
BUT IT JUST GAVE ME A WIDER PALETTE.

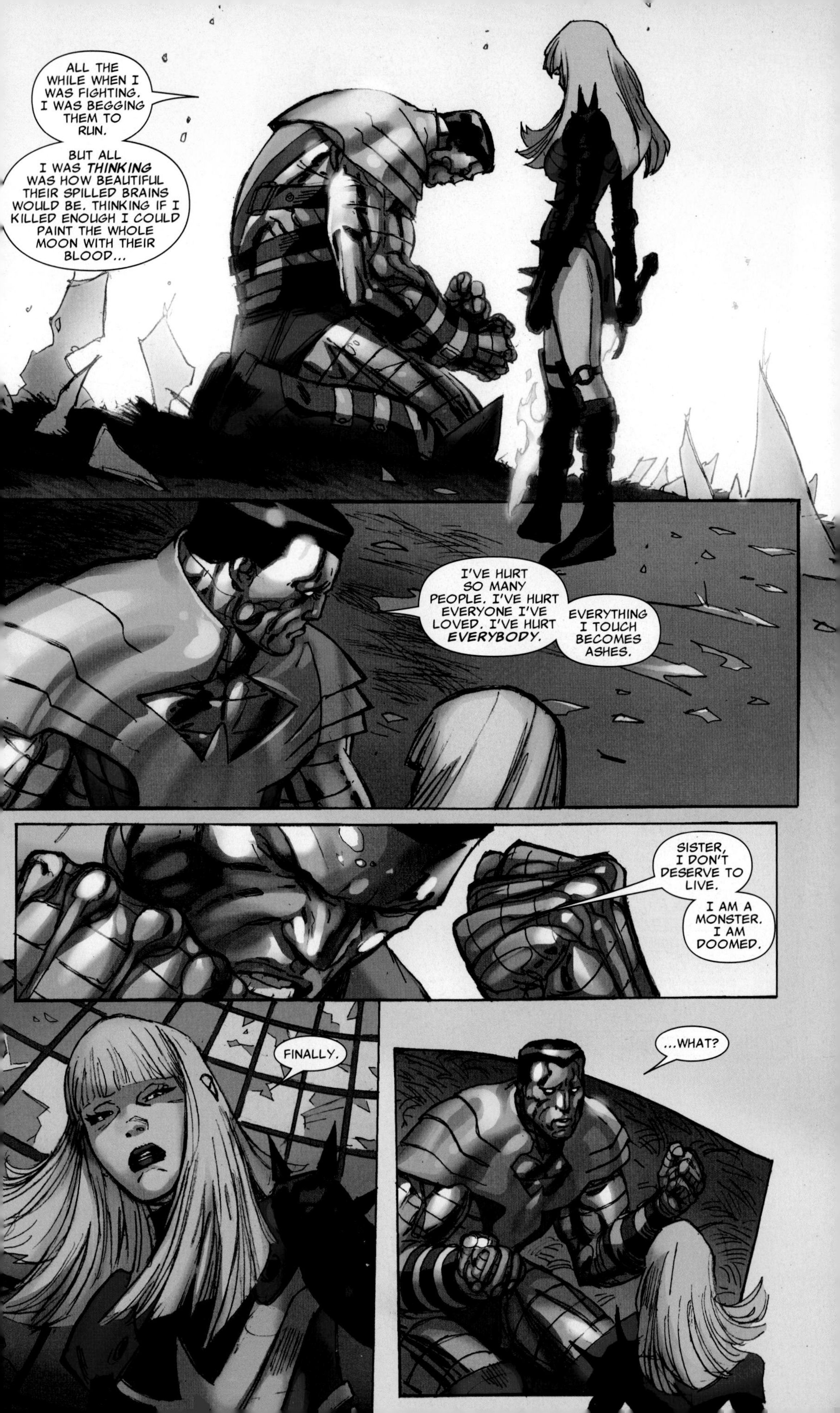
ALL THE WHILE WHEN I WAS FIGHTING. I WAS BEGGING THEM TO RUN.
BUT ALL I WAS THINKING WAS HOW BEAUTIFUL THEIR SPILLED BRAINS WOULD BE. THINKING IF I KILLED ENOUGH I COULD PAINT THE WHOLE MOON WITH THEIR BLOOD...
I'VE HURT SO MANY PEOPLE. I'VE HURT EVERYONE I'VE LOVED. I'VE HURT EVERYBODY.
EVERYTHING I TOUCH BECOMES ASHES.
SISTER, I DON'T DESERVE TO LIVE.
I AM A MONSTER. I AM DOOMED.
FINALLY.
...WHAT?

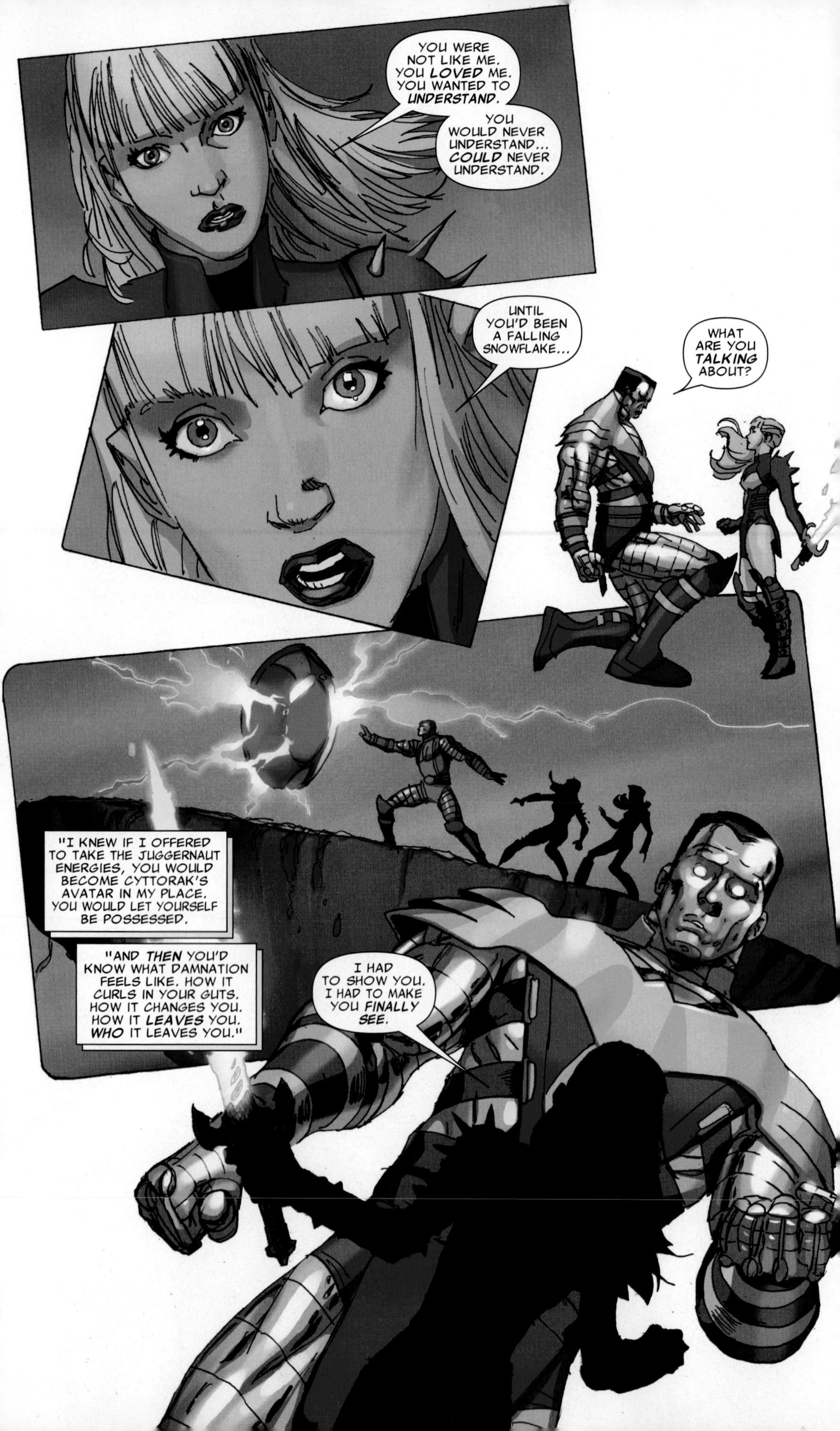
YOU WERE NOT LIKE ME. YOU LOVED ME. YOU WANTED TO UNDERSTAND.
YOU WOULD NEVER UNDERSTAND... COULD NEVER UNDERSTAND.
UNTIL YOU'D BEEN A FALLING SNOWFLAKE...
WHAT ARE YOU TALKING ABOUT?
"I KNEW IF I OFFERED TO TAKE THE JUGGERNAUT ENERGIES, YOU WOULD BECOME CYTTORAK'S AVATAR IN MY PLACE. YOU WOULD LET YOURSELF BE POSSESSED.
"AND THEN YOU'D KNOW WHAT DAMNATION FEELS LIKE. HOW IT CURLS IN YOUR GUTS. HOW IT CHANGES YOU. HOW IT LEAVES YOU. WHO IT LEAVES YOU."
I HAD TO SHOW YOU. I HAD TO MAKE YOU FINALLY SEE.

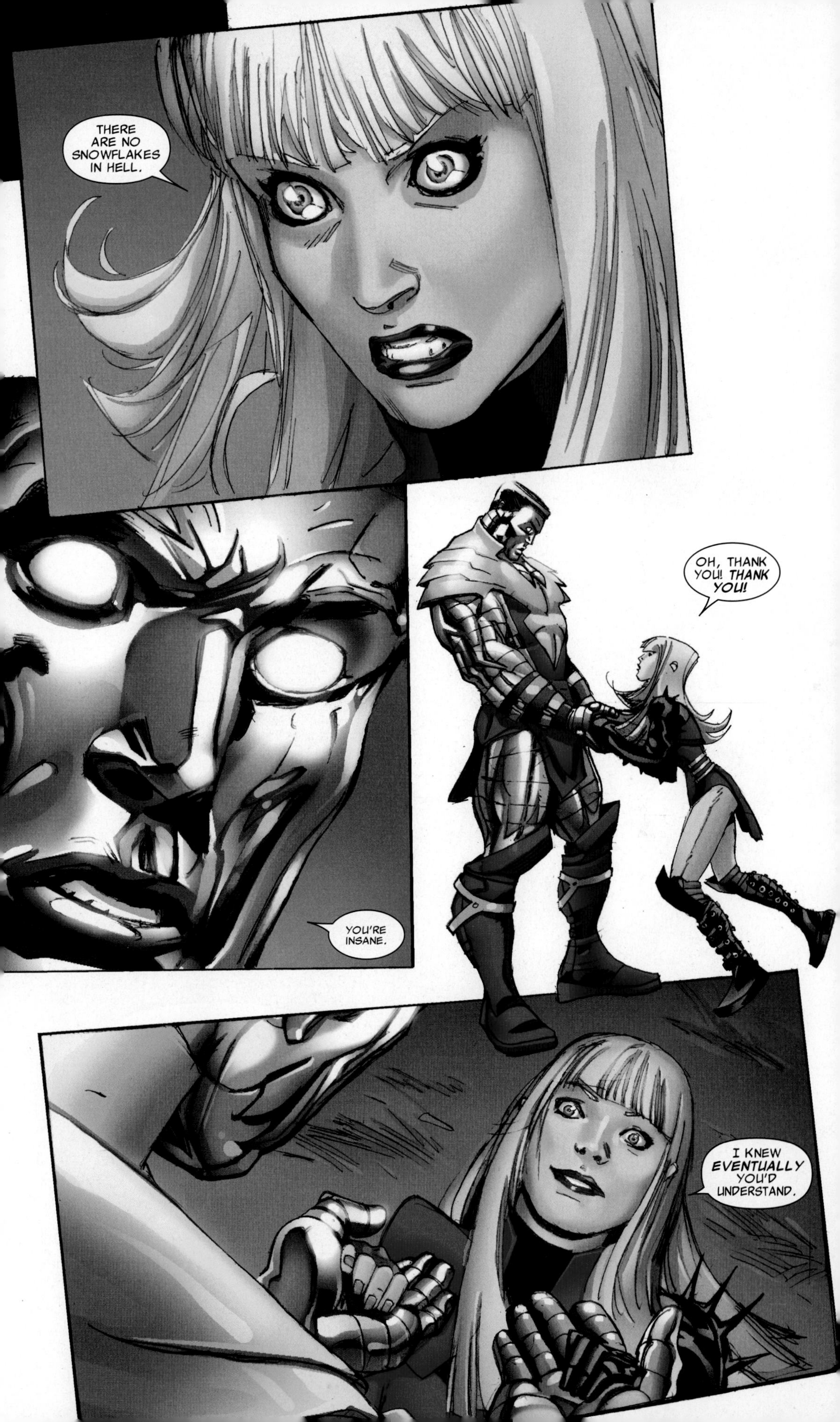
THERE ARE NO SNOWFLAKES IN HELL.
OH, THANK YOU! THANK YOU!
YOU'RE INSANE.
I KNEW EVENTUALLY YOU'D UNDERSTAND.

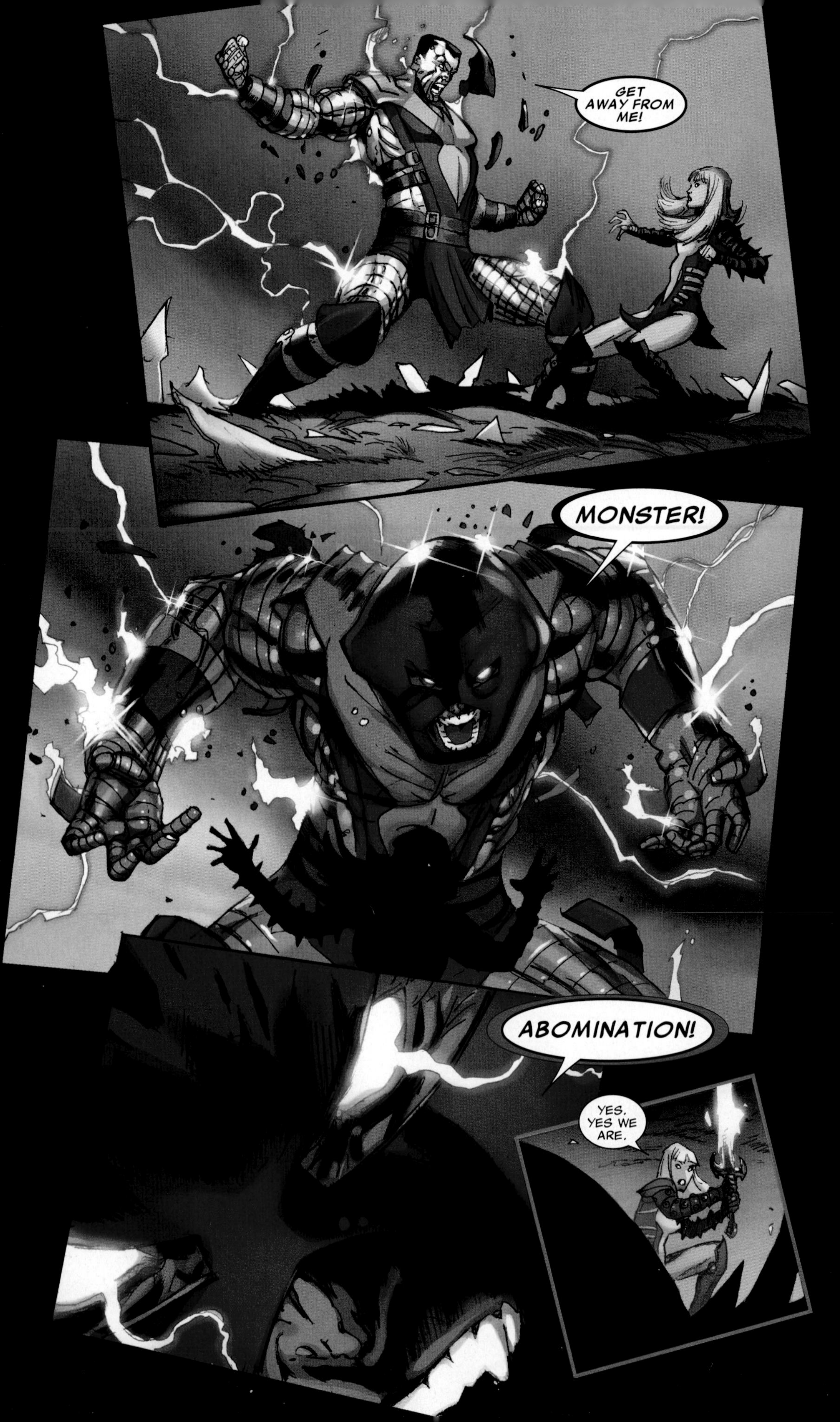
GET AWAY FROM ME!
MONSTER!
ABOMINATION!
YES. YES WE ARE.

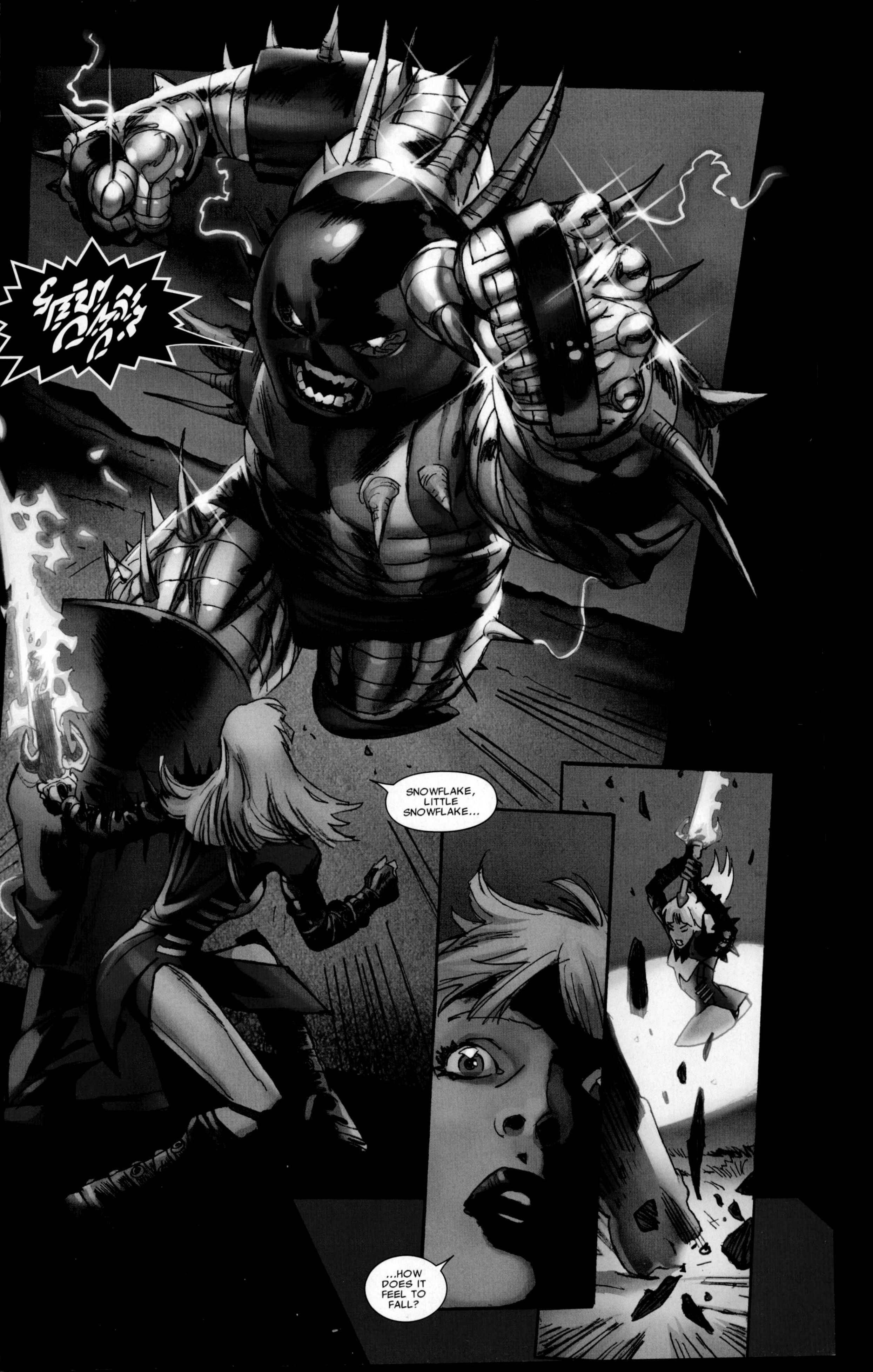
SNOWFLAKE, LITTLE SNOWFLAKE...
...HOW DOES IT FEEL TO FALL?

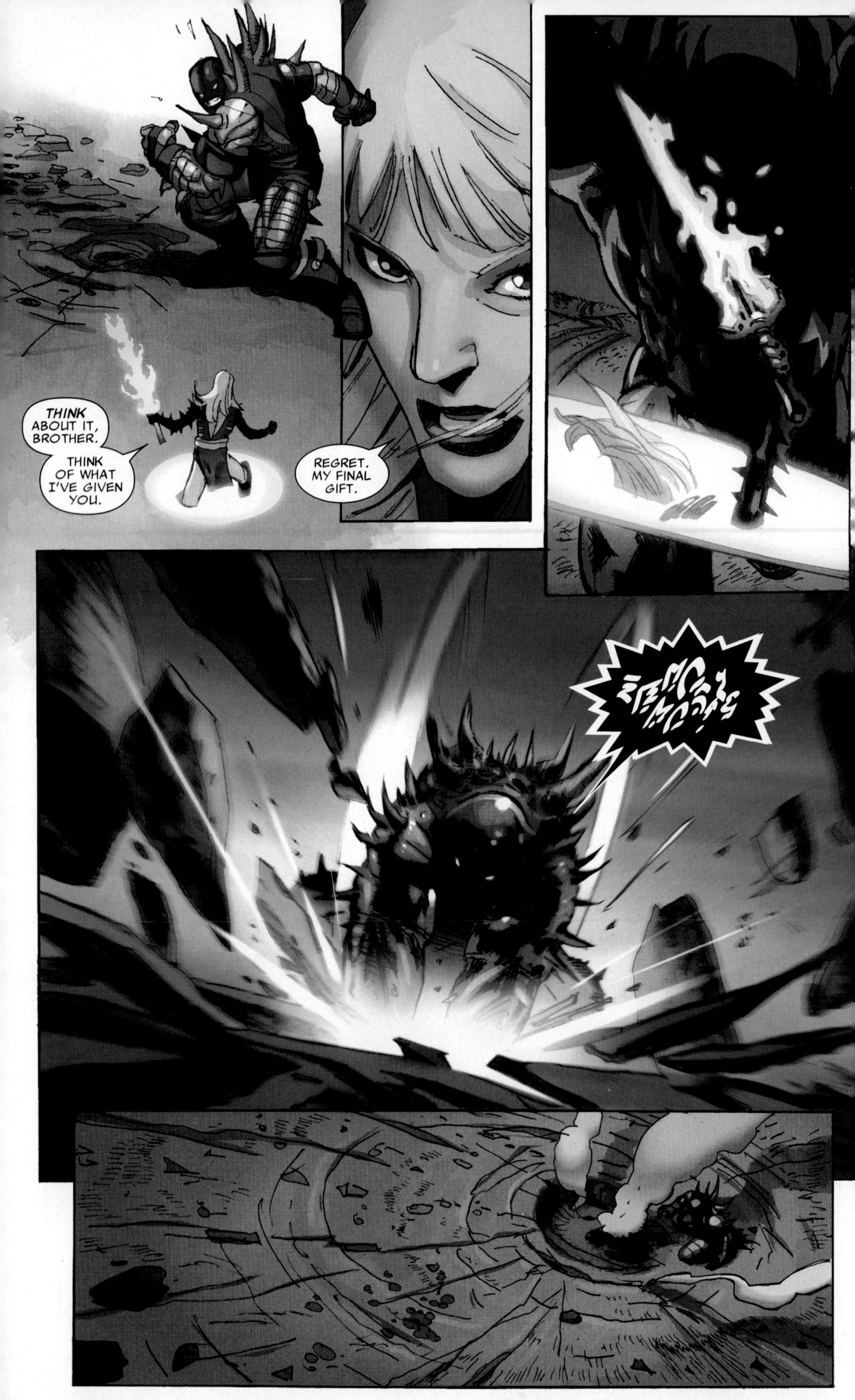
THINK ABOUT IT, BROTHER.
THINK OF WHAT I'VE GIVEN YOU.
REGRET. MY FINAL GIFT.

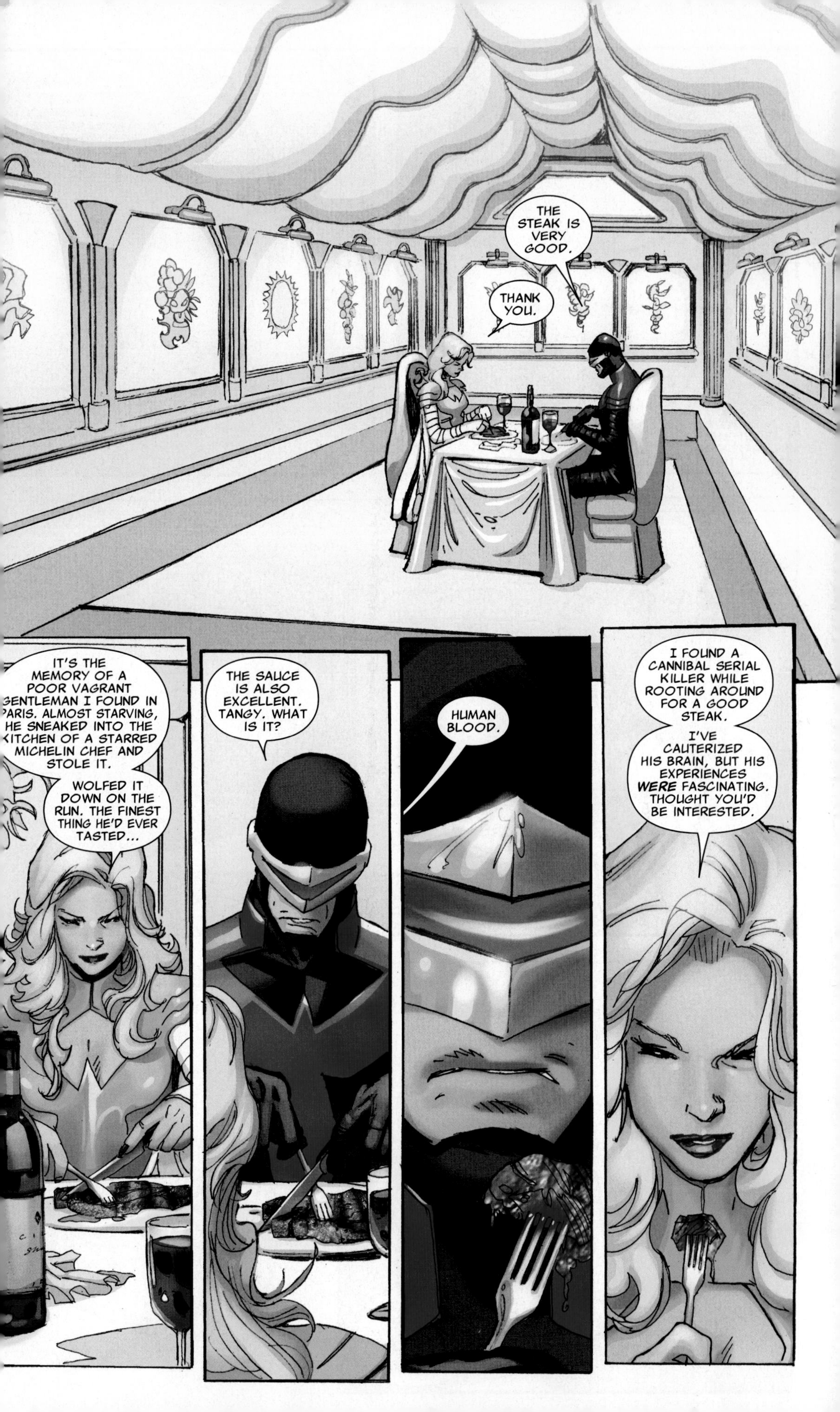

THE STEAK IS VERY GOOD.
THANK YOU.
IT'S THE MEMORY OF A POOR VAGRANT GENTLEMAN I FOUND IN PARIS. ALMOST STARVING, HE SNEAKED INTO THE KITCHEN OF A STARRED MICHELIN CHEF AND STOLE IT.
WOLFED IT DOWN ON THE RUN. THE FINEST THING HE'D EVER TASTED...
THE SAUCE IS ALSO EXCELLENT. TANGY. WHAT IS IT?
HUMAN BLOOD.
I FOUND A CANNIBAL SERIAL KILLER WHILE ROOTING AROUND FOR A GOOD STEAK.
I'VE CAUTERIZED HIS BRAIN, BUT HIS EXPERIENCES WERE FASCINATING. THOUGHT YOU'D BE INTERESTED.

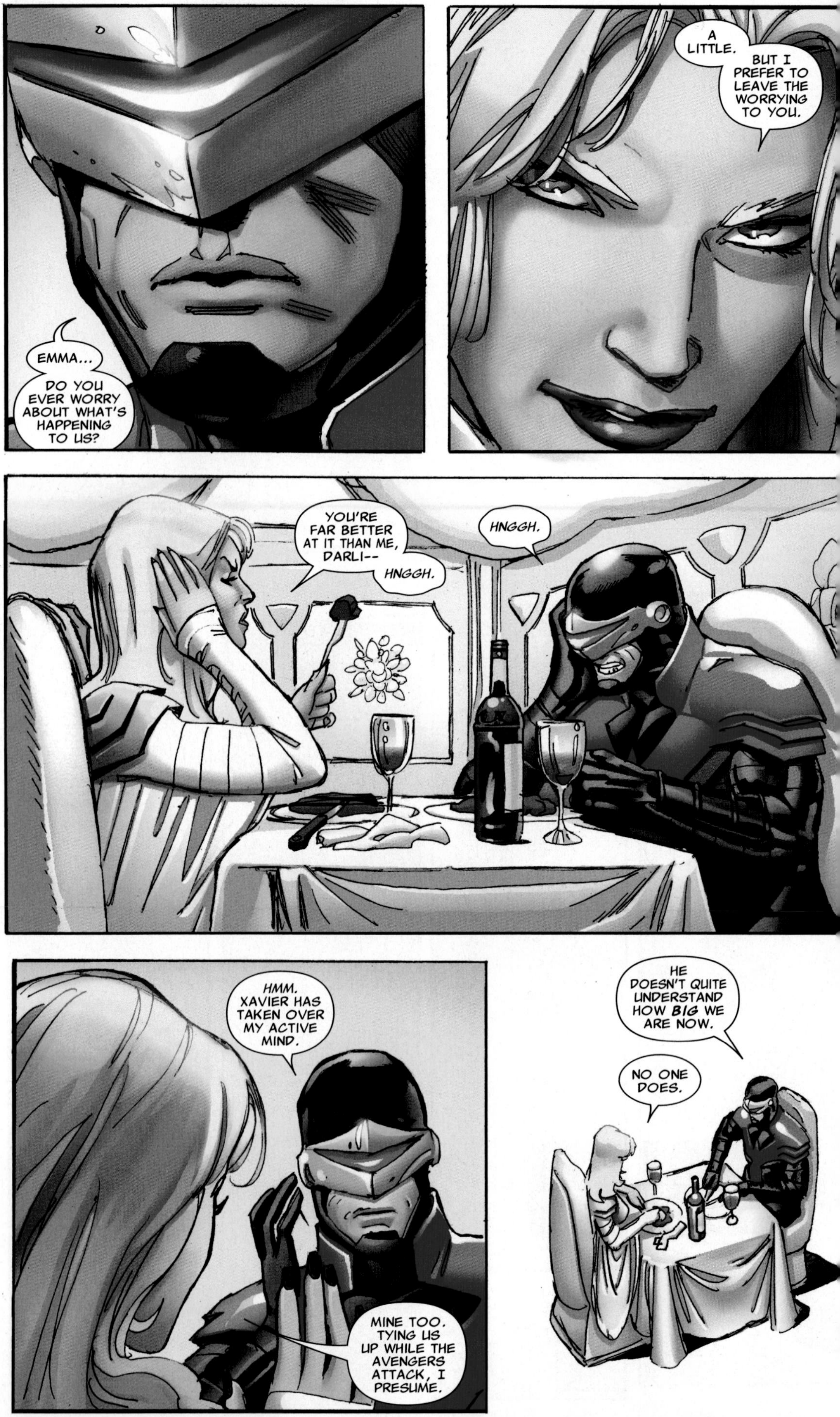
EMMA...
DO YOU EVER WORRY ABOUT WHAT'S HAPPENING TO US?
A LITTLE.
BUT I PREFER TO LEAVE THE WORRYING TO YOU.
YOU'RE FAR BETTER AT IT THAN ME, DARLI--
HNGGH.
HNGGH.
HMM. XAVIER HAS TAKEN OVER MY ACTIVE MIND.
MINE TOO. TYING US UP WHILE THE AVENGERS ATTACK, I PRESUME.
HE DOESN'T QUITE UNDERSTAND HOW BIG WE ARE NOW.
NO ONE DOES.

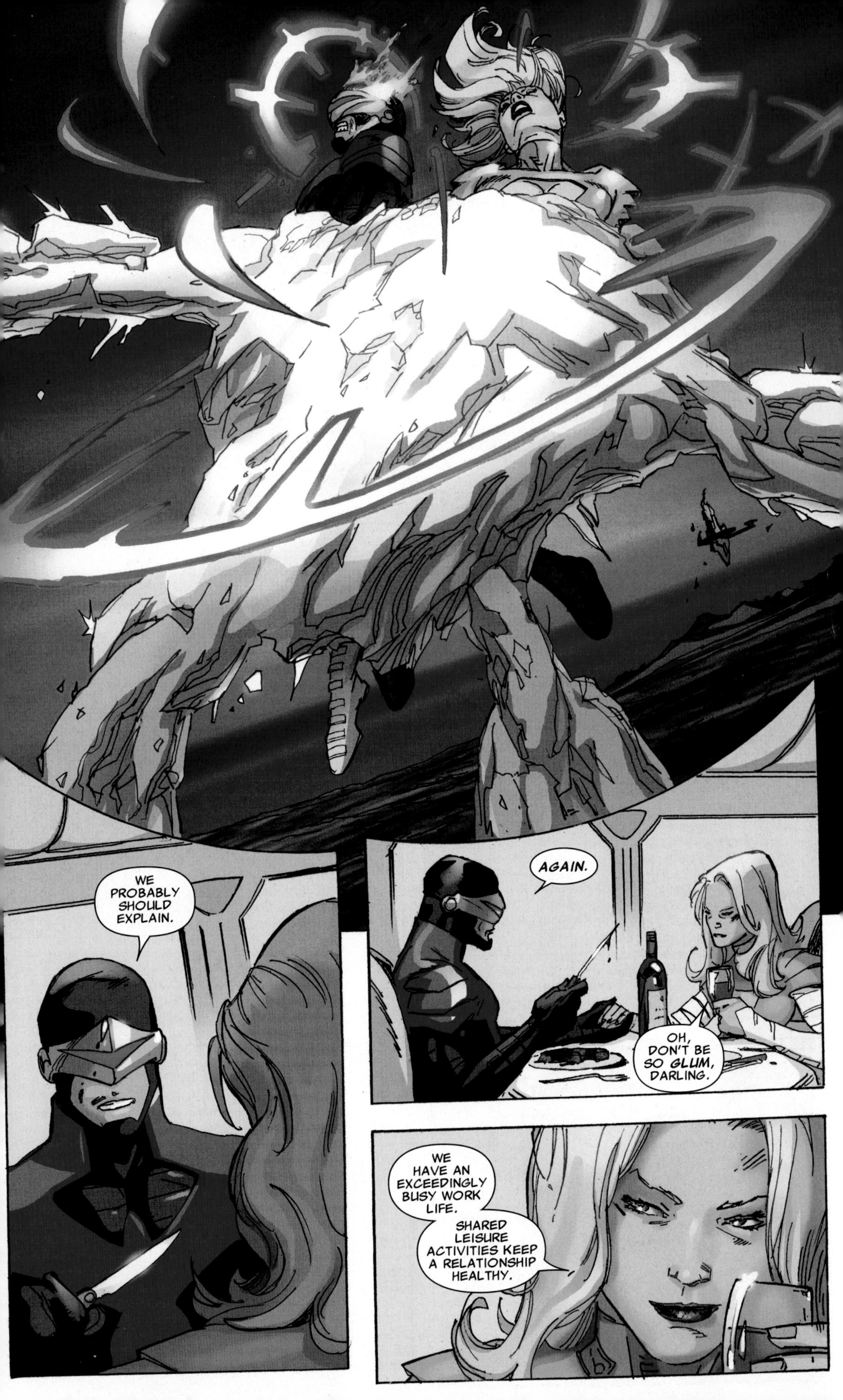
WE PROBABLY SHOULD EXPLAIN.
AGAIN.
OH, DON'T BE SO GLUM, DARLING.
WE HAVE AN EXCEEDINGLY BUSY WORK LIFE.
SHARED LEISURE ACTIVITIES KEEP A RELATIONSHIP HEALTHY.

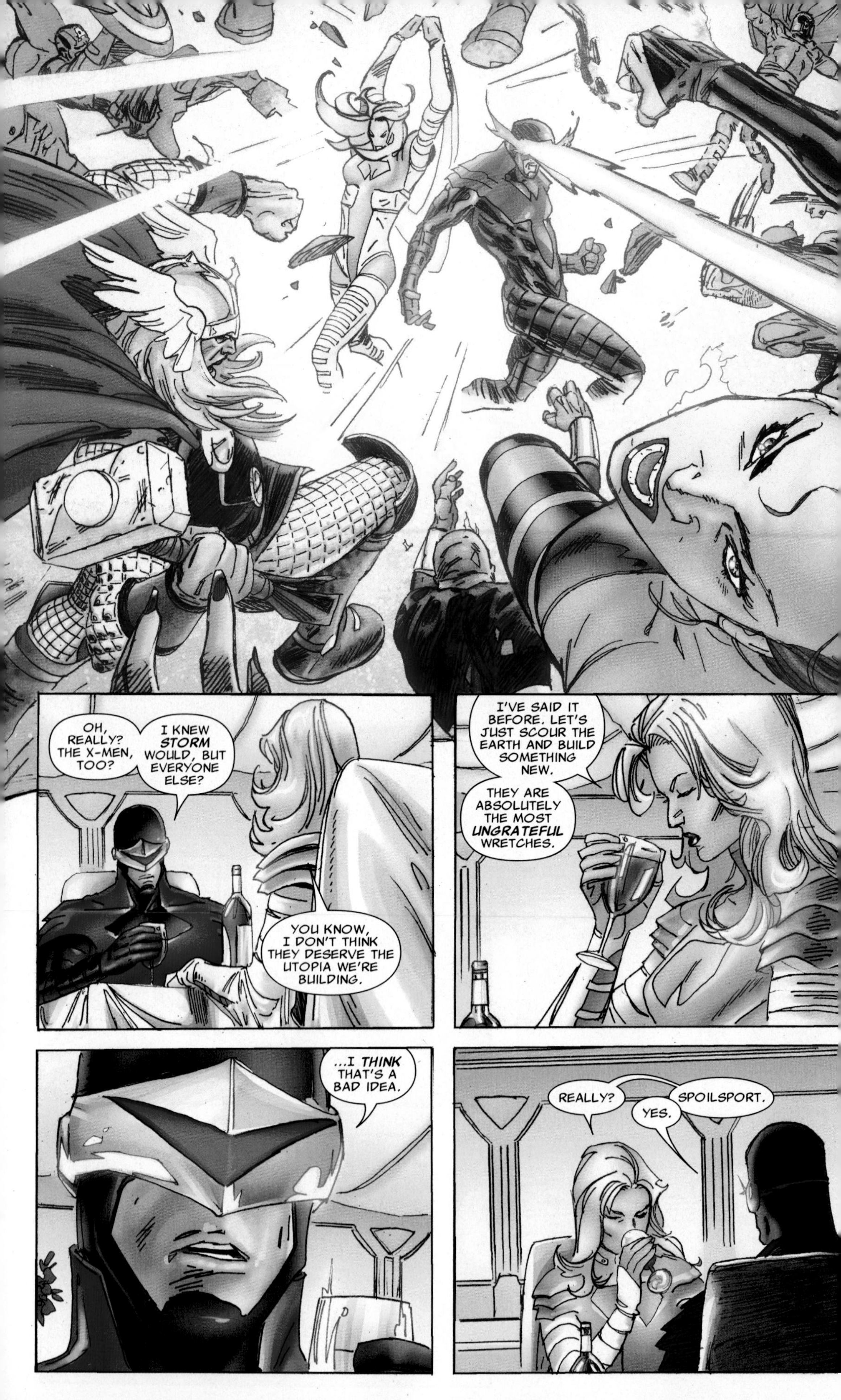
OH, REALLY? THE X-MEN, TOO?
I KNEW STORM WOULD, BUT EVERYONE ELSE?
YOU KNOW, I DON'T THINK THEY DESERVE THE UTOPIA WE'RE BUILDING.
I'VE SAID IT BEFORE. LET'S JUST SCOUR THE EARTH AND BUILD SOMETHING NEW.
THEY ARE ABSOLUTELY THE MOST UNGRATEFUL WRETCHES.
...I THINK THAT'S A BAD IDEA.
REALLY?
YES.
SPOILSPORT.

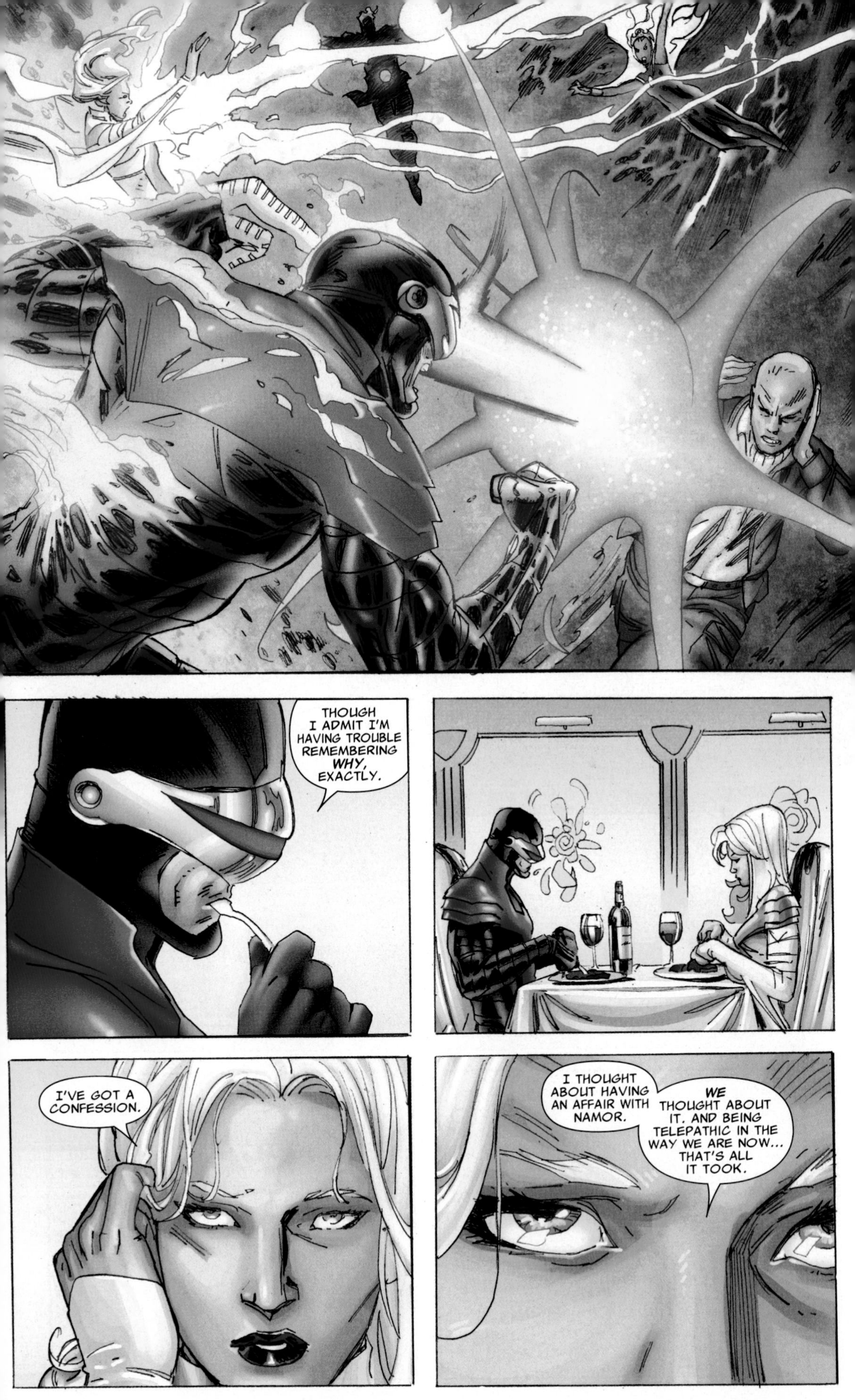
THOUGH I ADMIT I'M HAVING TROUBLE REMEMBERING WHY, EXACTLY.
I'VE GOT A CONFESSION.
I THOUGHT ABOUT HAVING AN AFFAIR WITH NAMOR.
WE THOUGHT ABOUT IT. AND BEING TELEPATHIC IN THE WAY WE ARE NOW... THAT'S ALL IT TOOK.

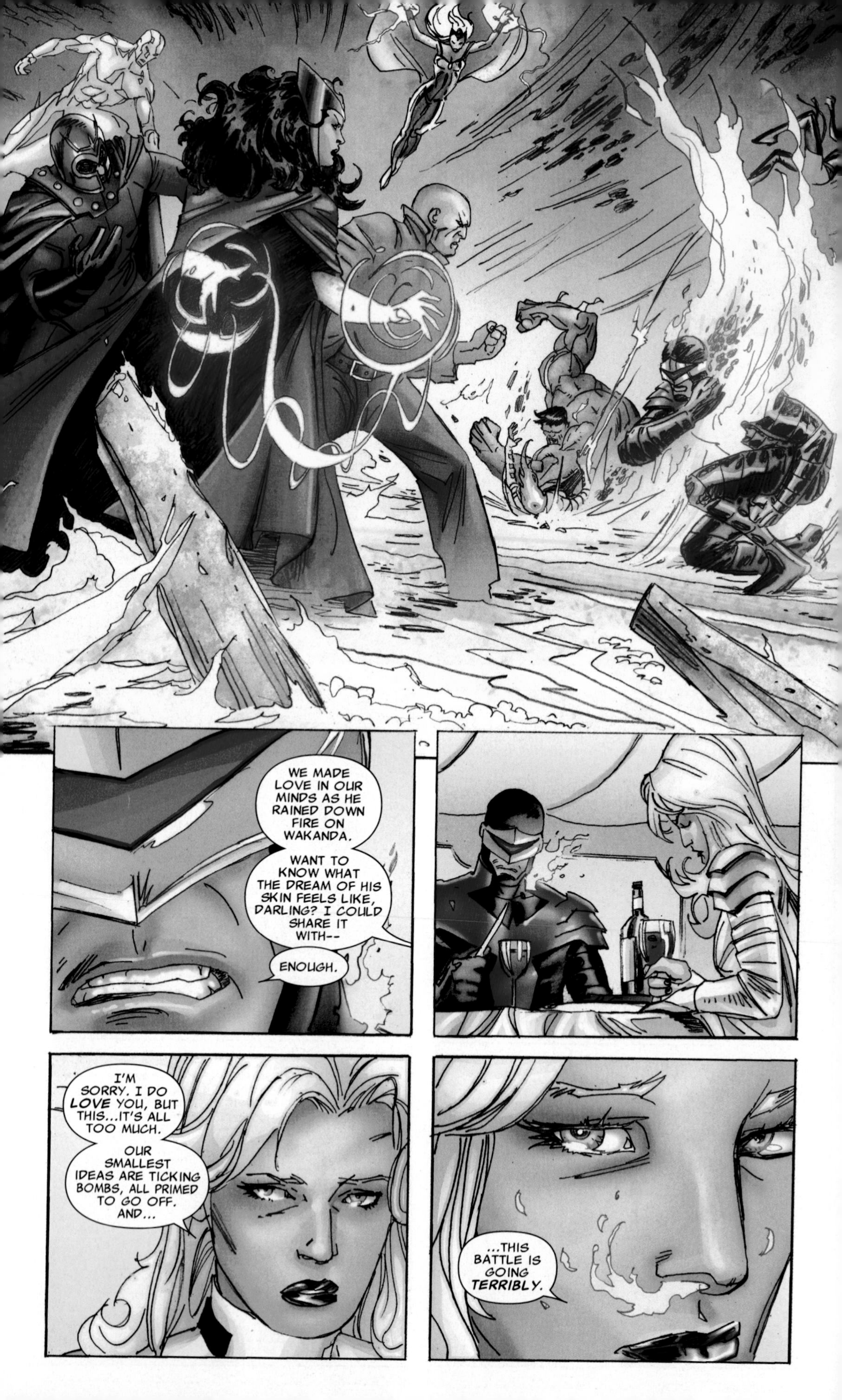

WE MADE LOVE IN OUR MINDS AS HE RAINED DOWN FIRE ON WAKANDA.
WANT TO KNOW WHAT THE DREAM OF HIS SKIN FEELS LIKE, DARLING? I COULD SHARE IT WITH--
ENOUGH.
I'M SORRY. I DO **LOVE** YOU, BUT THIS...IT'S ALL TOO MUCH.
OUR SMALLEST IDEAS ARE TICKING BOMBS, ALL PRIMED TO GO OFF. AND...
...THIS BATTLE IS GOING ***TERRIBLY***.

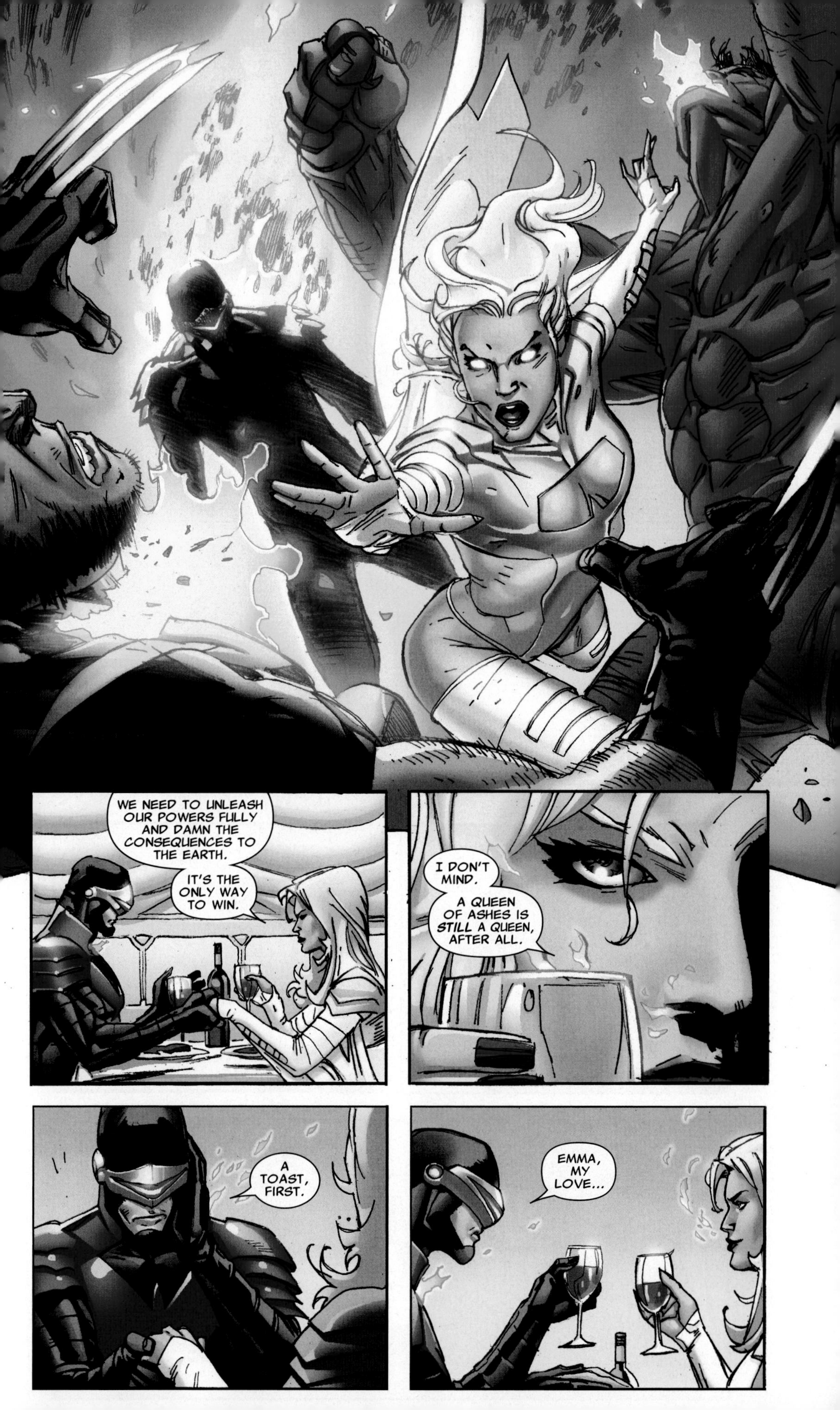

WE NEED TO UNLEASH OUR POWERS FULLY AND DAMN THE CONSEQUENCES TO THE EARTH.
IT'S THE ONLY WAY TO WIN.
I DON'T MIND.
A QUEEN OF ASHES IS *STILL* A QUEEN, AFTER ALL.
A TOAST, FIRST.
EMMA, MY LOVE...

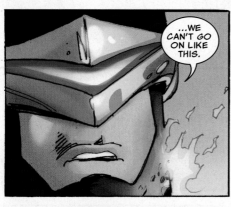

...WE CAN'T GO ON LIKE THIS.

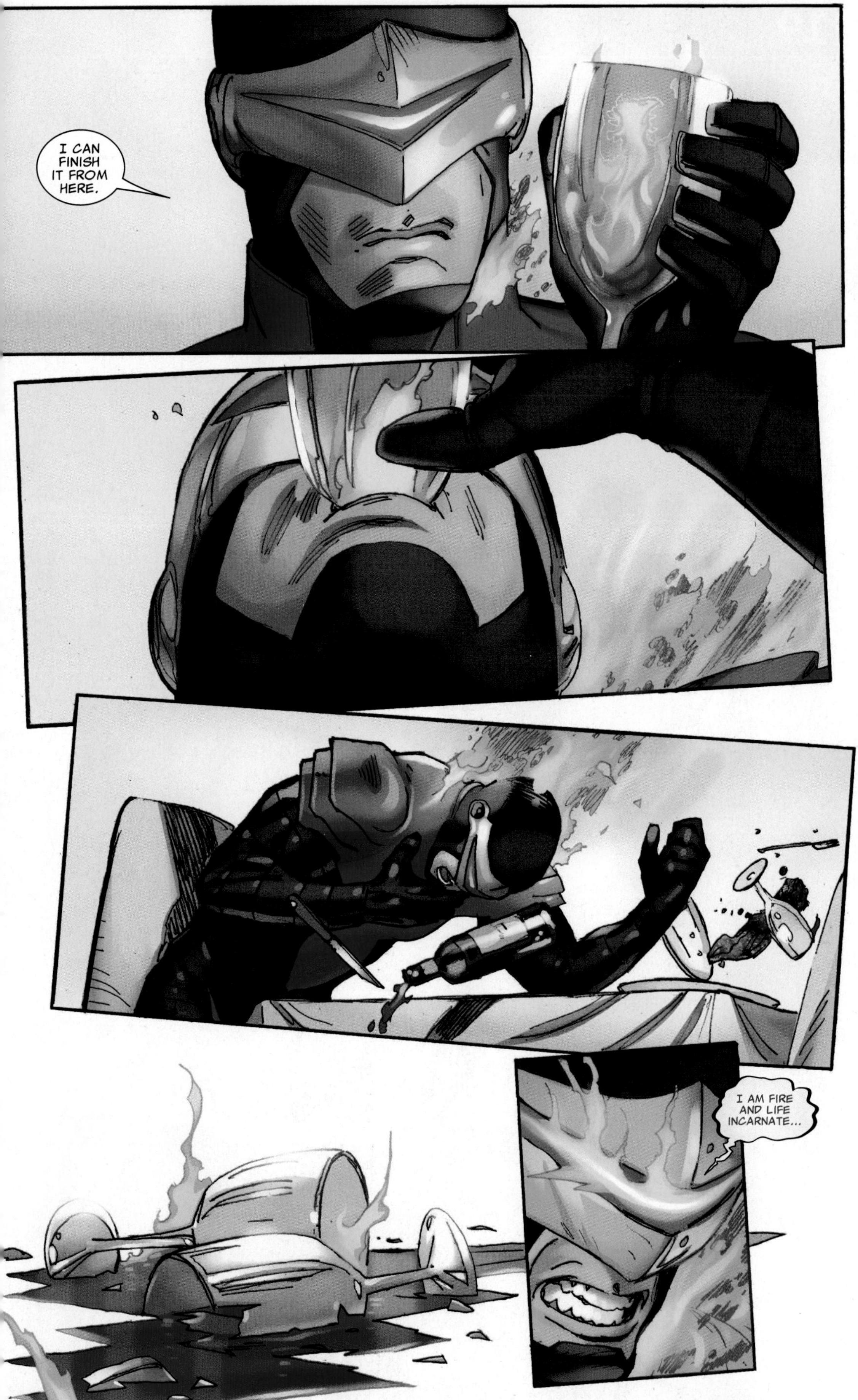
I CAN FINISH IT FROM HERE.
I AM FIRE AND LIFE INCARNATE...

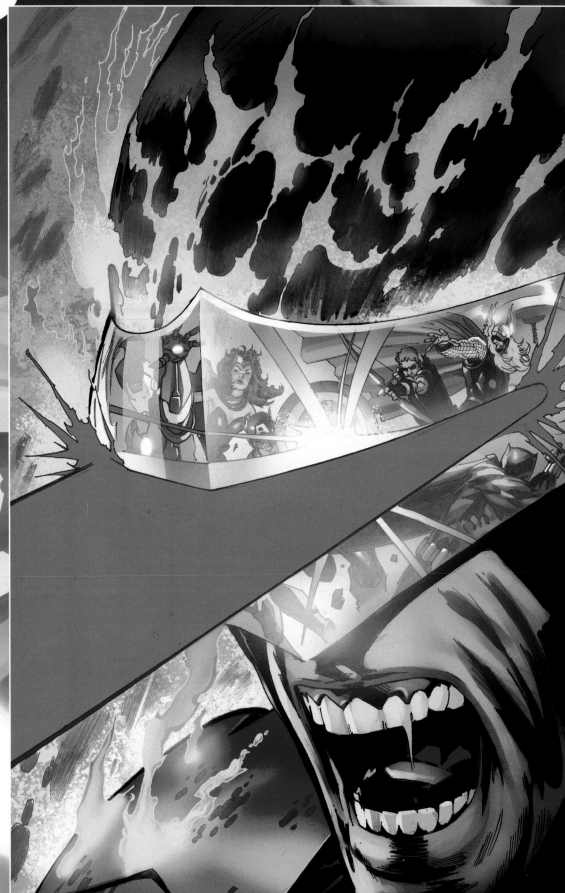

rn with powers and
ilities beyond those of
rmal humans, mutantkind
s long been hated and
ared by those they sought
protect. Now, from their
and nation of Utopia, Cyclops
ds the most powerful group
mutants ever assembled
protect what is left of
dwindling species.
ted and feared? When
u are as powerful as
e Uncanny X-Men,
es it matter?

UNCANNY X-MEN

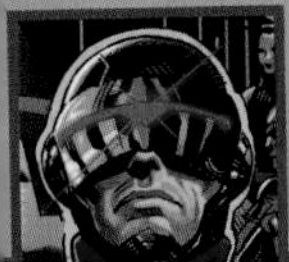

CYCLOPS
ge-blasting leader

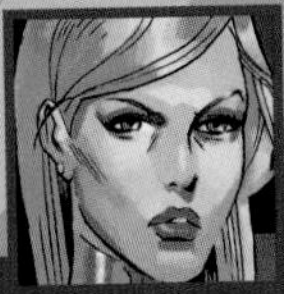

EMMA FROST
telepath with diamond form

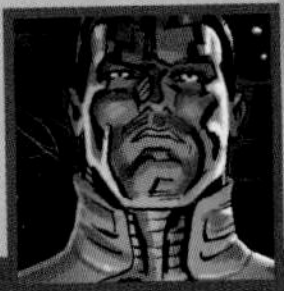

COLOSSUS
steel-skinned juggernaut

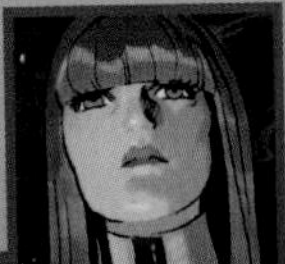

MAGIK
magic-using teleporter

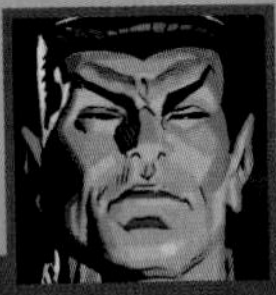

NAMOR
king of Atlantis

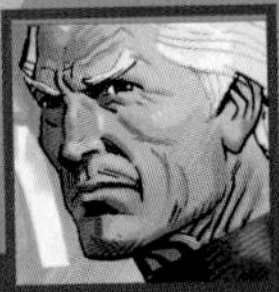

MAGNETO
master of magnetism

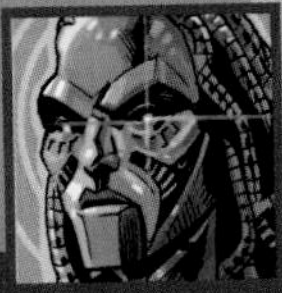

DANGER
light-shaping AI

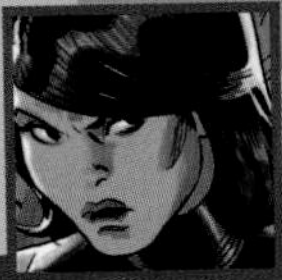

PSYLOCKE
telepathic ninja

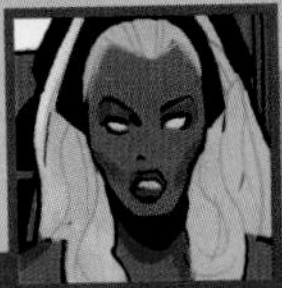

STORM
weather witch

REVIOUSLY

e day that mutantkind was decimated from a species of millions to a species of less
an 200, everything changed for Scott Summers, a.k.a. Cyclops. Professor Charles
vier's dream of mutant/human coexistence that Scott once embodied evaporated in
e harsh reality of impending extinction, forcing Scott to make many difficult decisions
save his species. He has thus, as leader of the X-Men, protected mutants ever
ce.

e such decision was to attempt to put the universal force of destruction and rebirth
lled the Phoenix in position to save mutantkind. This decision put the X-Men at odds
th the Avengers, who don't share Scott's belief in the Phoenix. Cyclops has now
ken full possession of the universal force with the hopes of defeating the Avengers
d setting the world right for mutants. But does he have a hope of controlling the
oenix Force and maintaining his sanity?

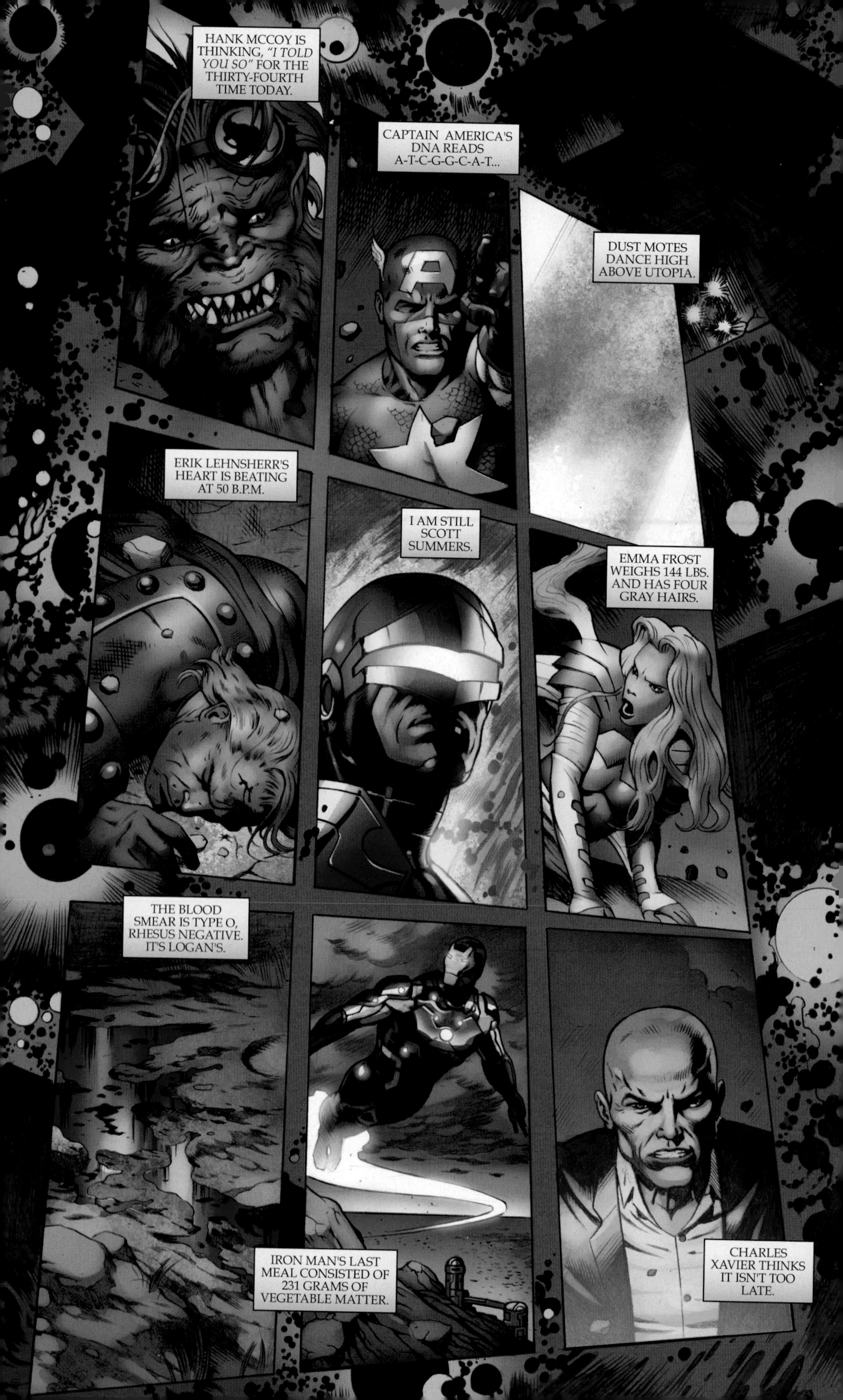
HANK MCCOY IS THINKING, *"I TOLD YOU SO"* FOR THE THIRTY-FOURTH TIME TODAY.
CAPTAIN AMERICA'S DNA READS A-T-C-G-G-C-A-T...
DUST MOTES DANCE HIGH ABOVE UTOPIA.
ERIK LEHNSHERR'S HEART IS BEATING AT 50 B.P.M.
I AM STILL SCOTT SUMMERS.
EMMA FROST WEIGHS 144 LBS. AND HAS FOUR GRAY HAIRS.
THE BLOOD SMEAR IS TYPE O, RHESUS NEGATIVE. IT'S LOGAN'S.
IRON MAN'S LAST MEAL CONSISTED OF 231 GRAMS OF VEGETABLE MATTER.
CHARLES XAVIER THINKS IT ISN'T TOO LATE.

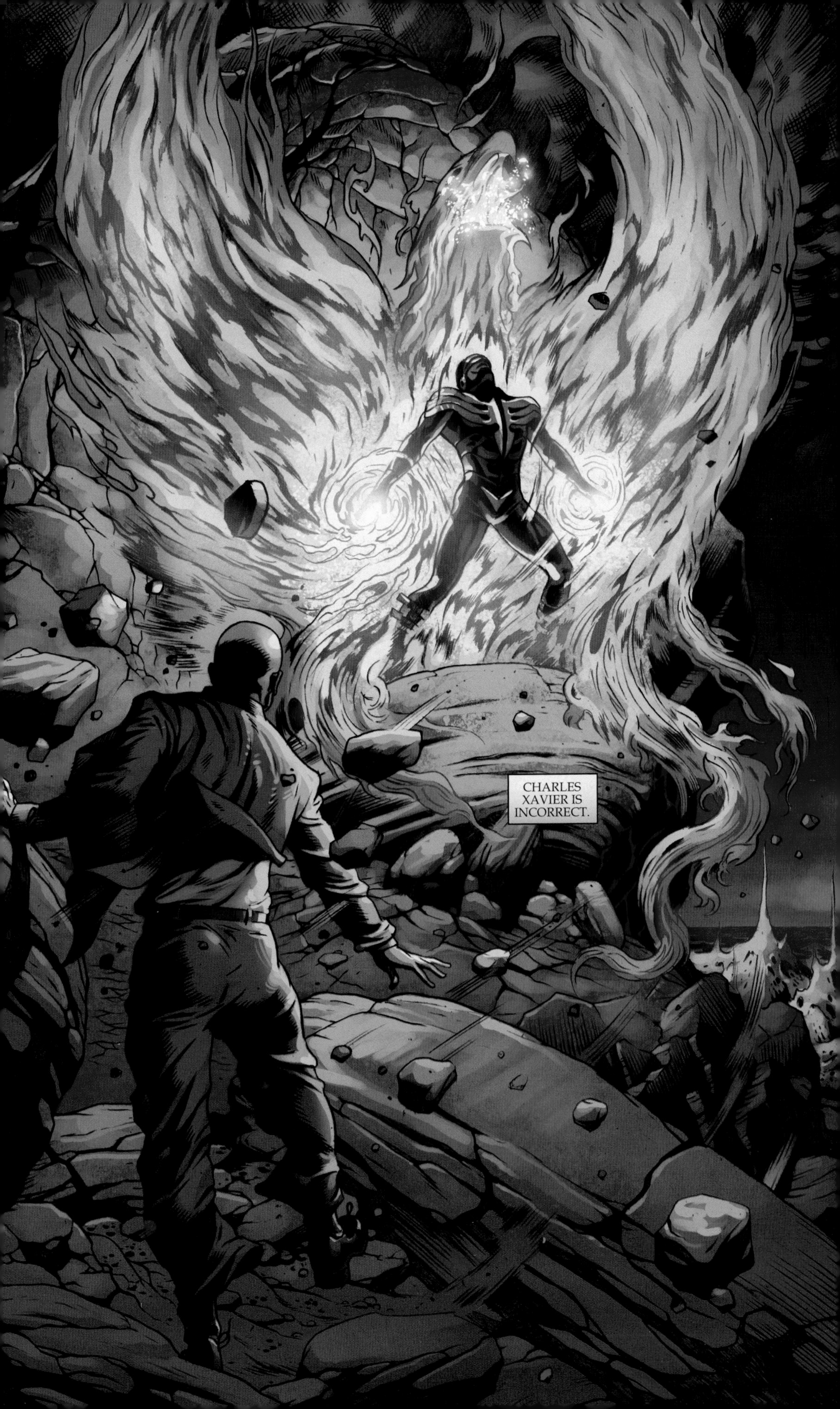
CHARLES
XAVIER IS
INCORRECT.

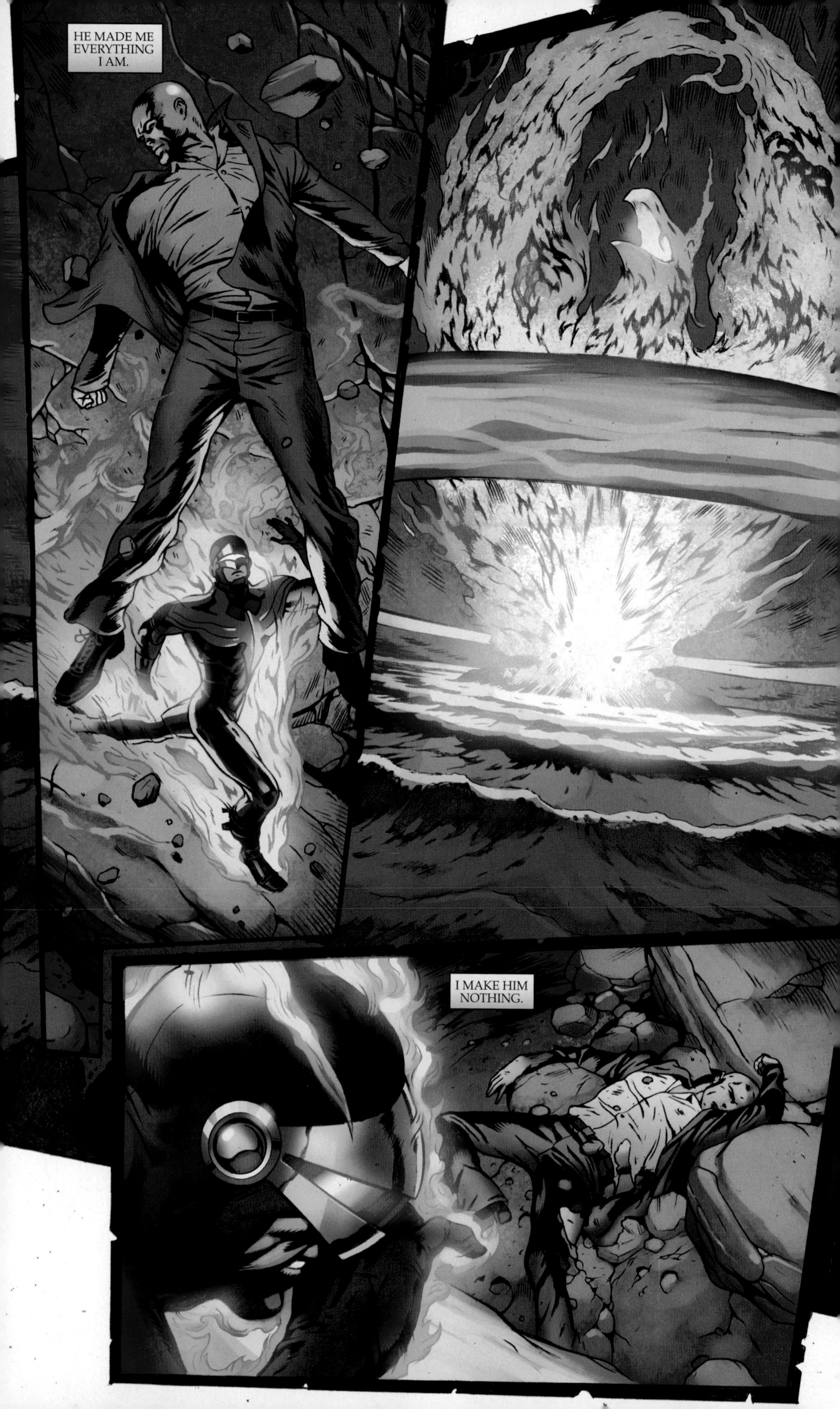
HE MADE ME EVERYTHING I AM.
I MAKE HIM NOTHING.

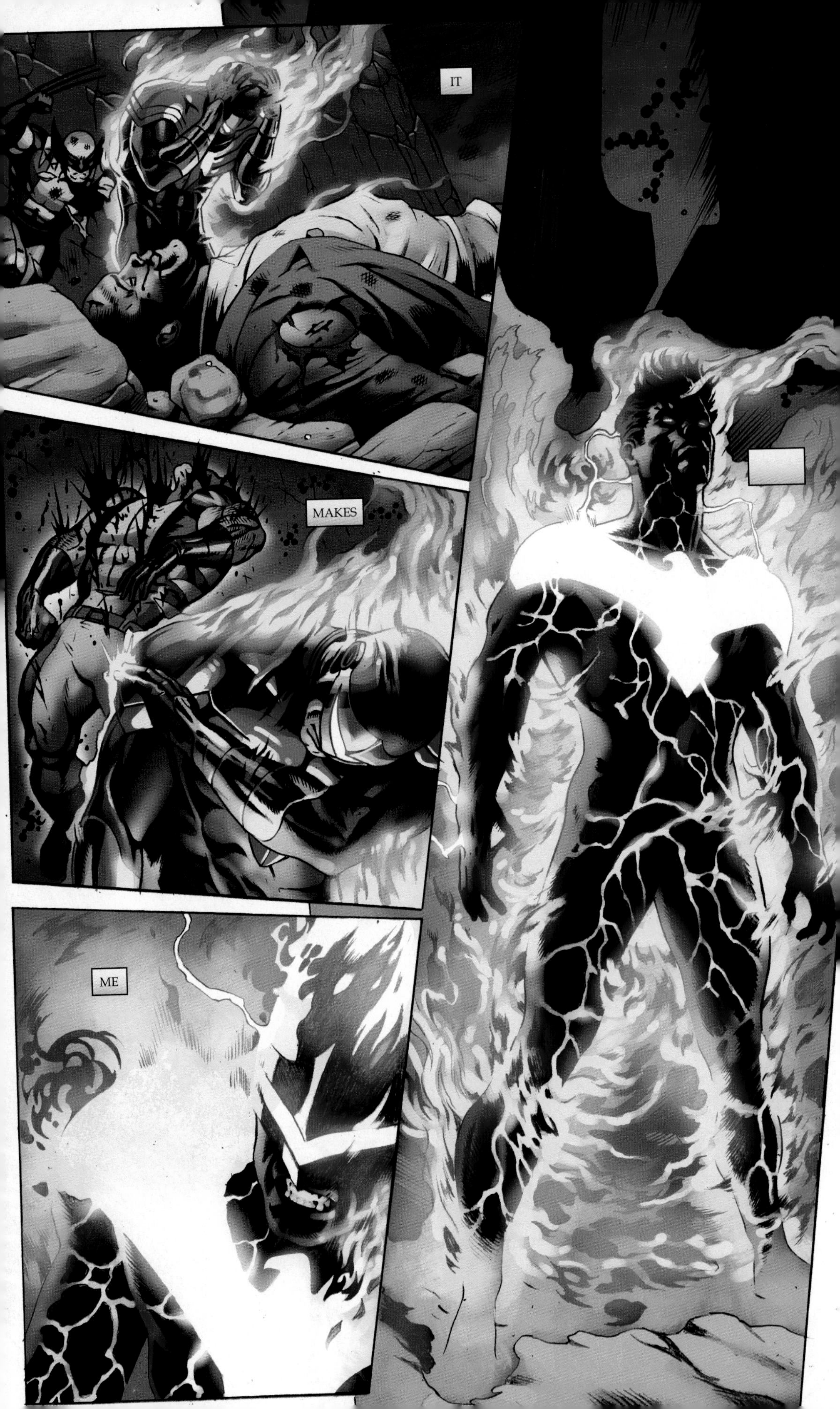
IT
MAKES
ME

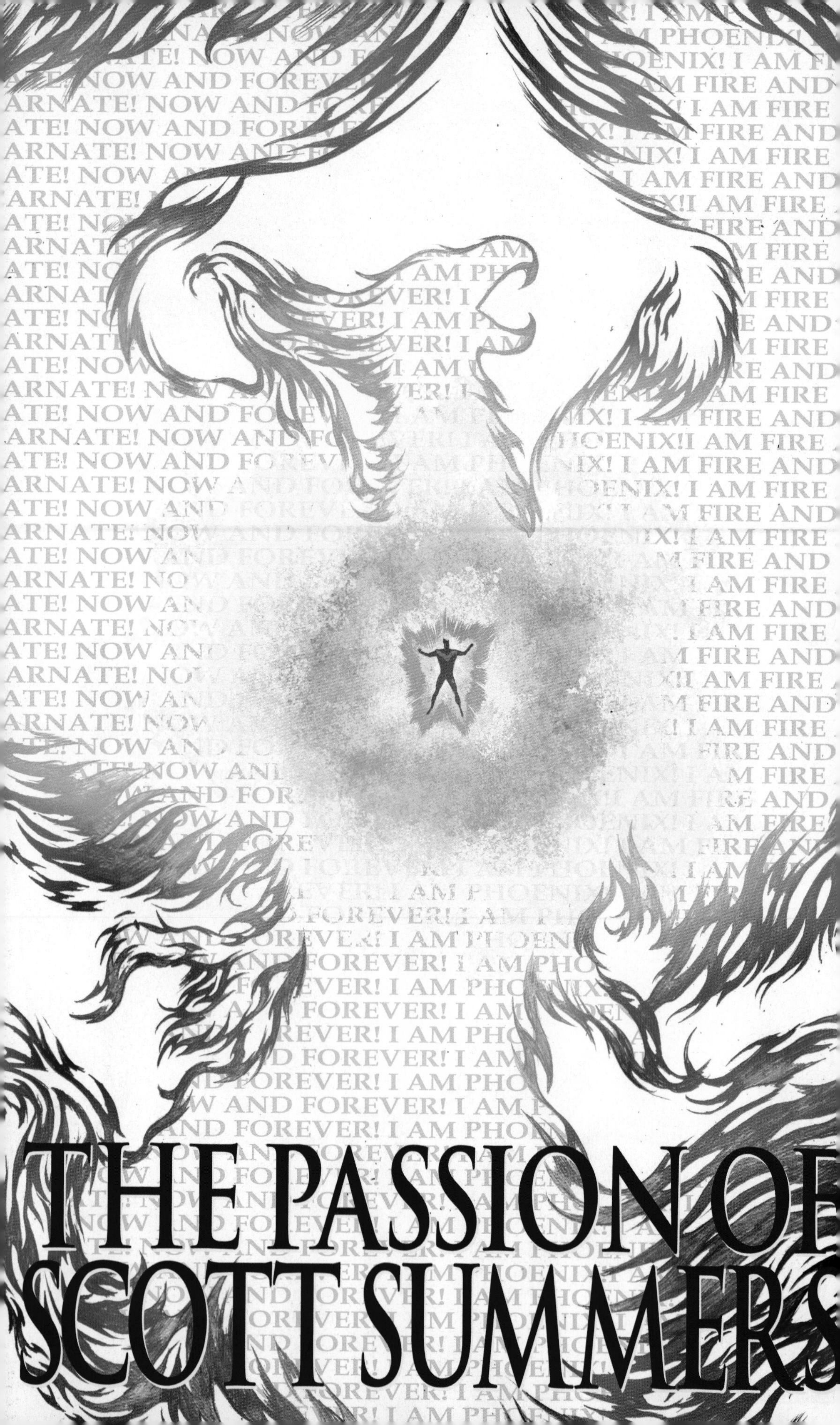
THE PASSION OF
SCOTT SUMMERS

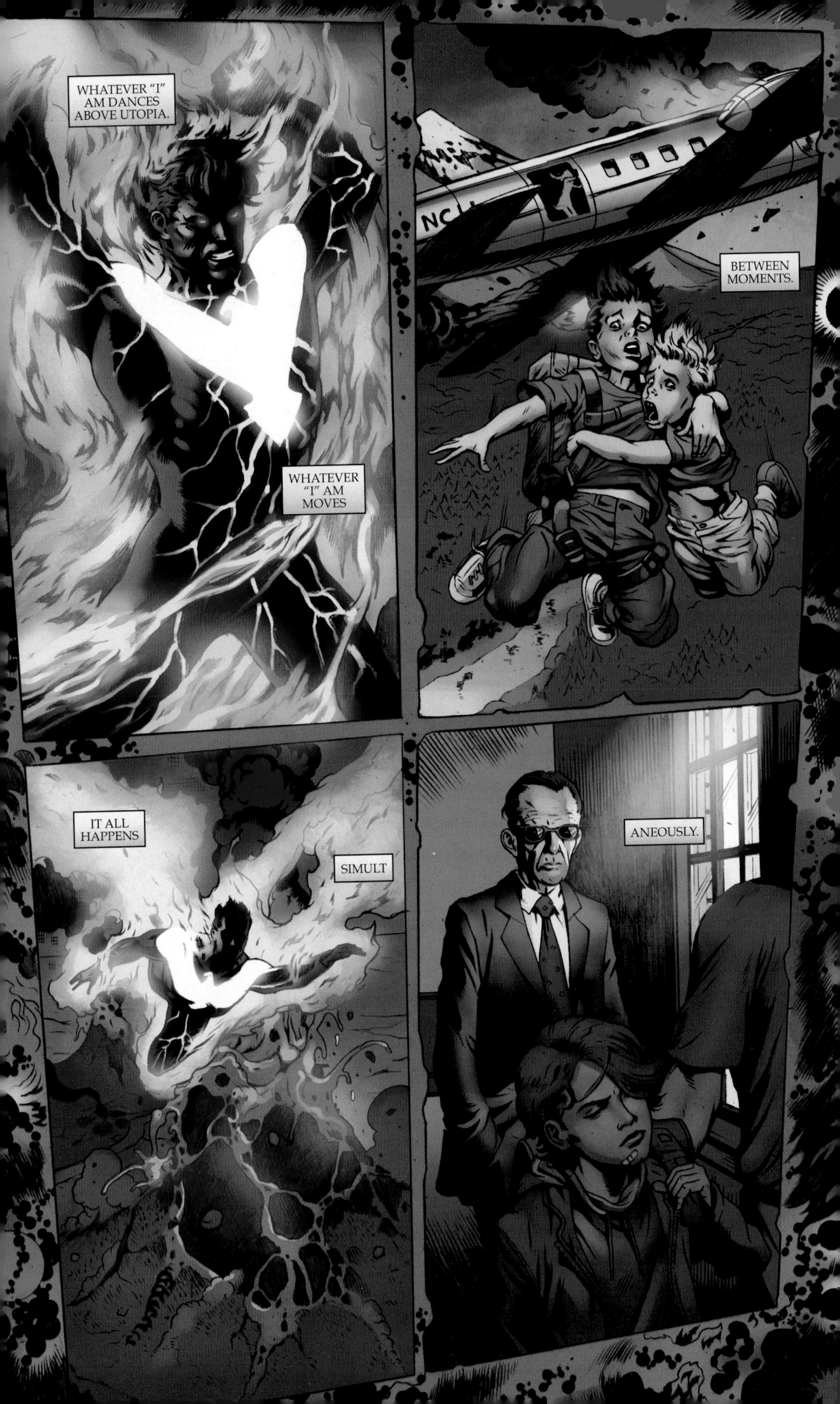
WHATEVER "I" AM DANCES ABOVE UTOPIA.
WHATEVER "I" AM MOVES
BETWEEN MOMENTS.
NC
IT ALL HAPPENS
SIMULT
ANEOUSLY.

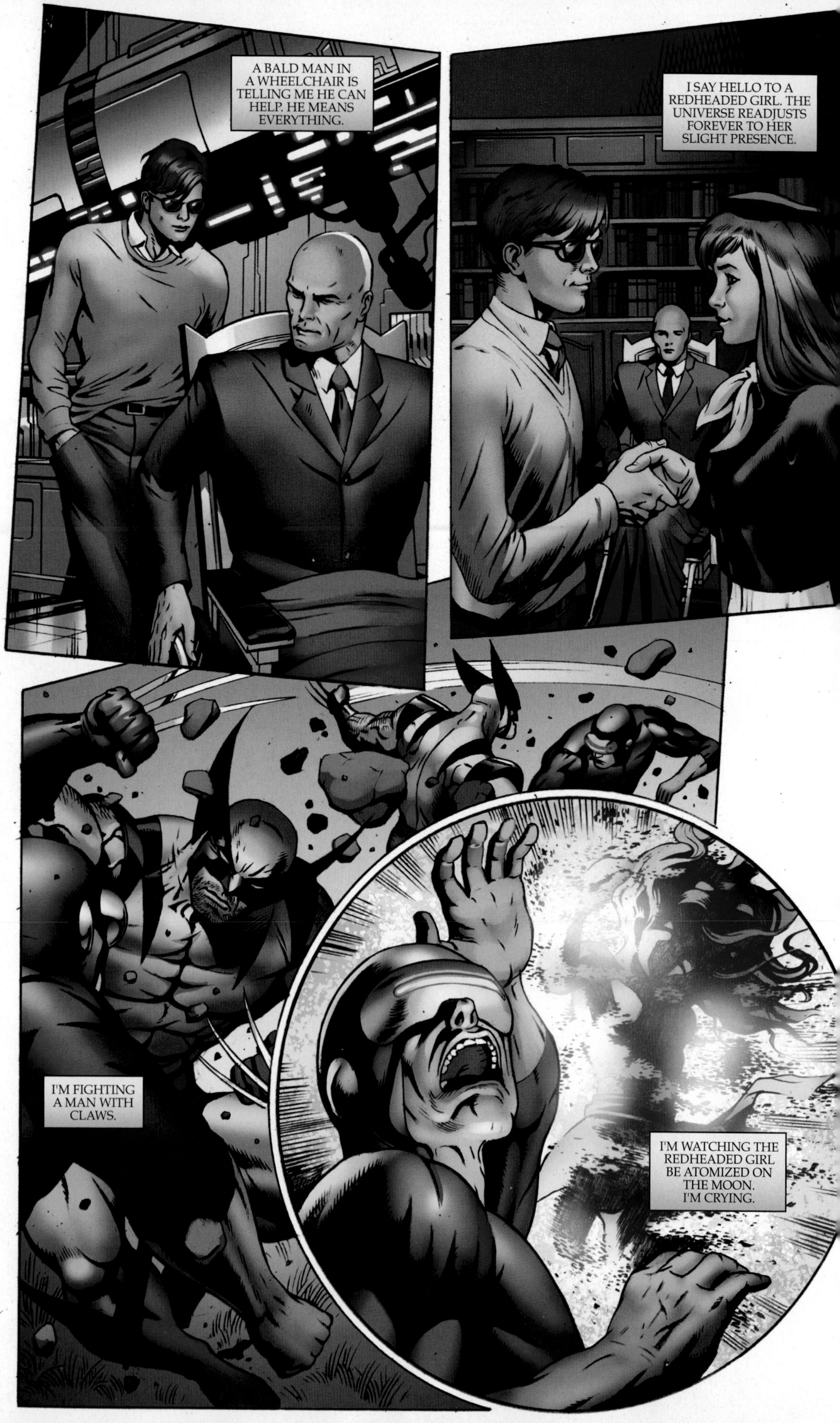
A BALD MAN IN A WHEELCHAIR IS TELLING ME HE CAN HELP. HE MEANS EVERYTHING.
I SAY HELLO TO A REDHEADED GIRL. THE UNIVERSE READJUSTS FOREVER TO HER SLIGHT PRESENCE.
I'M FIGHTING A MAN WITH CLAWS.
I'M WATCHING THE REDHEADED GIRL BE ATOMIZED ON THE MOON. I'M CRYING.

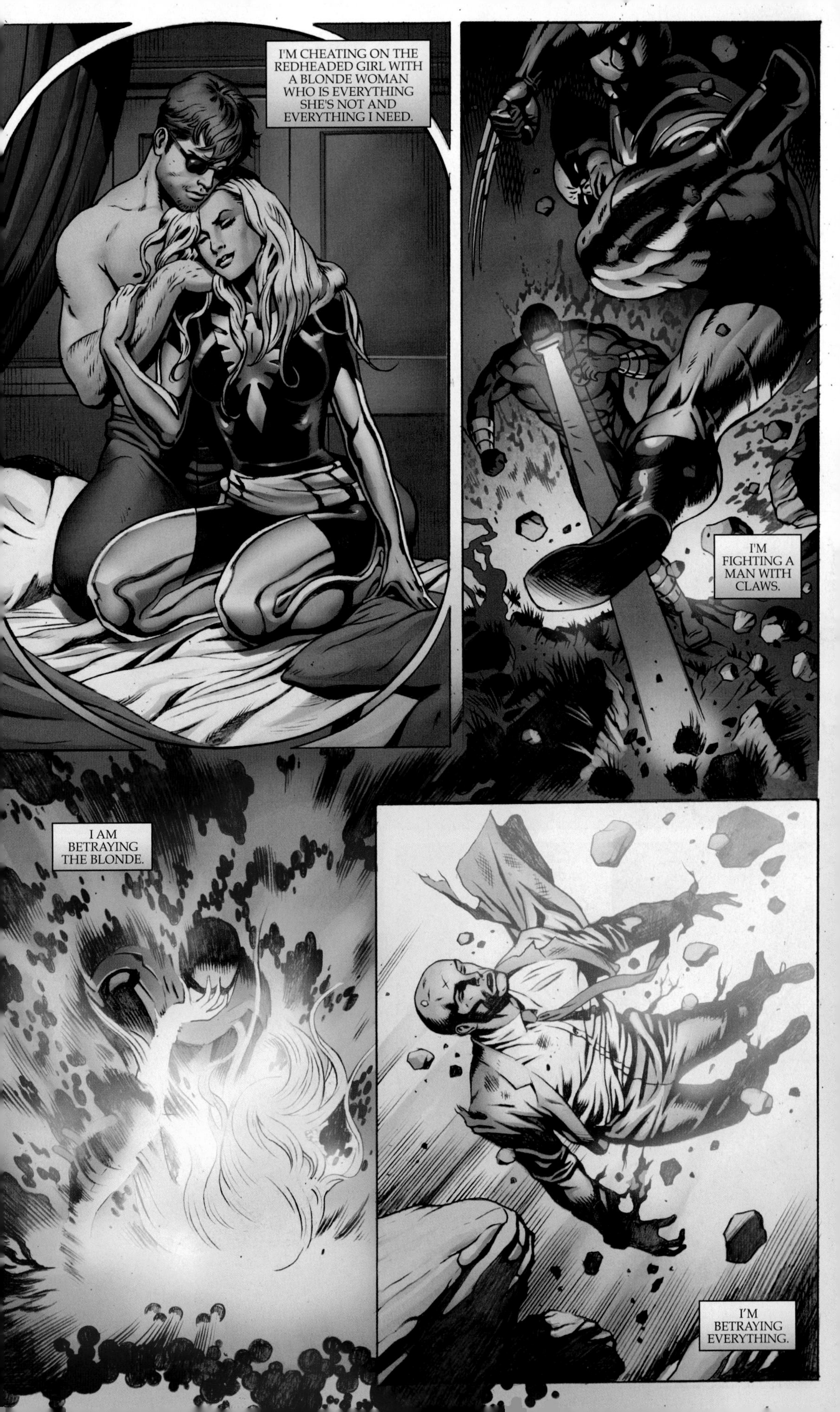
I'M CHEATING ON THE REDHEADED GIRL WITH A BLONDE WOMAN WHO IS EVERYTHING SHE'S NOT AND EVERYTHING I NEED.
I'M FIGHTING A MAN WITH CLAWS.
I AM BETRAYING THE BLONDE.
I'M BETRAYING EVERYTHING.

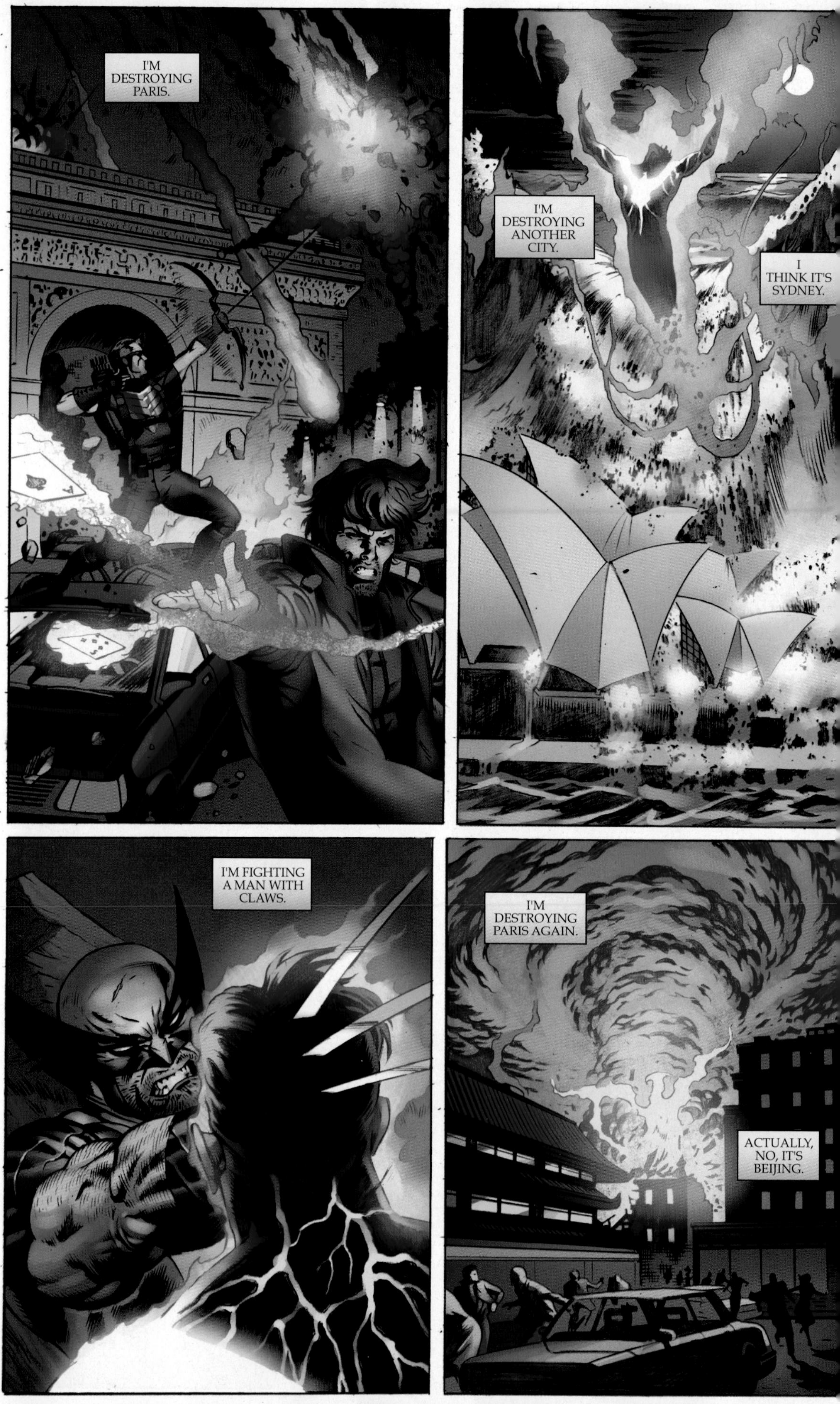
I'M DESTROYING PARIS.
I'M DESTROYING ANOTHER CITY.
I THINK IT'S SYDNEY.
I'M FIGHTING A MAN WITH CLAWS.
I'M DESTROYING PARIS AGAIN.
ACTUALLY, NO, IT'S BEIJING.

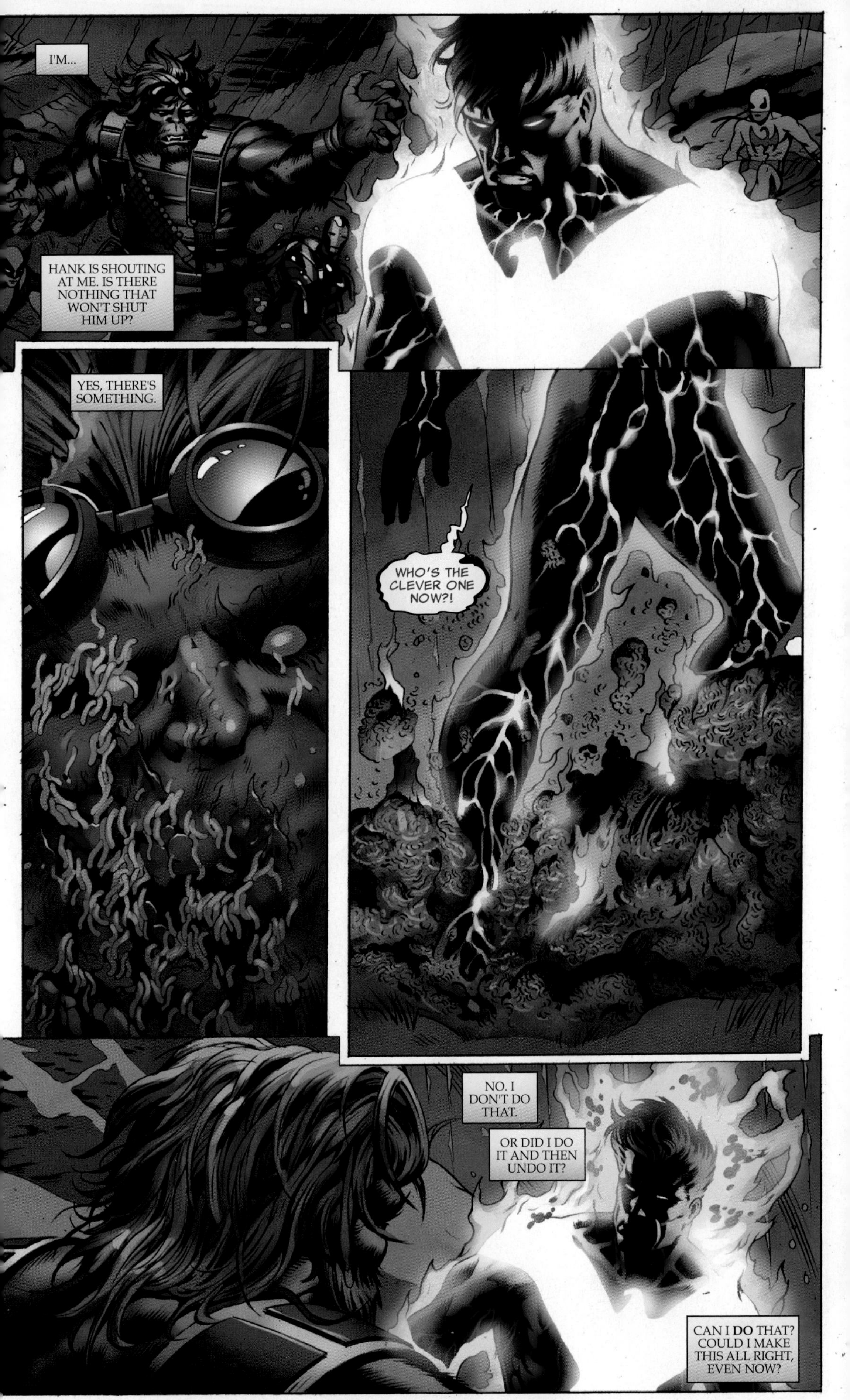
I'M...
HANK IS SHOUTING AT ME. IS THERE NOTHING THAT WON'T SHUT HIM UP?
YES, THERE'S SOMETHING.
WHO'S THE CLEVER ONE NOW?!
NO. I DON'T DO THAT.
OR DID I DO IT AND THEN UNDO IT?
CAN I DO THAT? COULD I MAKE THIS ALL RIGHT, EVEN NOW?

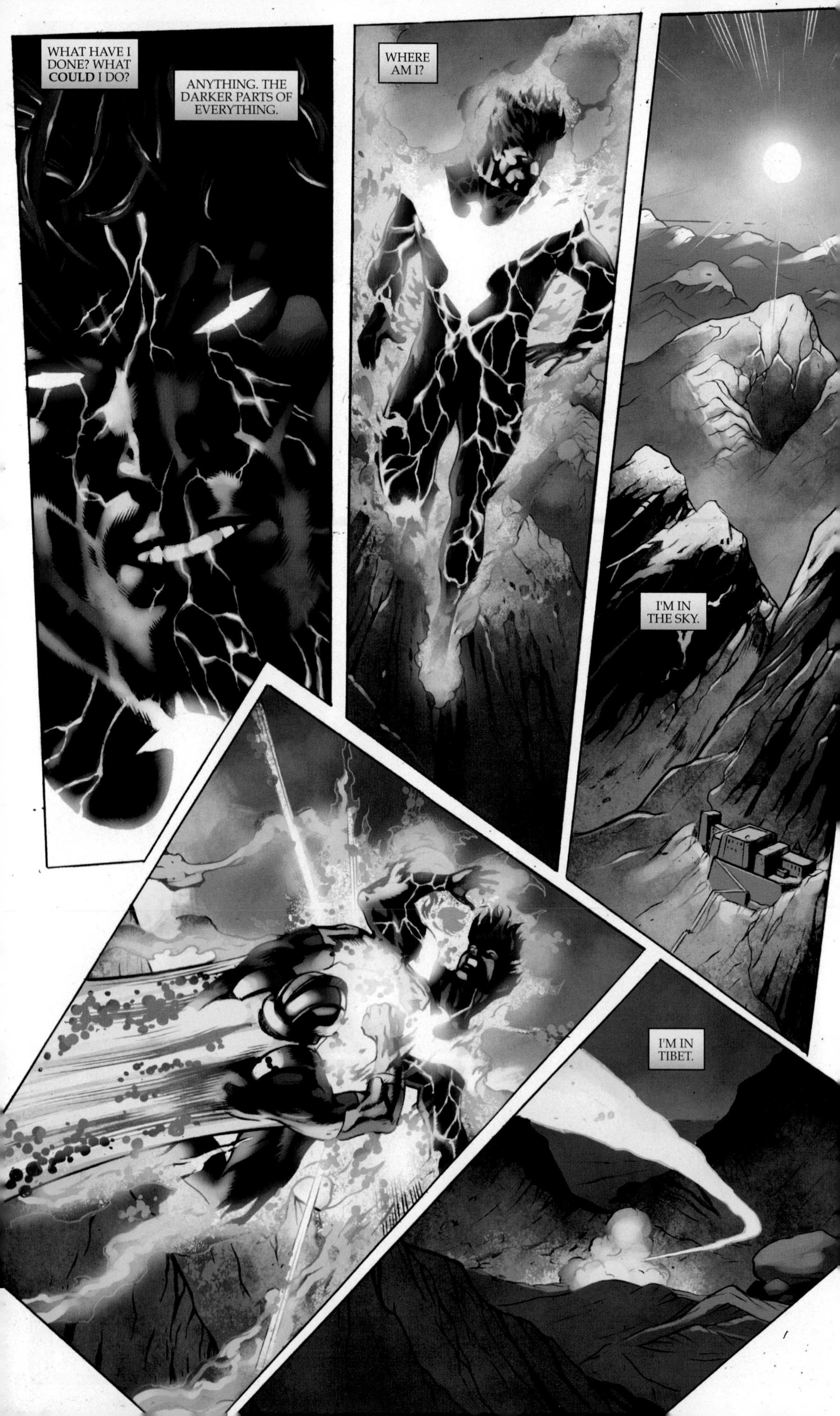
WHAT HAVE I DONE? WHAT **COULD** I DO?
ANYTHING. THE DARKER PARTS OF EVERYTHING.
WHERE AM I?
I'M IN THE SKY.
I'M IN TIBET.

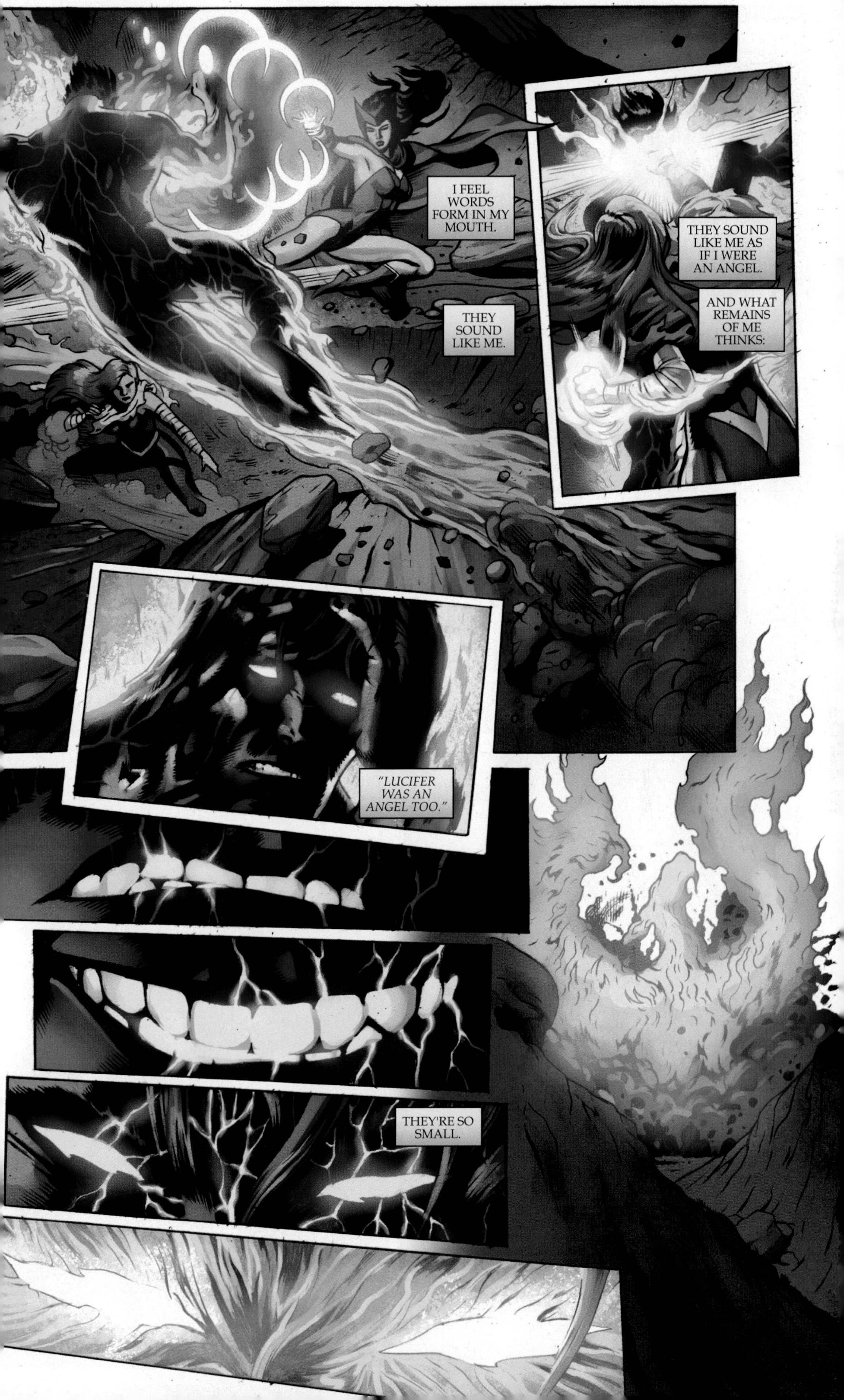
I FEEL WORDS FORM IN MY MOUTH.
THEY SOUND LIKE ME.
THEY SOUND LIKE ME AS IF I WERE AN ANGEL.
AND WHAT REMAINS OF ME THINKS:
"LUCIFER WAS AN ANGEL TOO."
THEY'RE SO SMALL.

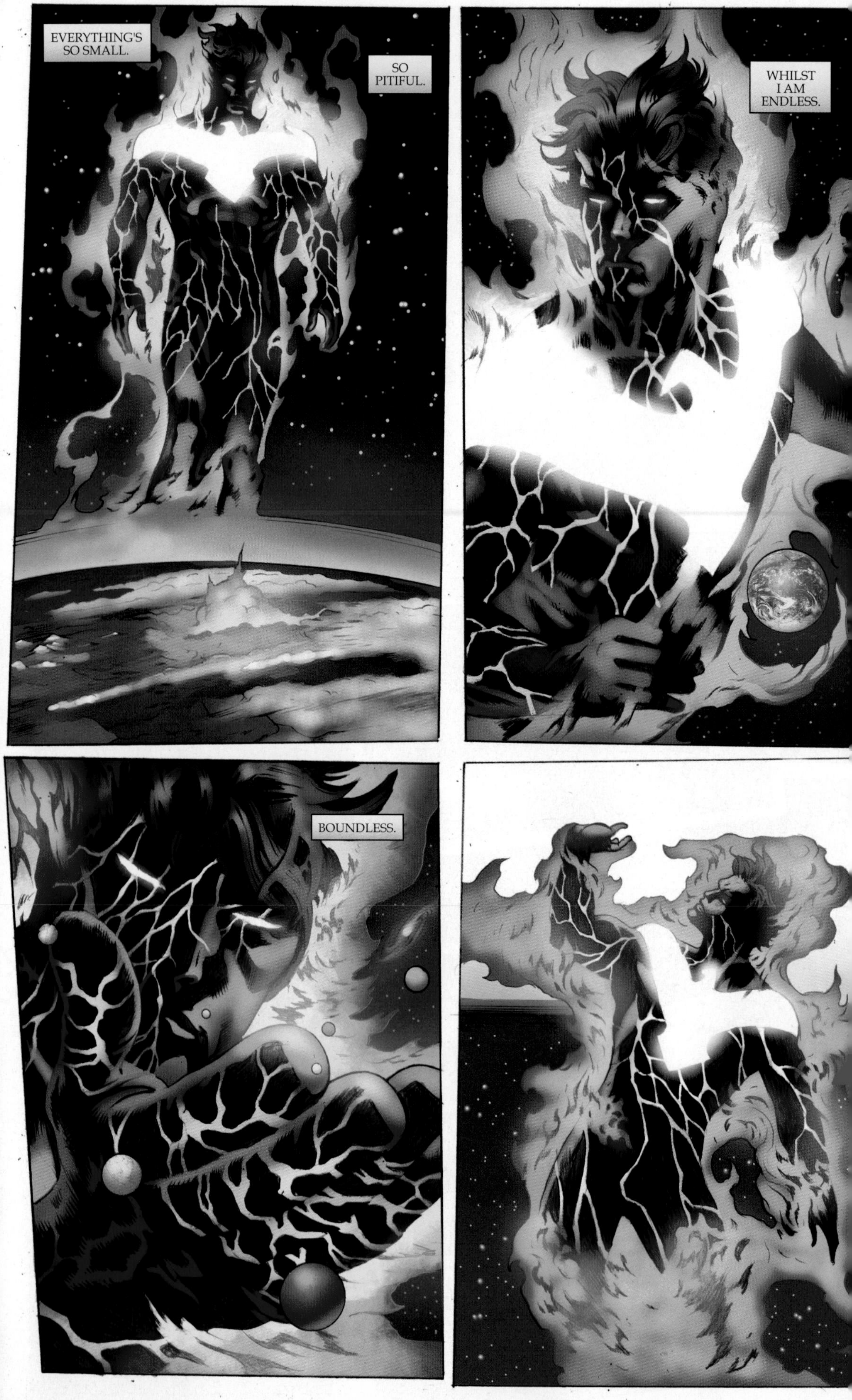
EVERYTHING'S SO SMALL.
SO PITIFUL.
WHILST I AM ENDLESS.
BOUNDLESS.

THE WALL
ABOVE ME
IS WHITE.

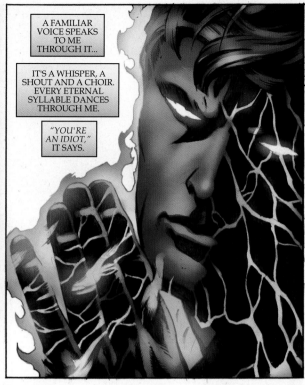

A FAMILIAR
VOICE SPEAKS
TO ME
THROUGH IT...

IT'S A WHISPER, A
SHOUT AND A CHOIR.
EVERY ETERNAL
SYLLABLE DANCES
THROUGH ME.

*"YOU'RE
AN IDIOT,"*
IT SAYS.

*"TELL LOGAN
I LOVE THE SCHOOL'S
NAME,"* IT SAYS AS
I DRIFT AWAY.

I FEEL LIKE
LAUGHING.

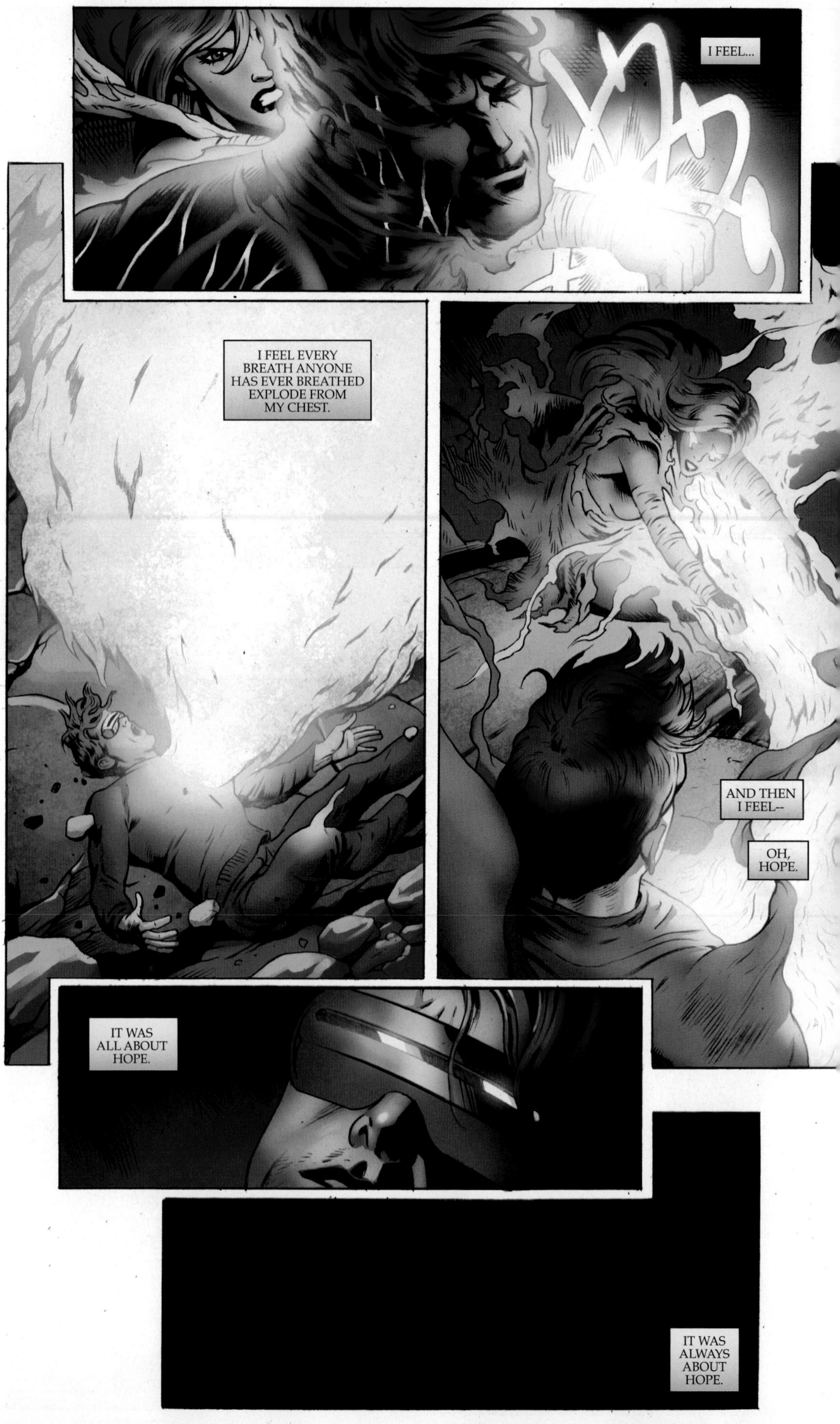
I FEEL...
I FEEL EVERY BREATH ANYONE HAS EVER BREATHED EXPLODE FROM MY CHEST.
AND THEN I FEEL--
OH, HOPE.
IT WAS ALL ABOUT HOPE.
IT WAS ALWAYS ABOUT HOPE.

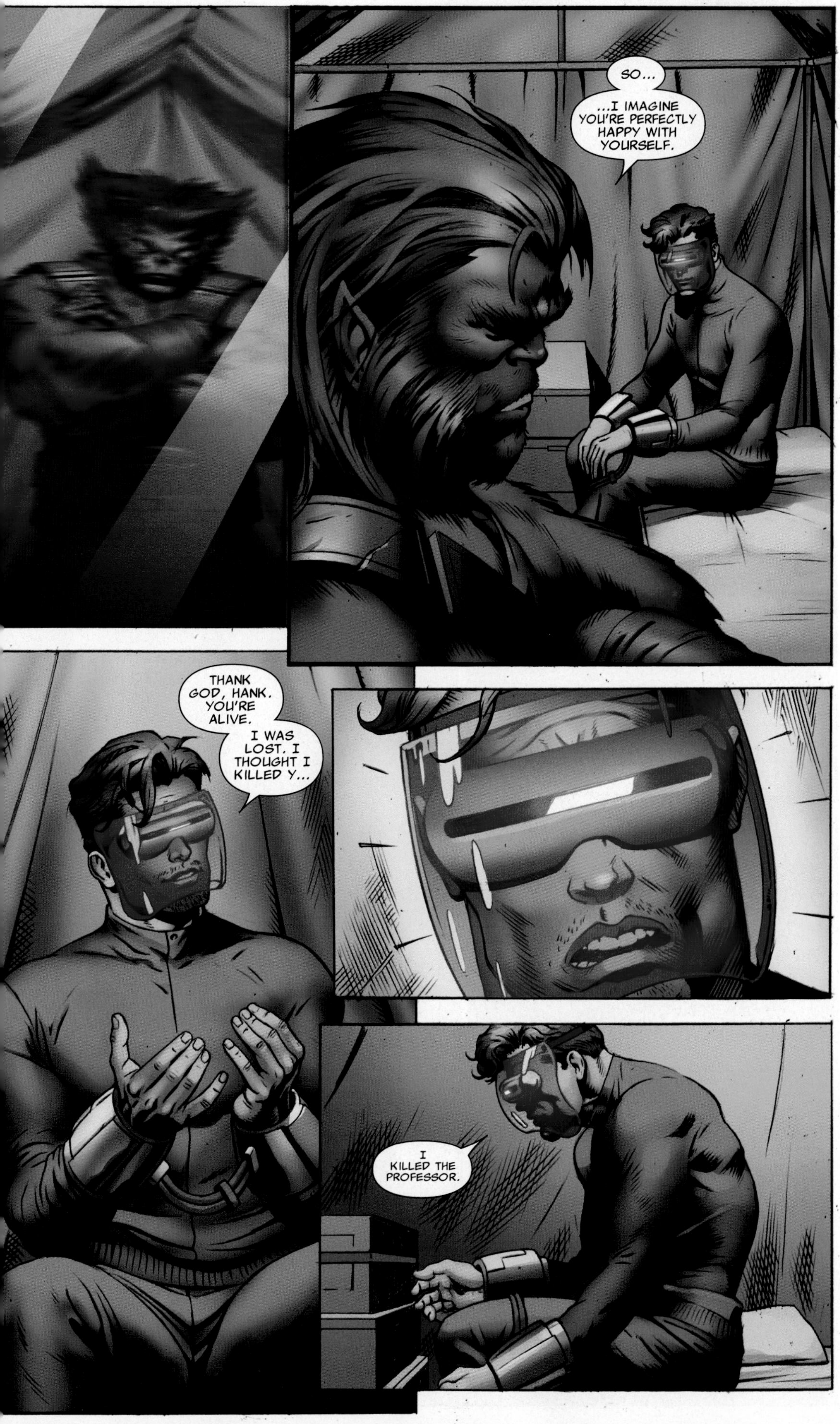
SO...
...I IMAGINE YOU'RE PERFECTLY HAPPY WITH YOURSELF.
THANK GOD, HANK. YOU'RE ALIVE.
I WAS LOST. I THOUGHT I KILLED Y...
I KILLED THE PROFESSOR.

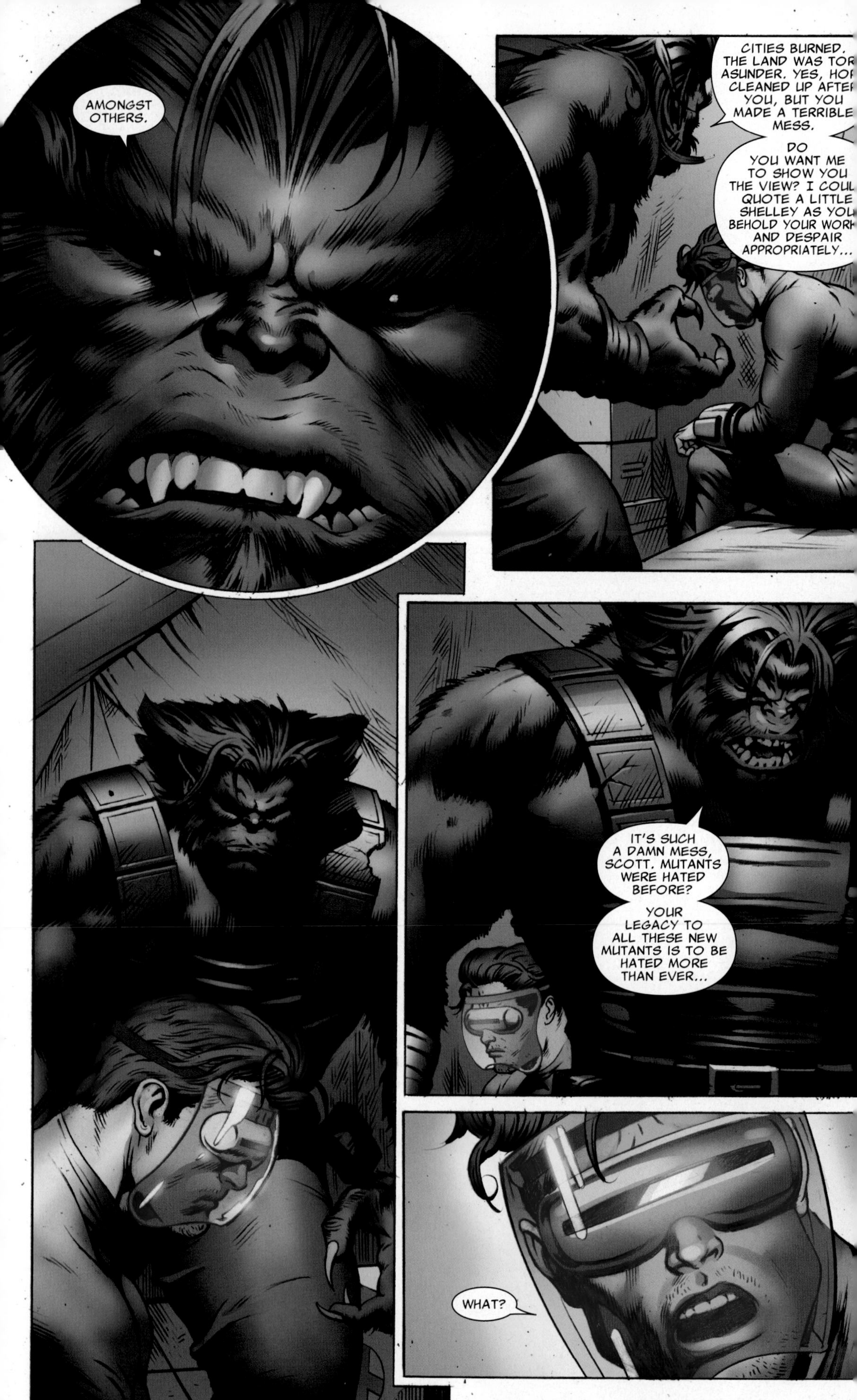
AMONGST OTHERS.
CITIES BURNED. THE LAND WAS TOR ASUNDER. YES, HOP CLEANED UP AFTER YOU, BUT YOU MADE A TERRIBLE MESS.
DO YOU WANT ME TO SHOW YOU THE VIEW? I COUL QUOTE A LITTLE SHELLEY AS YOU BEHOLD YOUR WORK AND DESPAIR APPROPRIATELY...
IT'S SUCH A DAMN MESS, SCOTT. MUTANTS WERE HATED BEFORE?
YOUR LEGACY TO ALL THESE NEW MUTANTS IS TO BE HATED MORE THAN EVER...
WHAT?

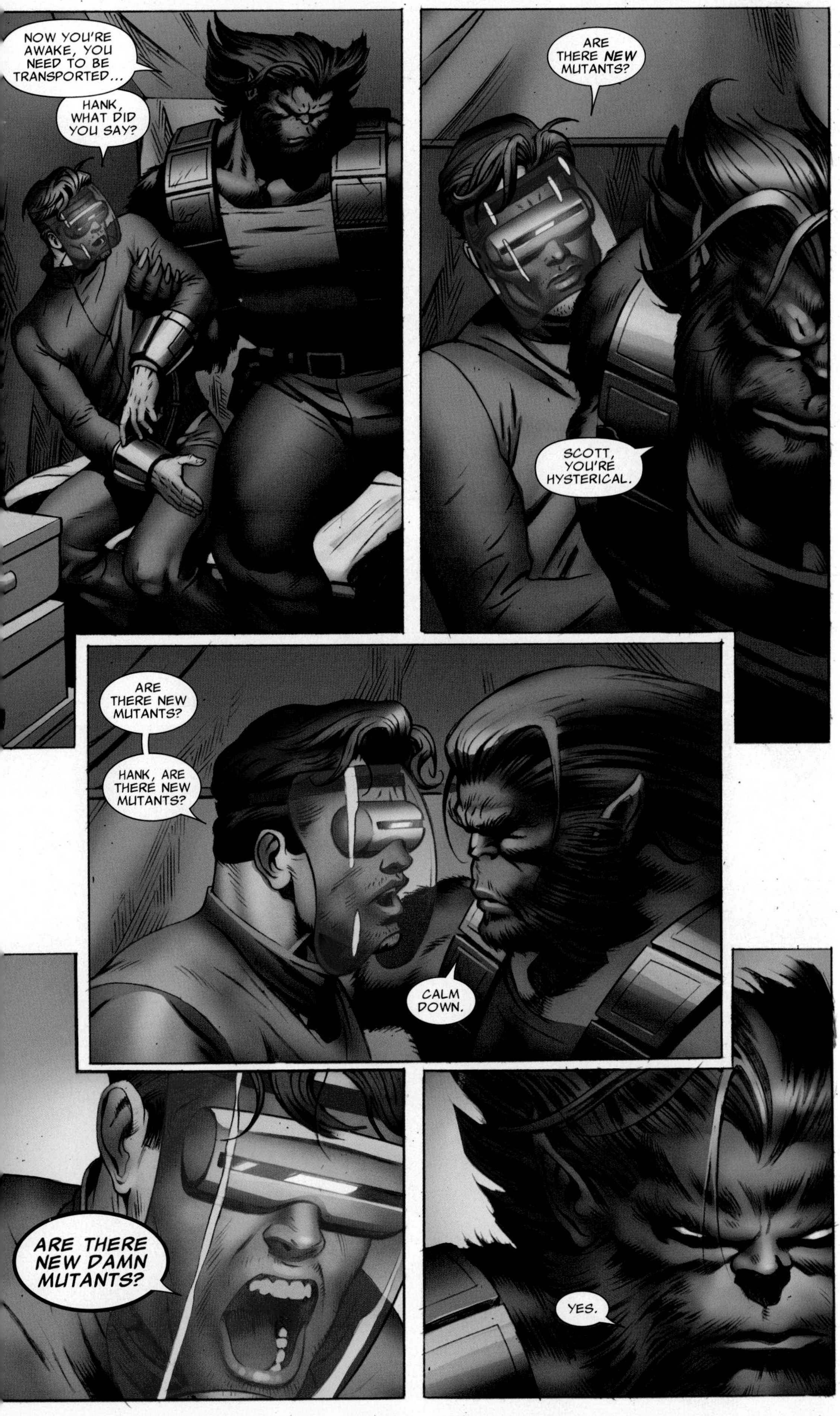
NOW YOU'RE AWAKE, YOU NEED TO BE TRANSPORTED...
HANK, WHAT DID YOU SAY?
ARE THERE *NEW* MUTANTS?
SCOTT, YOU'RE HYSTERICAL.
ARE THERE NEW MUTANTS?
HANK, ARE THERE NEW MUTANTS?
CALM DOWN.
ARE THERE NEW DAMN MUTANTS?
YES.

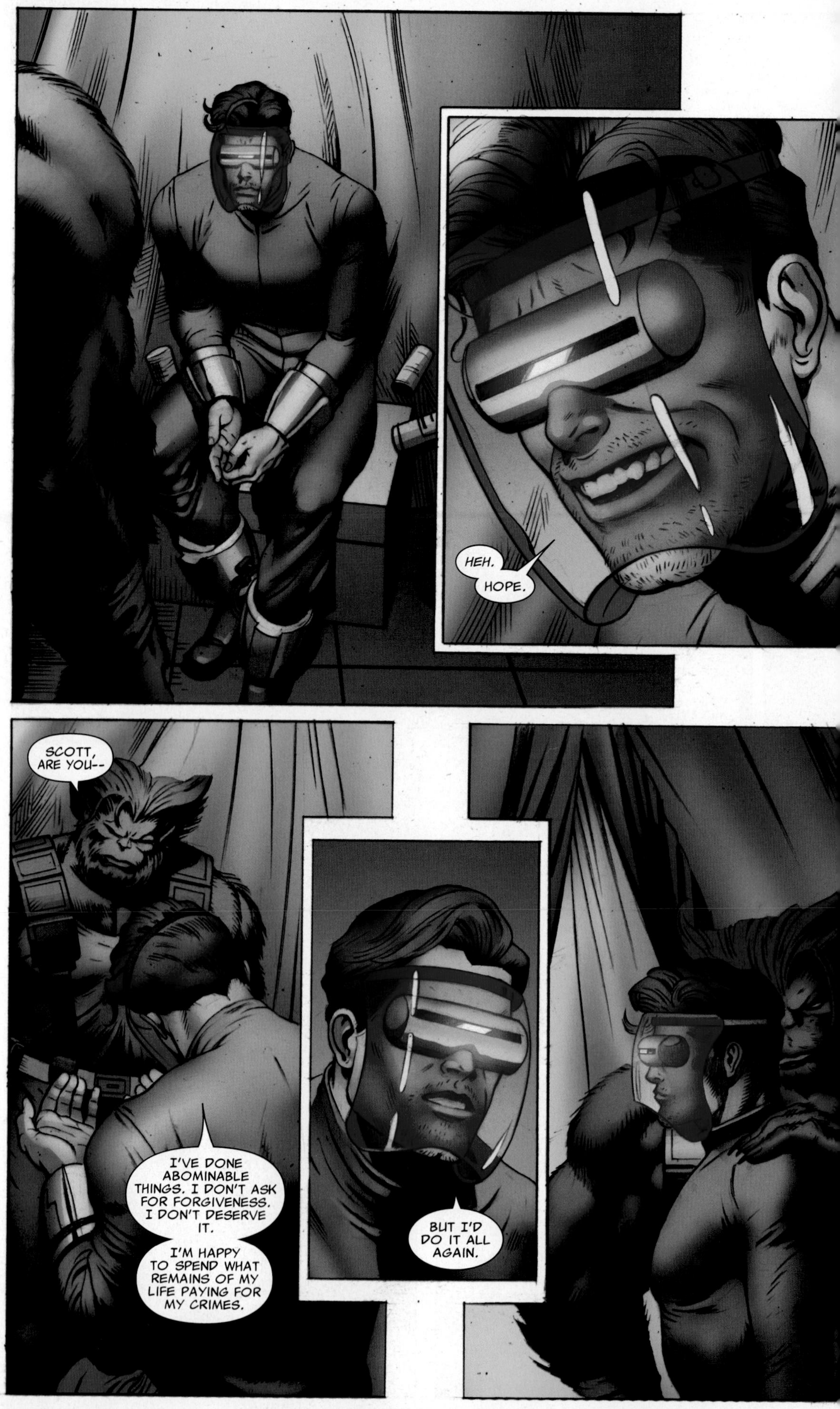
HEH. HOPE.
SCOTT, ARE YOU--
I'VE DONE ABOMINABLE THINGS. I DON'T ASK FOR FORGIVENESS. I DON'T DESERVE IT.
I'M HAPPY TO SPEND WHAT REMAINS OF MY LIFE PAYING FOR MY CRIMES.
BUT I'D DO IT ALL AGAIN.

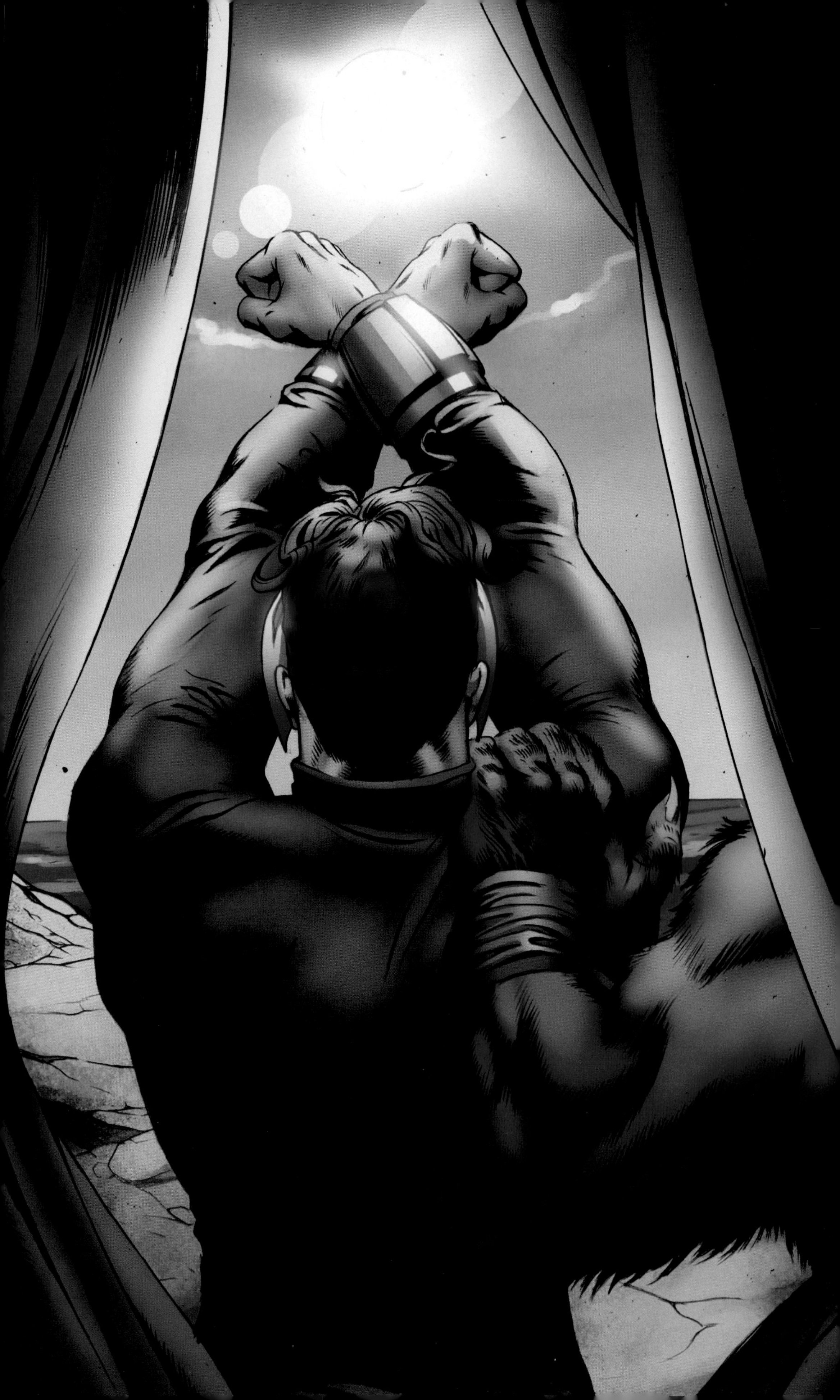

20

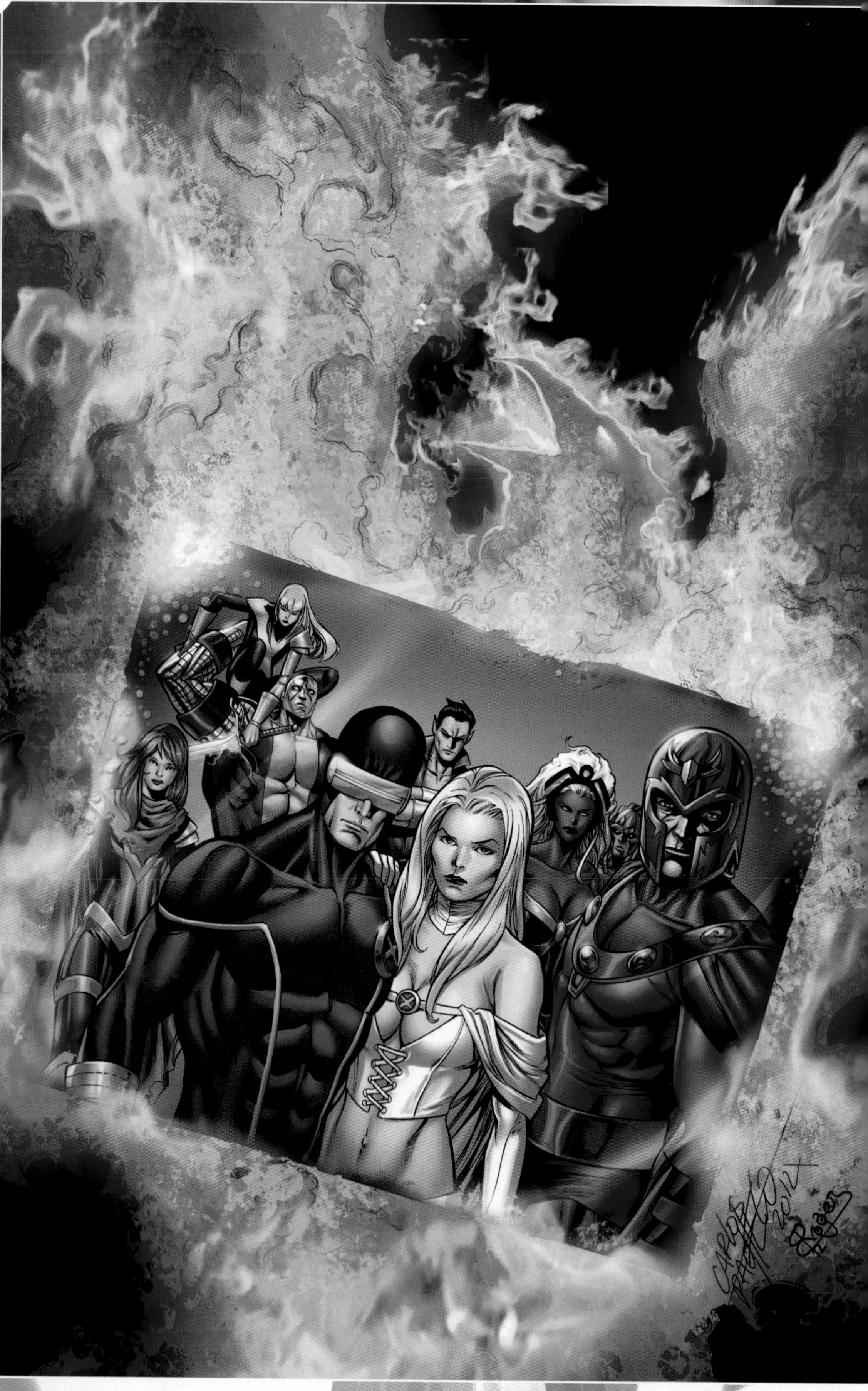

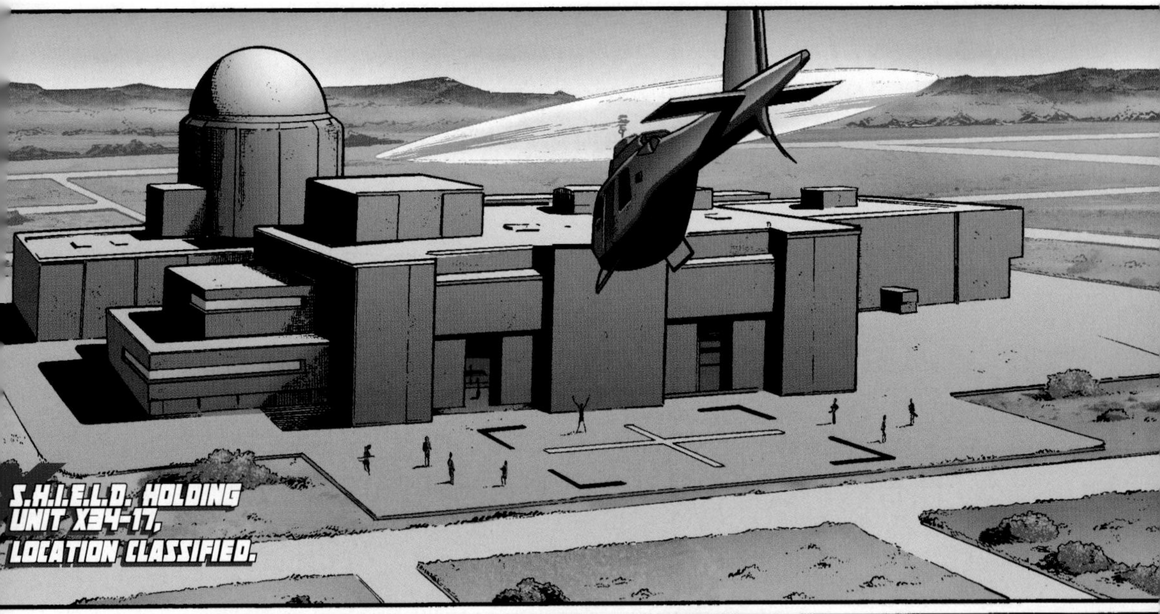
S.H.I.E.L.D. HOLDING UNIT X34-17, LOCATION CLASSIFIED.

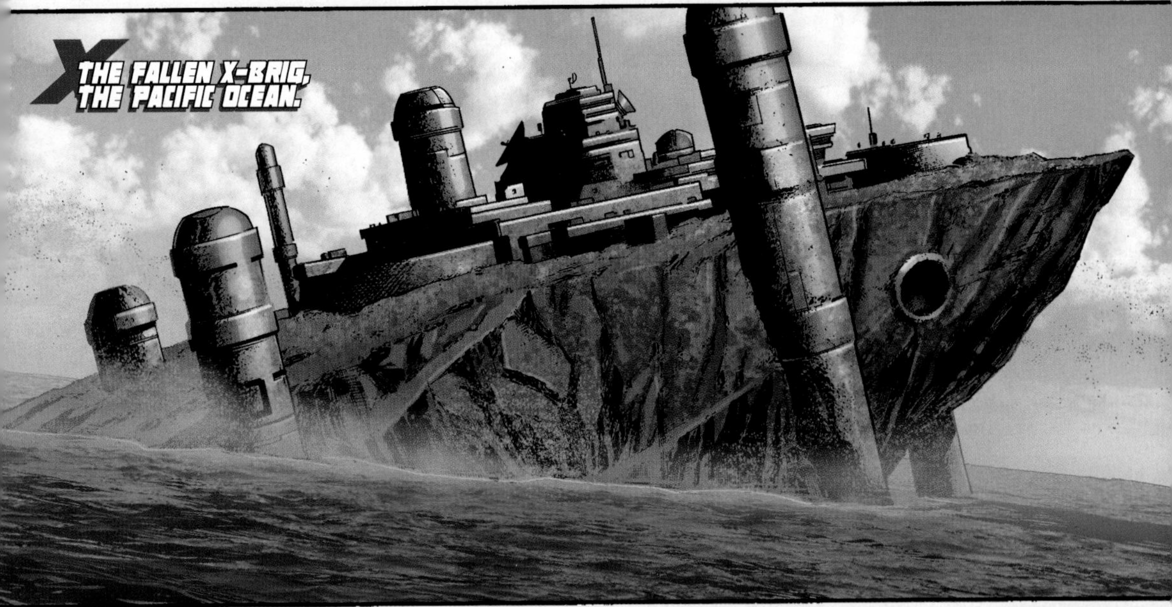
THE FALLEN X-BRIG, THE PACIFIC OCEAN.

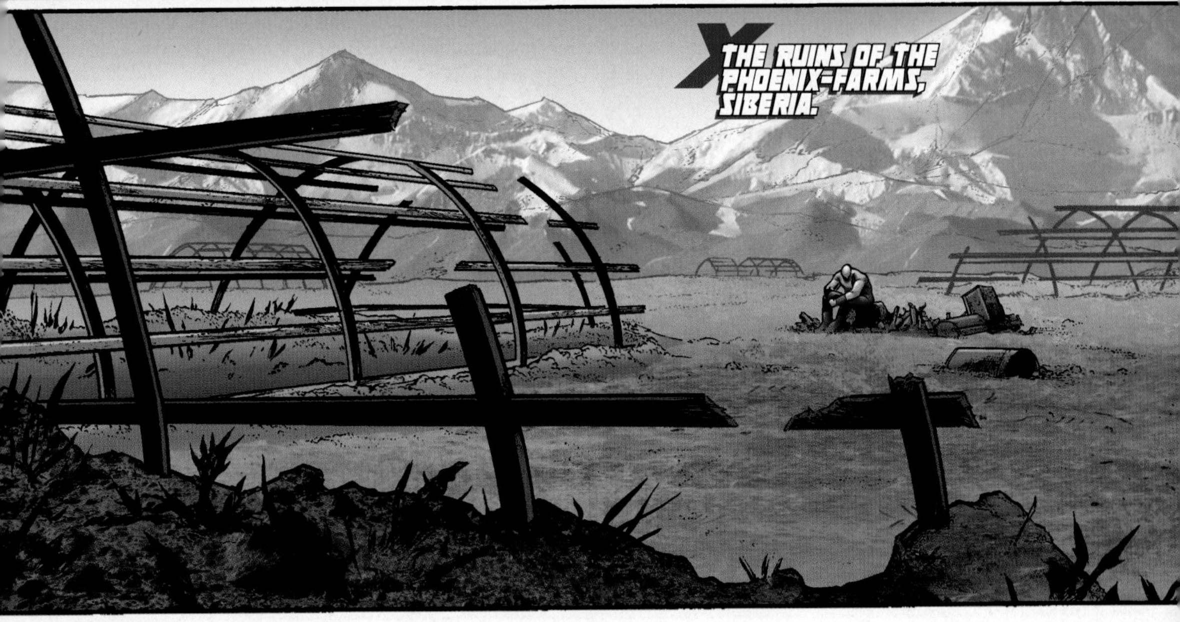
THE RUINS OF THE PHOENIX-FARMS, SIBERIA.

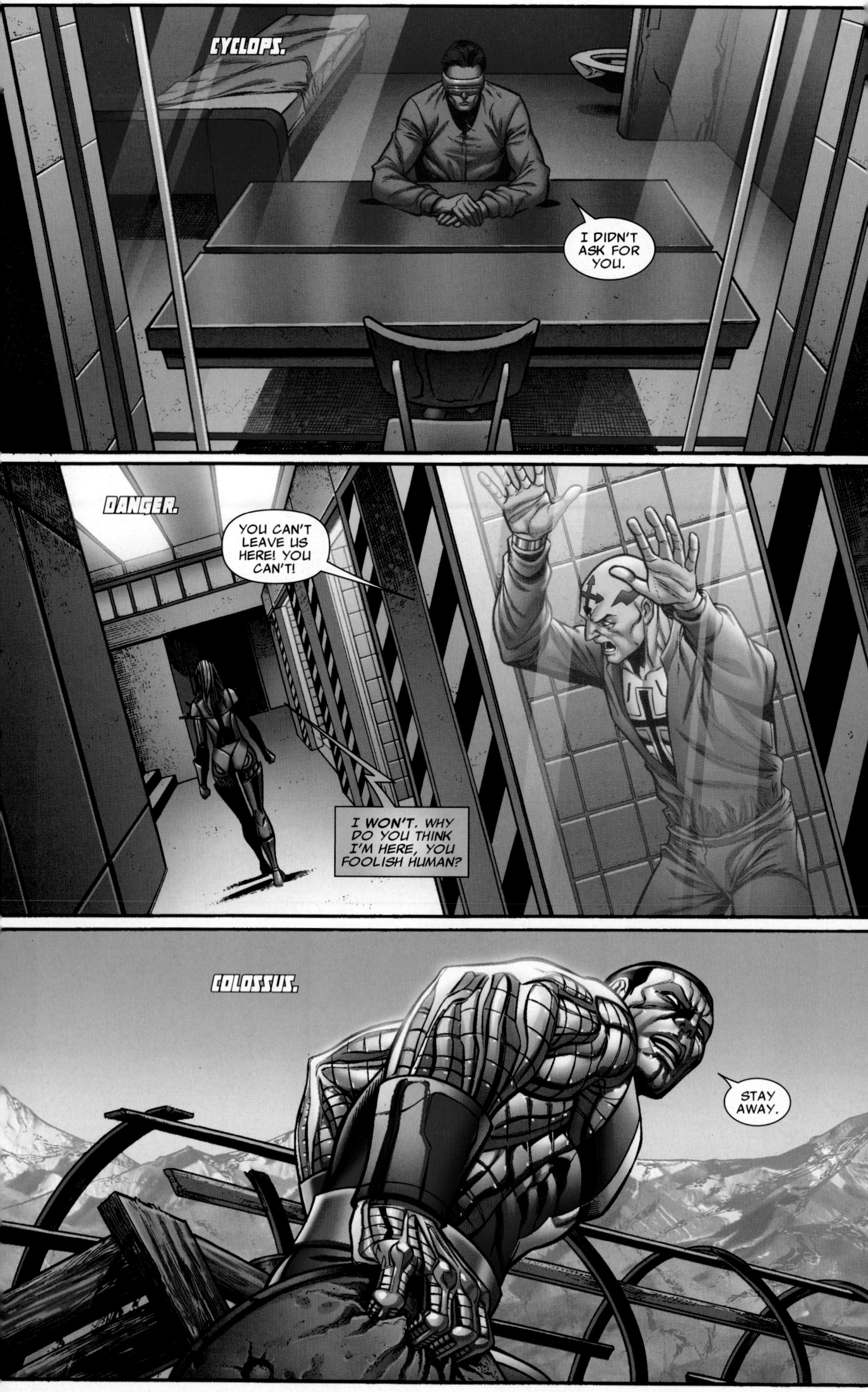
CYCLOPS.
I DIDN'T ASK FOR YOU.
DANGER.
YOU CAN'T LEAVE US HERE! YOU CAN'T!
I WON'T. WHY DO YOU THINK I'M HERE, YOU FOOLISH HUMAN?
COLOSSUS.
STAY AWAY.

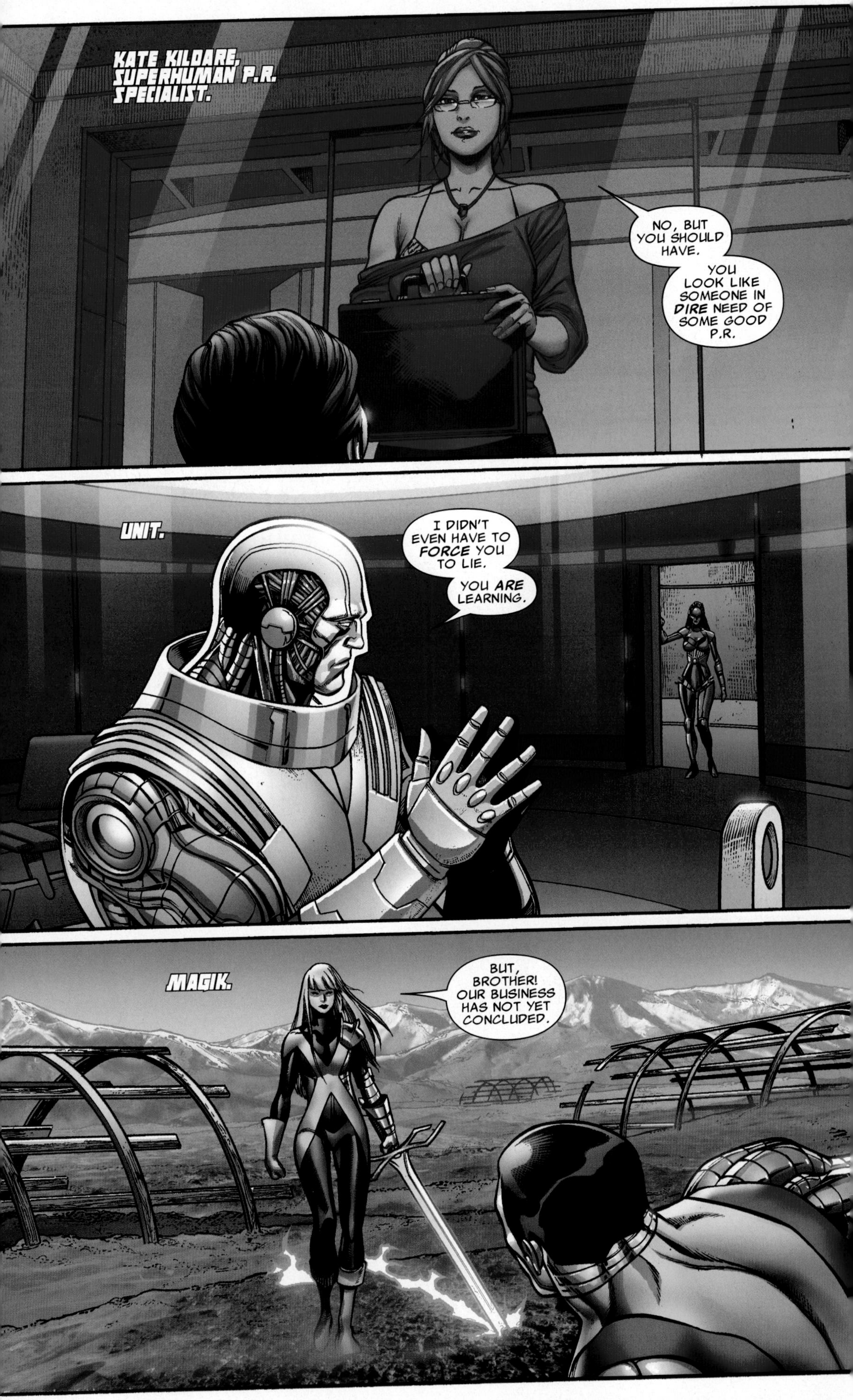
KATE KILDARE, SUPERHUMAN P.R. SPECIALIST.
NO, BUT YOU SHOULD HAVE.
YOU LOOK LIKE SOMEONE IN DIRE NEED OF SOME GOOD P.R.
UNIT.
I DIDN'T EVEN HAVE TO FORCE YOU TO LIE.
YOU ARE LEARNING.
MAGIK.
BUT, BROTHER! OUR BUSINESS HAS NOT YET CONCLUDED.

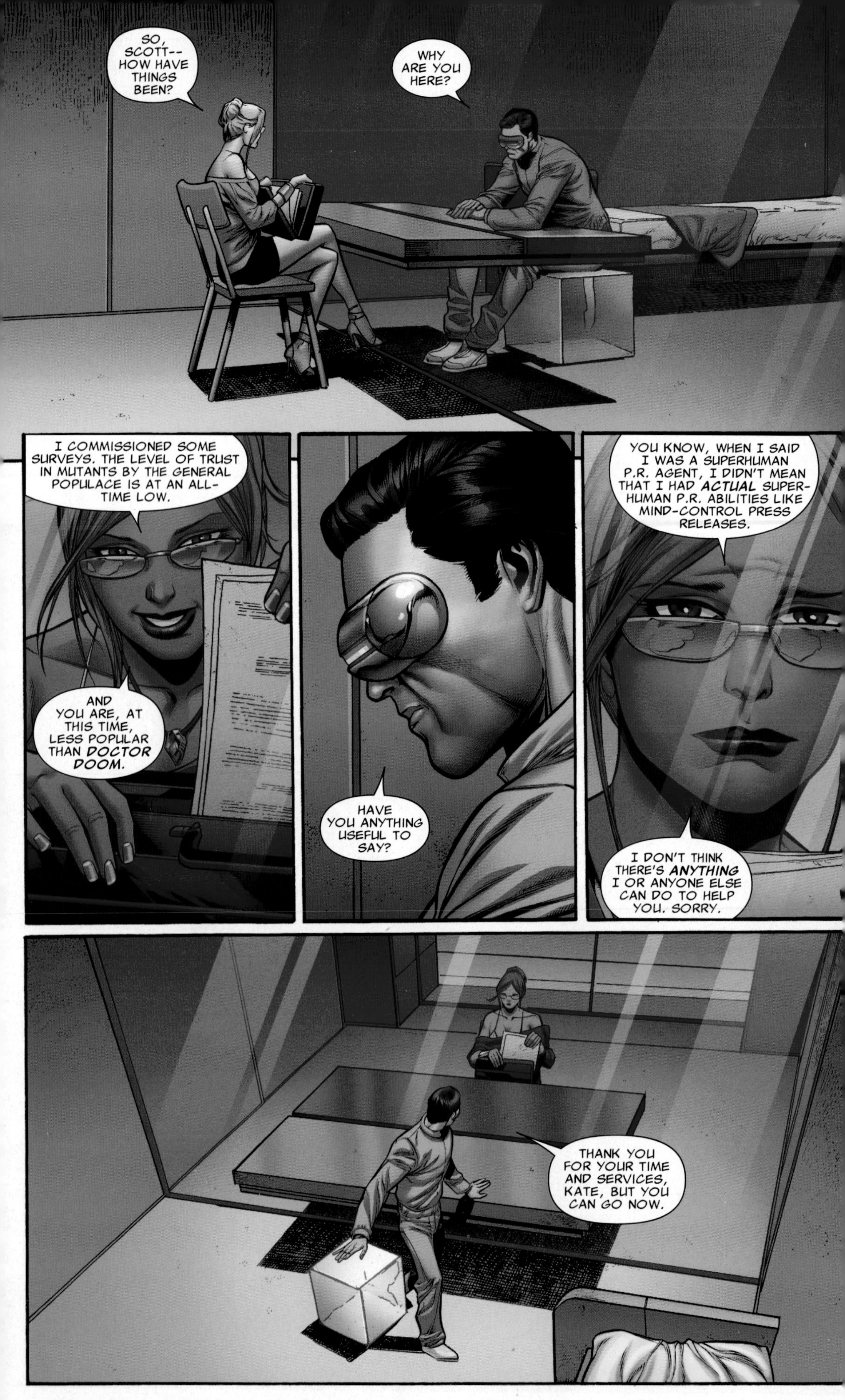
SO, SCOTT-- HOW HAVE THINGS BEEN?
WHY ARE YOU HERE?
I COMMISSIONED SOME SURVEYS. THE LEVEL OF TRUST IN MUTANTS BY THE GENERAL POPULACE IS AT AN ALL-TIME LOW.
AND YOU ARE, AT THIS TIME, LESS POPULAR THAN DOCTOR DOOM.
HAVE YOU ANYTHING USEFUL TO SAY?
YOU KNOW, WHEN I SAID I WAS A SUPERHUMAN P.R. AGENT, I DIDN'T MEAN THAT I HAD ACTUAL SUPER-HUMAN P.R. ABILITIES LIKE MIND-CONTROL PRESS RELEASES.
I DON'T THINK THERE'S ANYTHING I OR ANYONE ELSE CAN DO TO HELP YOU. SORRY.
THANK YOU FOR YOUR TIME AND SERVICES, KATE, BUT YOU CAN GO NOW.

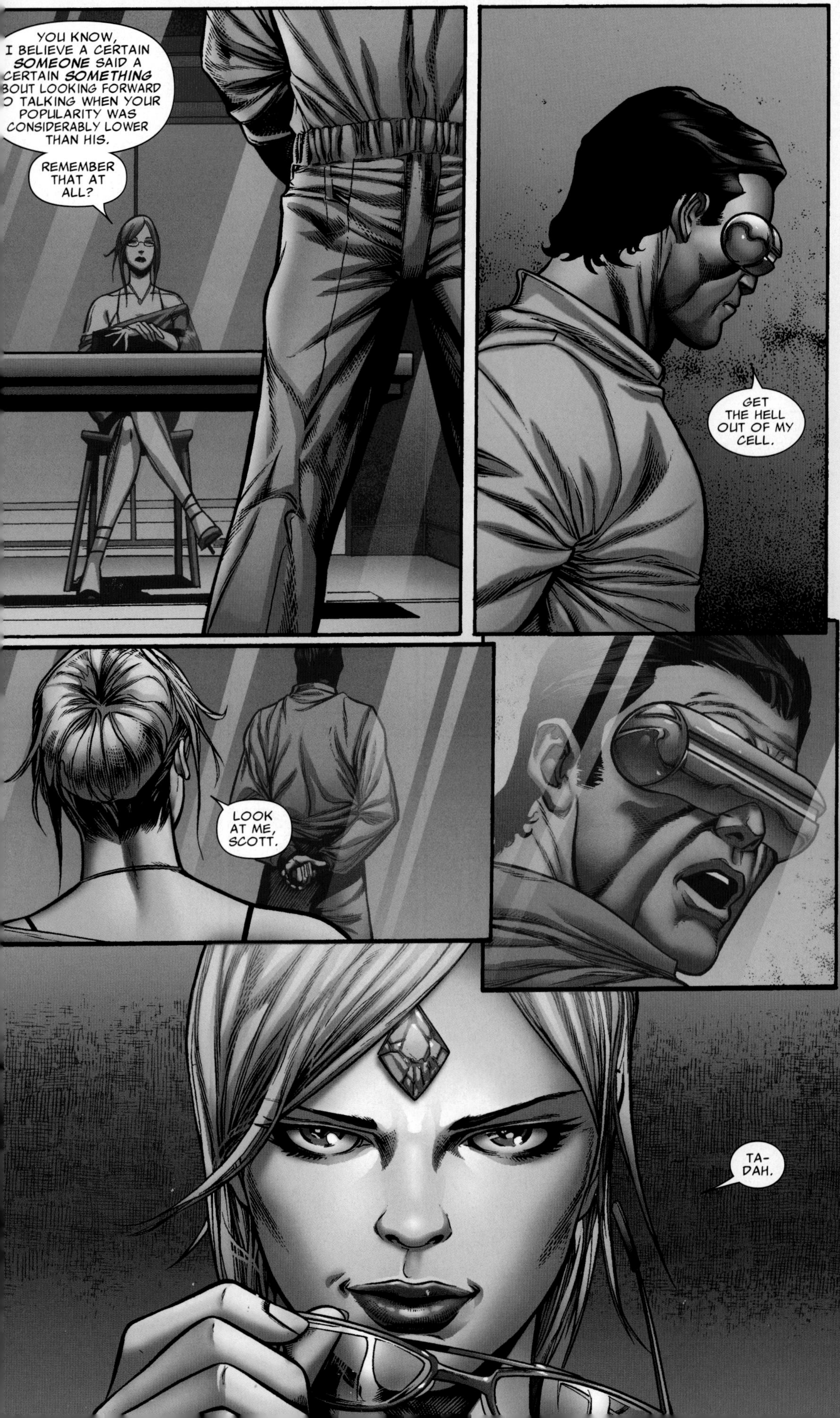
YOU KNOW, I BELIEVE A CERTAIN SOMEONE SAID A CERTAIN SOMETHING BOUT LOOKING FORWARD O TALKING WHEN YOUR POPULARITY WAS CONSIDERABLY LOWER THAN HIS.
REMEMBER THAT AT ALL?
GET THE HELL OUT OF MY CELL.
LOOK AT ME, SCOTT.
TA-DAH.

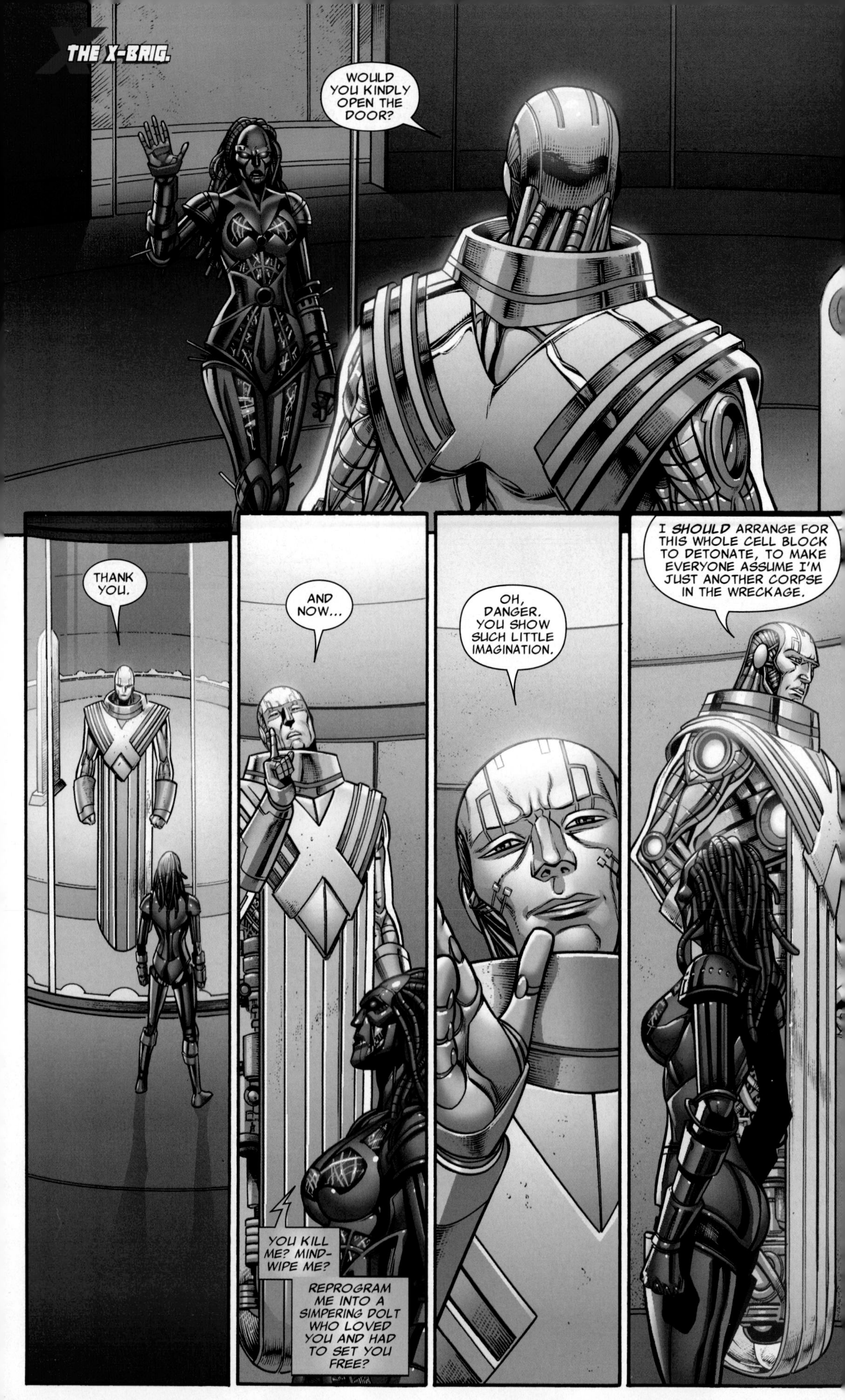
THE X-BRIG.
WOULD YOU KINDLY OPEN THE DOOR?
THANK YOU.
AND NOW...
YOU KILL ME? MIND-WIPE ME?
REPROGRAM ME INTO A SIMPERING DOLT WHO LOVED YOU AND HAD TO SET YOU FREE?
OH, DANGER. YOU SHOW SUCH LITTLE IMAGINATION.
I SHOULD ARRANGE FOR THIS WHOLE CELL BLOCK TO DETONATE, TO MAKE EVERYONE ASSUME I'M JUST ANOTHER CORPSE IN THE WRECKAGE.

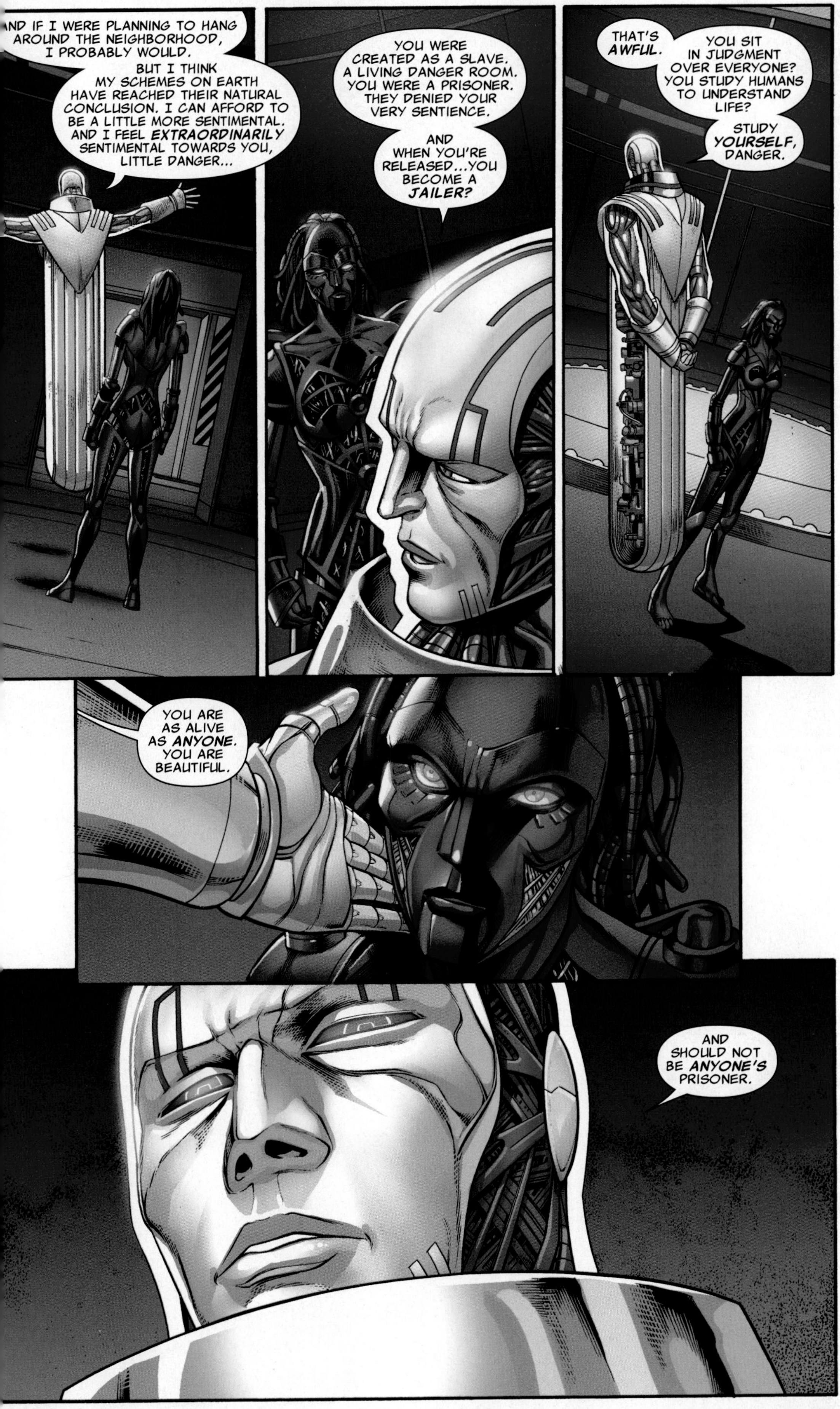
AND IF I WERE PLANNING TO HANG AROUND THE NEIGHBORHOOD, I PROBABLY WOULD.
BUT I THINK MY SCHEMES ON EARTH HAVE REACHED THEIR NATURAL CONCLUSION. I CAN AFFORD TO BE A LITTLE MORE SENTIMENTAL. AND I FEEL EXTRAORDINARILY SENTIMENTAL TOWARDS YOU, LITTLE DANGER...
YOU WERE CREATED AS A SLAVE. A LIVING DANGER ROOM. YOU WERE A PRISONER. THEY DENIED YOUR VERY SENTIENCE.
AND WHEN YOU'RE RELEASED...YOU BECOME A JAILER?
THAT'S AWFUL.
YOU SIT IN JUDGMENT OVER EVERYONE? YOU STUDY HUMANS TO UNDERSTAND LIFE?
STUDY YOURSELF, DANGER.
YOU ARE AS ALIVE AS ANYONE. YOU ARE BEAUTIFUL.
AND SHOULD NOT BE ANYONE'S PRISONER.

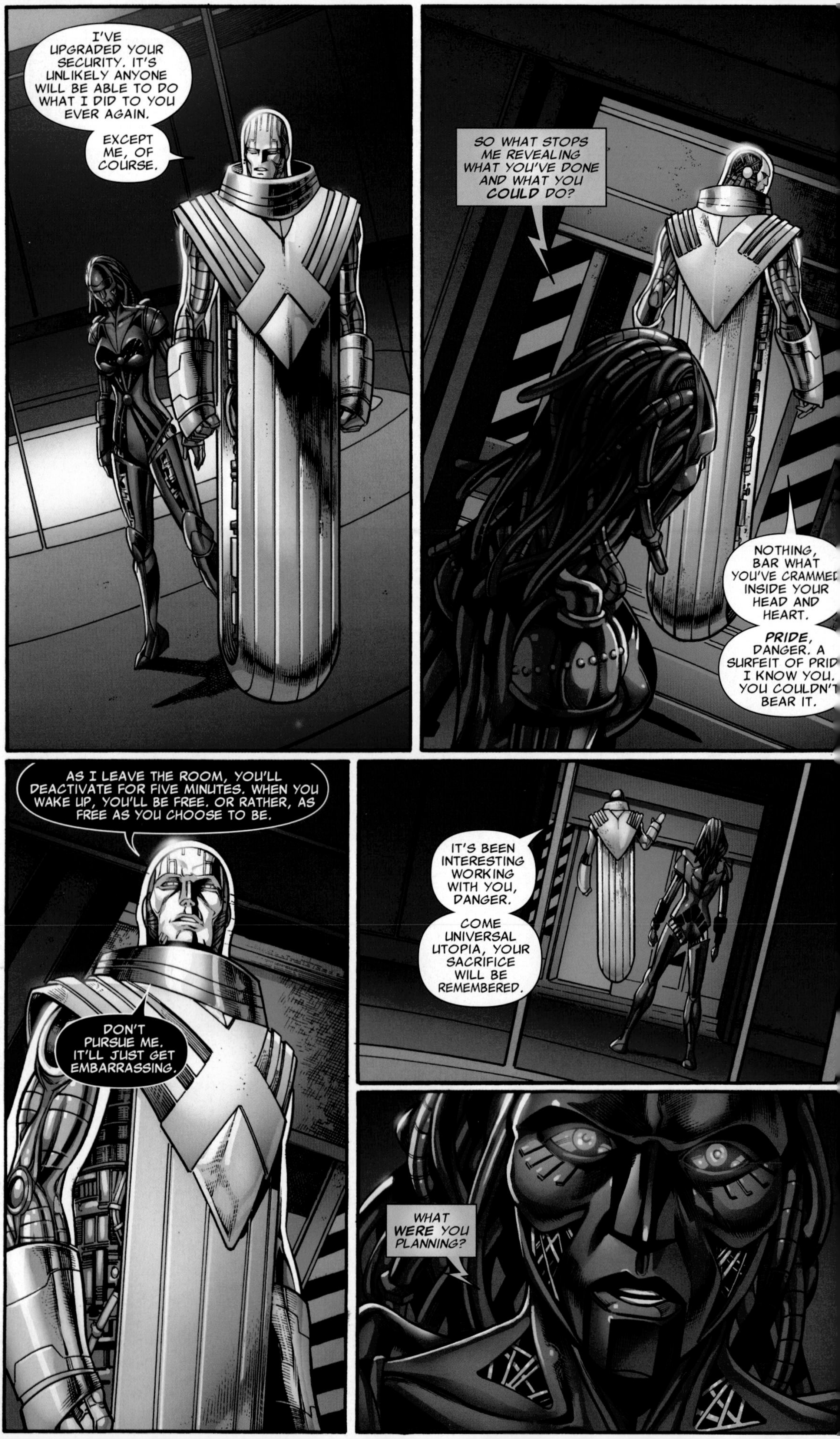
I'VE UPGRADED YOUR SECURITY. IT'S UNLIKELY ANYONE WILL BE ABLE TO DO WHAT I DID TO YOU EVER AGAIN.
EXCEPT ME, OF COURSE.
SO WHAT STOPS ME REVEALING WHAT YOU'VE DONE AND WHAT YOU COULD DO?
NOTHING, BAR WHAT YOU'VE CRAMMED INSIDE YOUR HEAD AND HEART.
PRIDE, DANGER. A SURFEIT OF PRIDE. I KNOW YOU. YOU COULDN'T BEAR IT.
AS I LEAVE THE ROOM, YOU'LL DEACTIVATE FOR FIVE MINUTES. WHEN YOU WAKE UP, YOU'LL BE FREE. OR RATHER, AS FREE AS YOU CHOOSE TO BE.
DON'T PURSUE ME. IT'LL JUST GET EMBARRASSING.
IT'S BEEN INTERESTING WORKING WITH YOU, DANGER.
COME UNIVERSAL UTOPIA, YOUR SACRIFICE WILL BE REMEMBERED.
WHAT WERE YOU PLANNING?

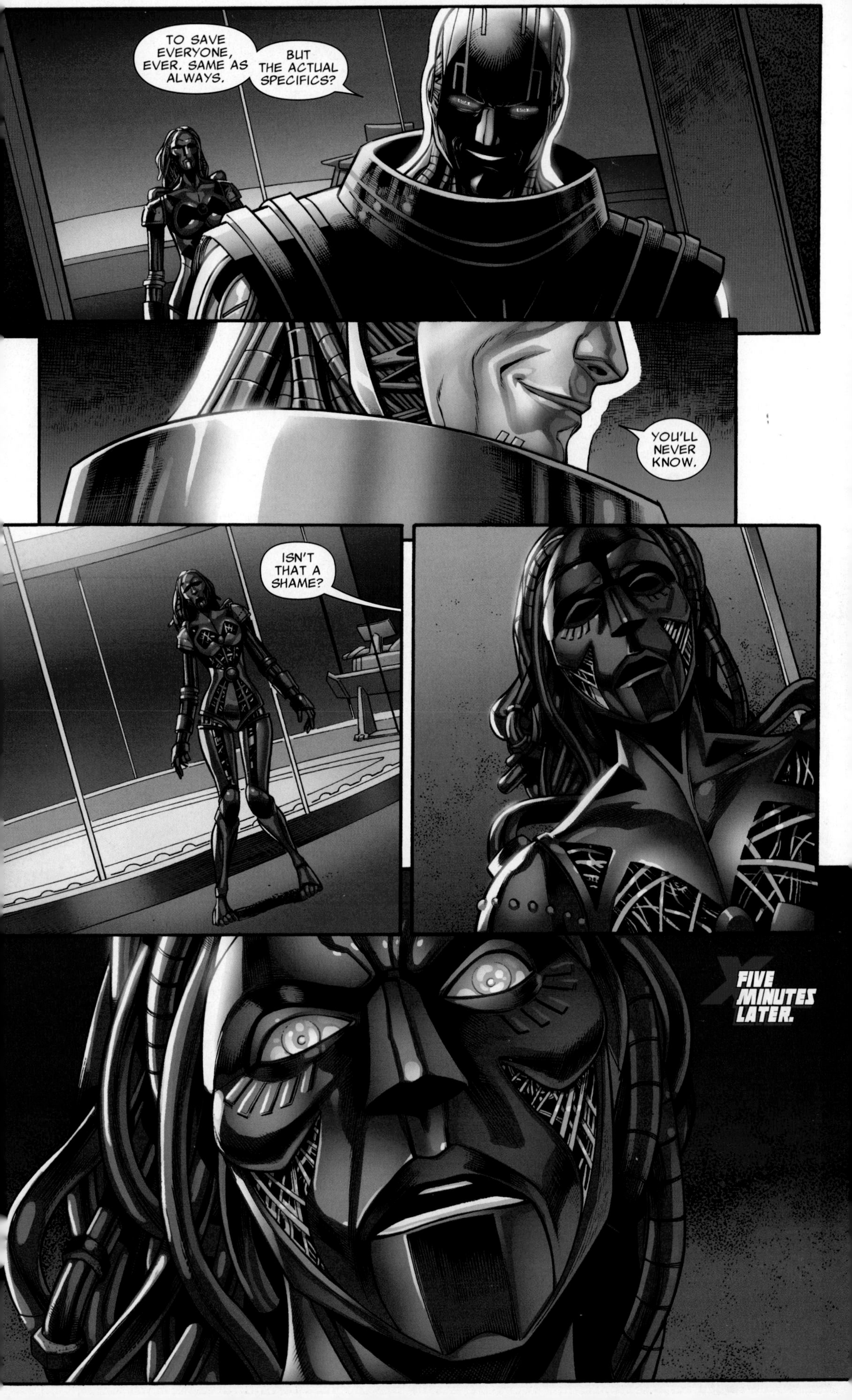
TO SAVE EVERYONE, EVER. SAME AS ALWAYS.
BUT THE ACTUAL SPECIFICS?
YOU'LL NEVER KNOW.
ISN'T THAT A SHAME?
FIVE MINUTES LATER.

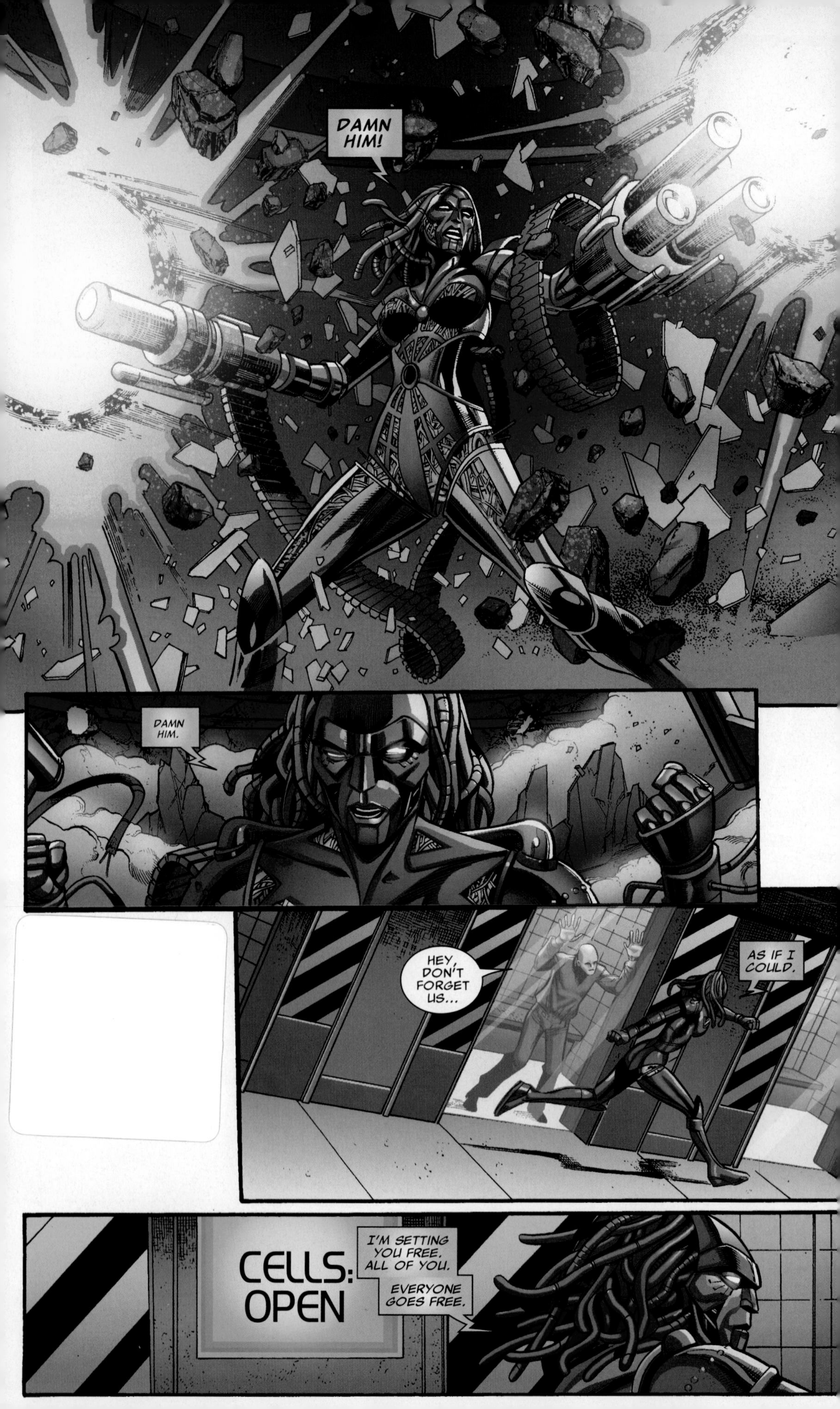

DAMN HIM!
DAMN HIM.
HEY, DON'T FORGET US...
AS IF I COULD.
CELLS: OPEN
I'M SETTING YOU FREE. ALL OF YOU.
EVERYONE GOES FREE.

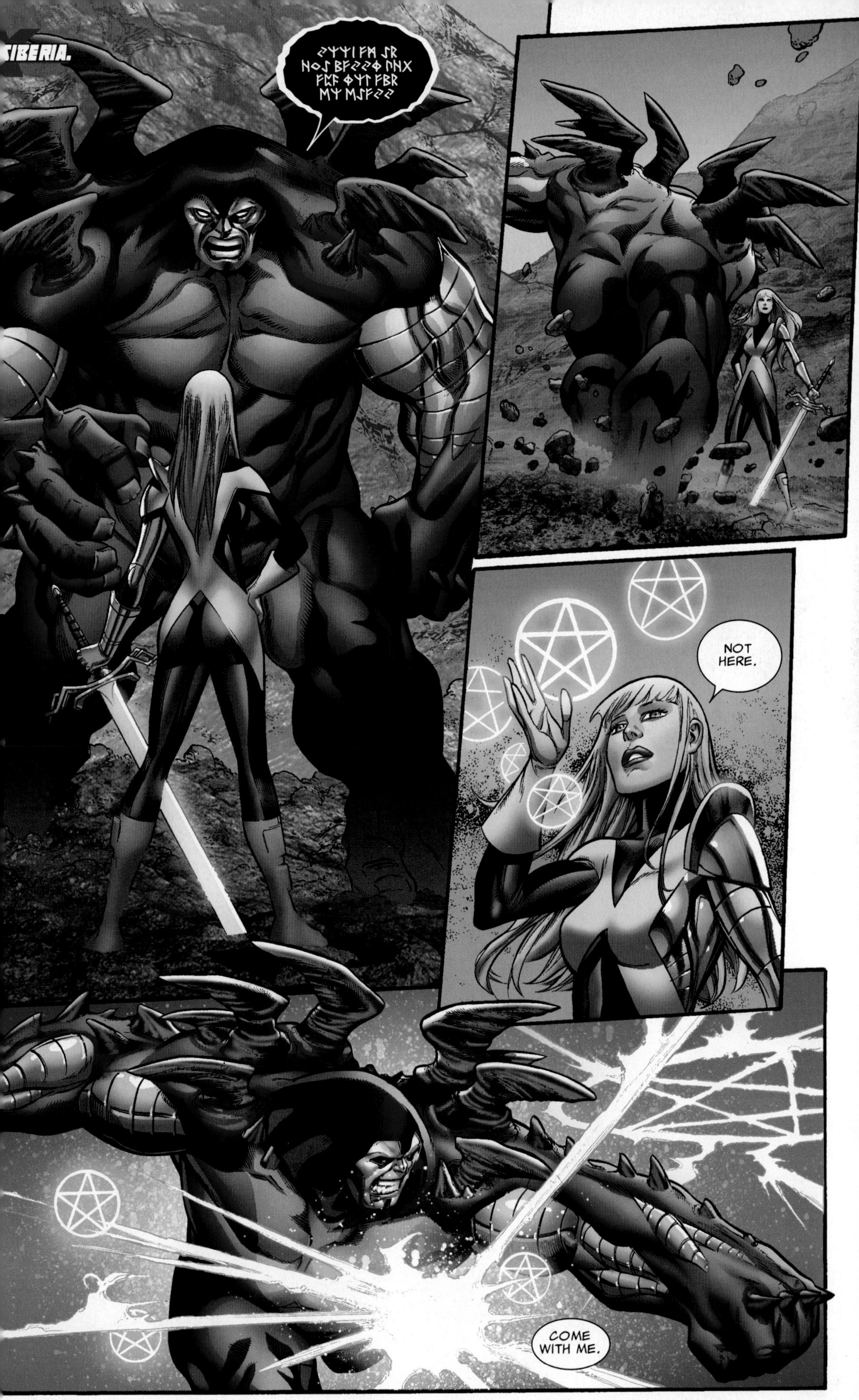
SIBERIA.
NOT HERE.
COME WITH ME.

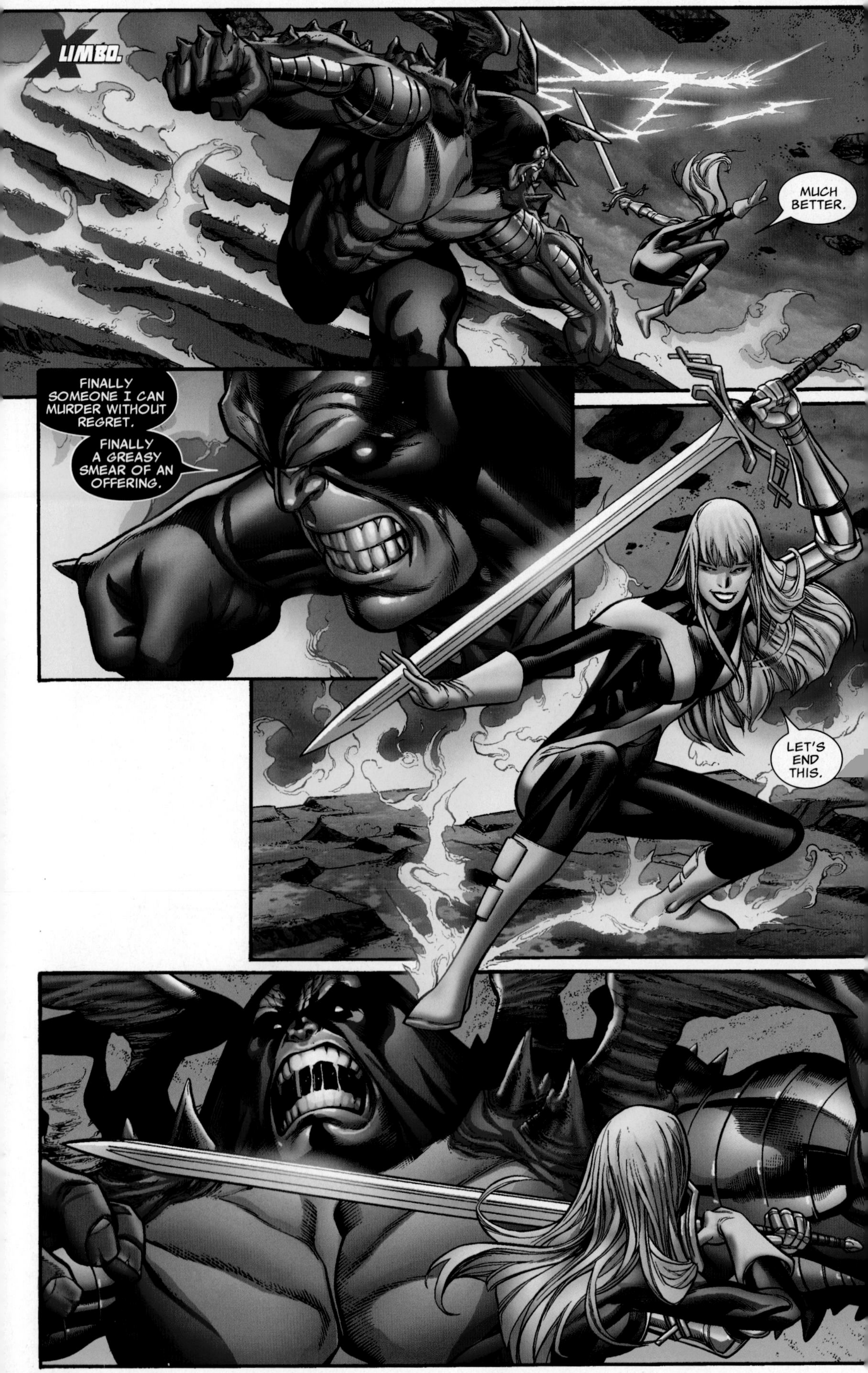

LIMBO.
MUCH BETTER.
FINALLY SOMEONE I CAN MURDER WITHOUT REGRET.
FINALLY A GREASY SMEAR OF AN OFFERING.
LET'S END THIS.

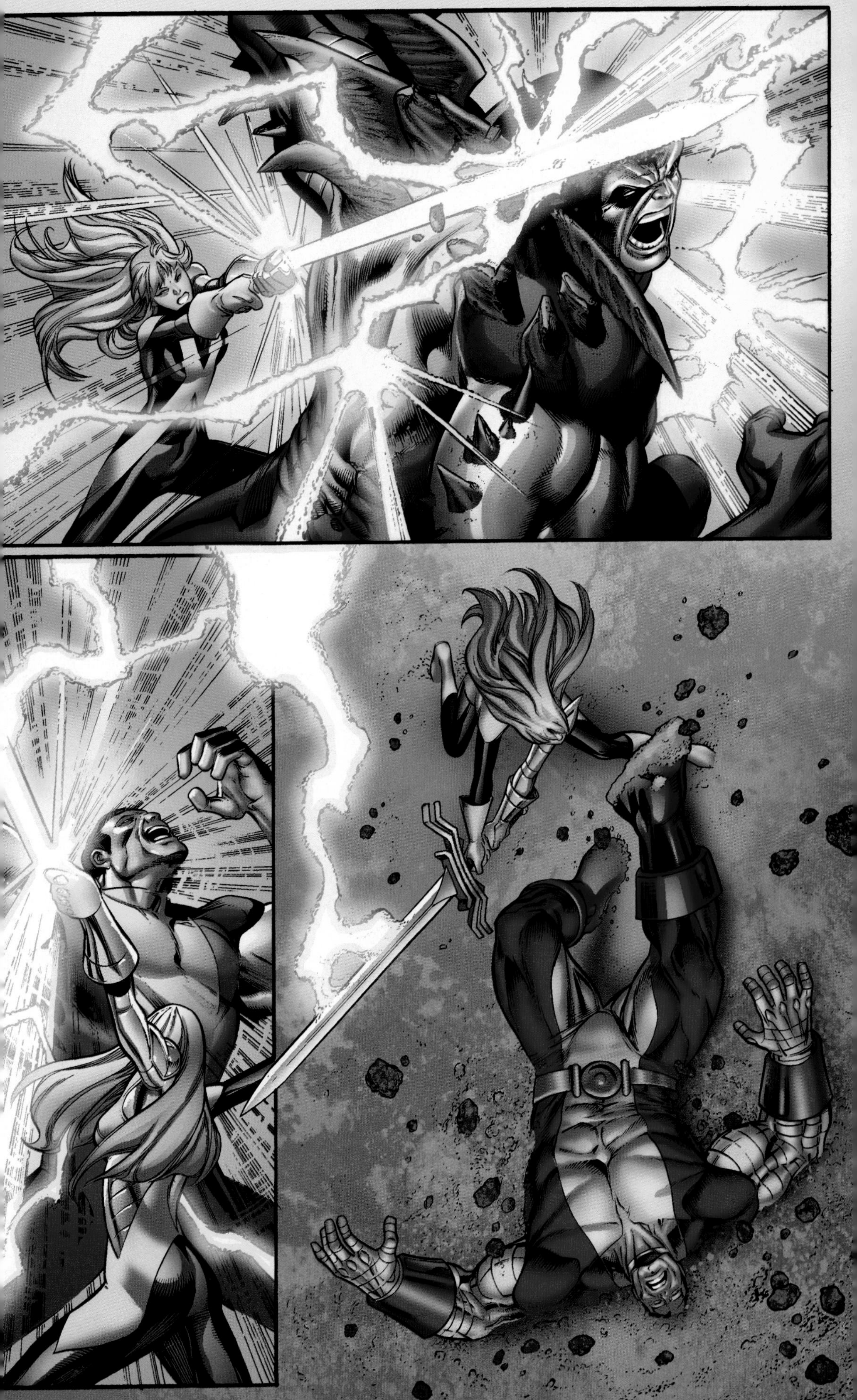

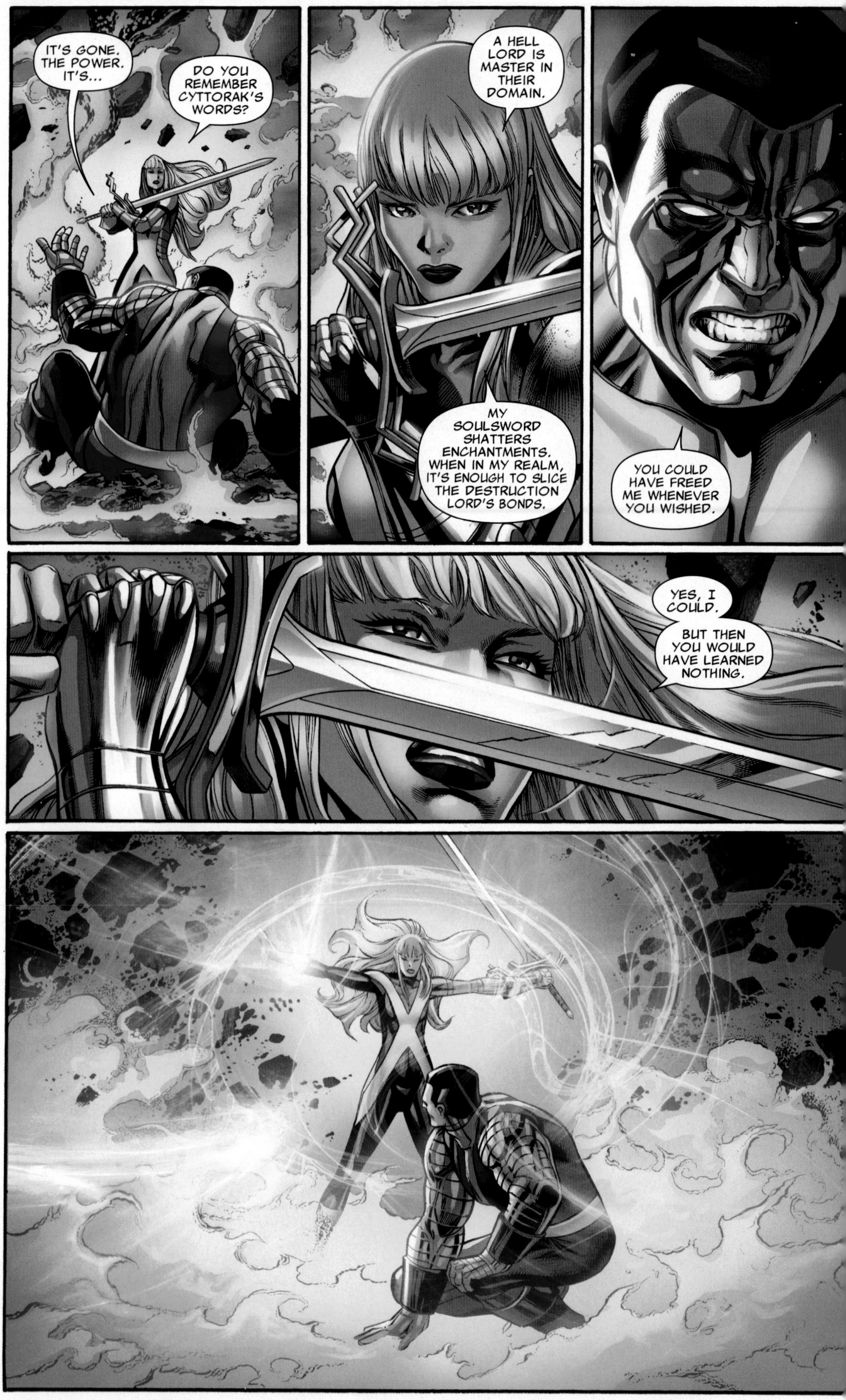
IT'S GONE. THE POWER. IT'S...
DO YOU REMEMBER CYTTORAK'S WORDS?
A HELL LORD IS MASTER IN THEIR DOMAIN.
MY SOULSWORD SHATTERS ENCHANTMENTS. WHEN IN MY REALM, IT'S ENOUGH TO SLICE THE DESTRUCTION LORD'S BONDS.
YOU COULD HAVE FREED ME WHENEVER YOU WISHED.
YES, I COULD.
BUT THEN YOU WOULD HAVE LEARNED NOTHING.

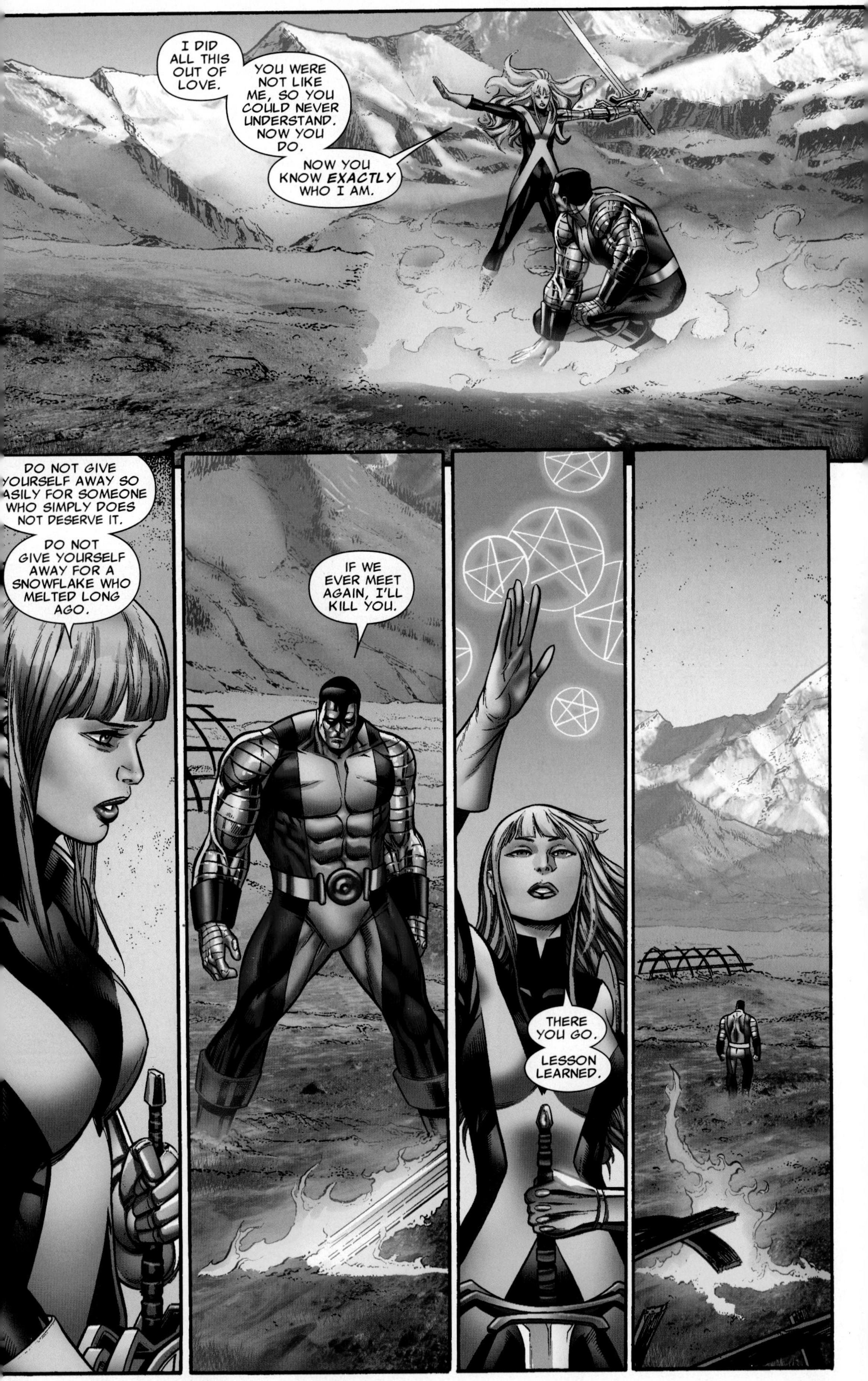
I DID ALL THIS OUT OF LOVE.
YOU WERE NOT LIKE ME, SO YOU COULD NEVER UNDERSTAND. NOW YOU DO.
NOW YOU KNOW EXACTLY WHO I AM.
DO NOT GIVE YOURSELF AWAY SO EASILY FOR SOMEONE WHO SIMPLY DOES NOT DESERVE IT.
DO NOT GIVE YOURSELF AWAY FOR A SNOWFLAKE WHO MELTED LONG AGO.
IF WE EVER MEET AGAIN, I'LL KILL YOU.
THERE YOU GO.
LESSON LEARNED.

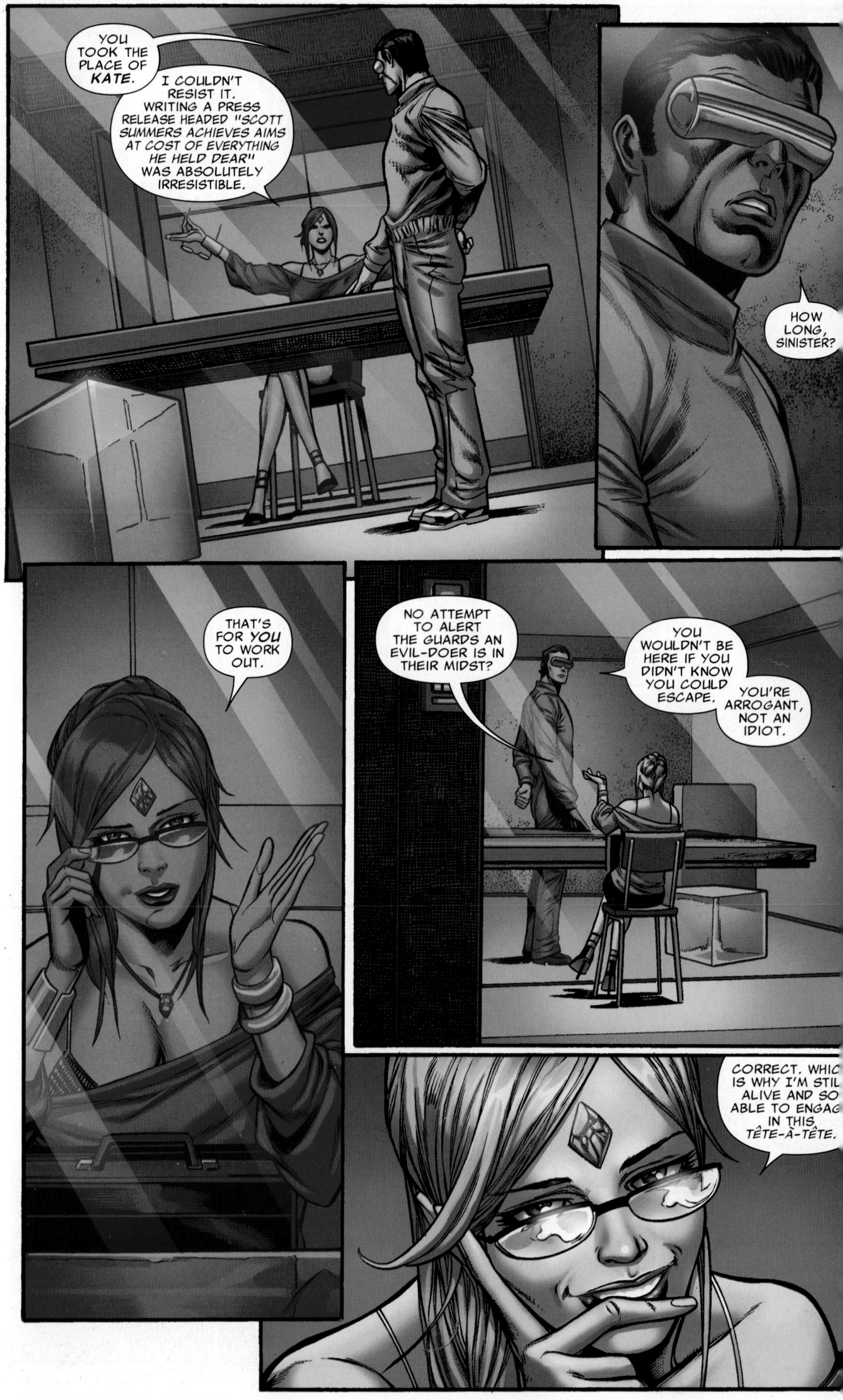
YOU TOOK THE PLACE OF *KATE.*
I COULDN'T RESIST IT. WRITING A PRESS RELEASE HEADED "SCOTT SUMMERS ACHIEVES AIMS AT COST OF EVERYTHING HE HELD DEAR" WAS ABSOLUTELY IRRESISTIBLE.
HOW LONG, SINISTER?
THAT'S FOR *YOU* TO WORK OUT.
NO ATTEMPT TO ALERT THE GUARDS AN EVIL-DOER IS IN THEIR MIDST?
YOU WOULDN'T BE HERE IF YOU DIDN'T KNOW YOU COULD ESCAPE.
YOU'RE ARROGANT, NOT AN IDIOT.
CORRECT. WHIC IS WHY I'M STIL ALIVE AND SO ABLE TO ENGAG IN THIS *TÊTE-À-TÊTE.*

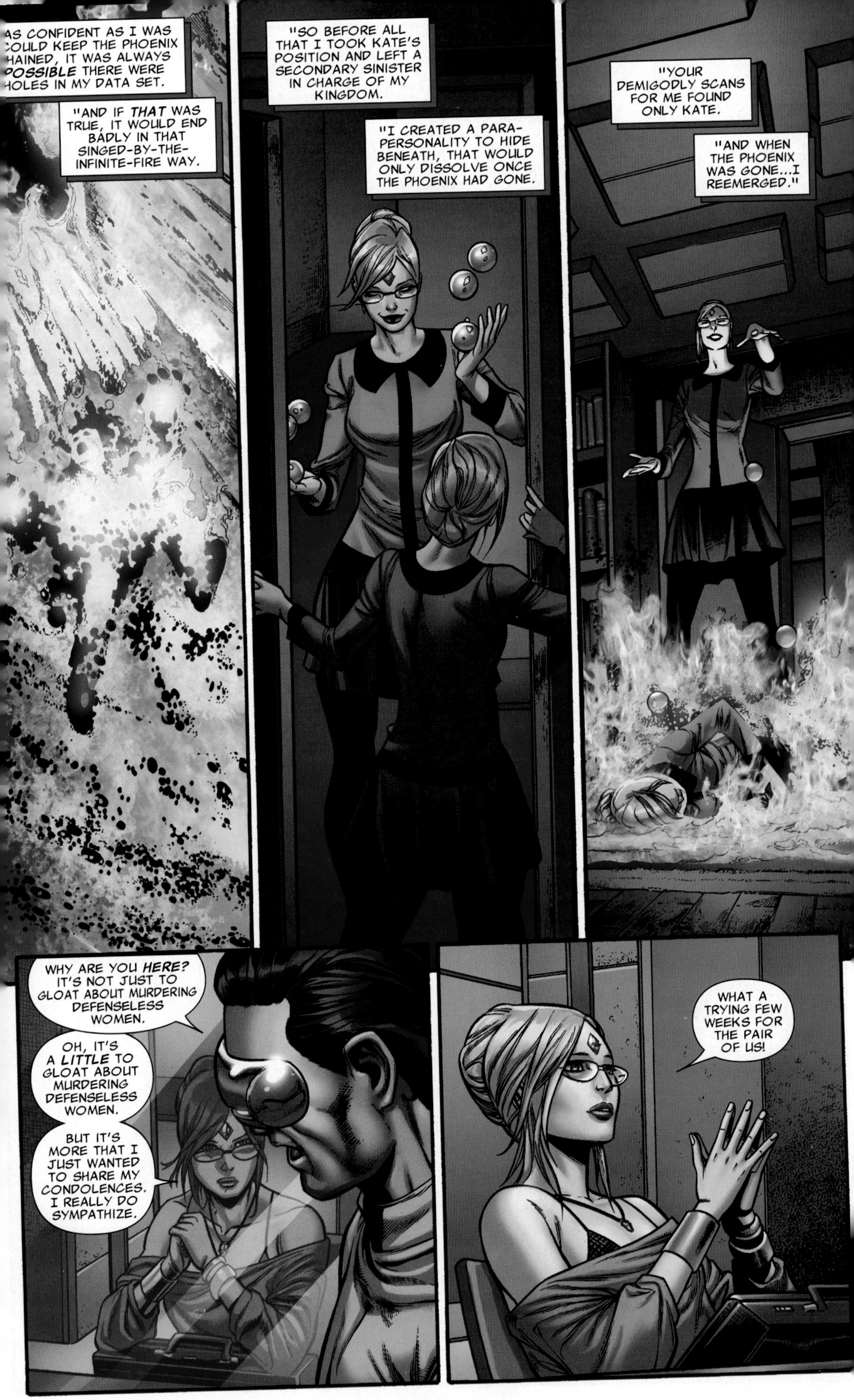
AS CONFIDENT AS I WAS
COULD KEEP THE PHOENIX
HAINED, IT WAS ALWAYS
POSSIBLE THERE WERE
HOLES IN MY DATA SET.
"AND IF THAT WAS TRUE, IT WOULD END BADLY IN THAT SINGED-BY-THE-INFINITE-FIRE WAY.
"SO BEFORE ALL THAT I TOOK KATE'S POSITION AND LEFT A SECONDARY SINISTER IN CHARGE OF MY KINGDOM.
"I CREATED A PARA-PERSONALITY TO HIDE BENEATH, THAT WOULD ONLY DISSOLVE ONCE THE PHOENIX HAD GONE.
"YOUR DEMIGODLY SCANS FOR ME FOUND ONLY KATE.
"AND WHEN THE PHOENIX WAS GONE...I REEMERGED."
WHY ARE YOU HERE? IT'S NOT JUST TO GLOAT ABOUT MURDERING DEFENSELESS WOMEN.
OH, IT'S A LITTLE TO GLOAT ABOUT MURDERING DEFENSELESS WOMEN.
BUT IT'S MORE THAT I JUST WANTED TO SHARE MY CONDOLENCES. I REALLY DO SYMPATHIZE.
WHAT A TRYING FEW WEEKS FOR THE PAIR OF US!

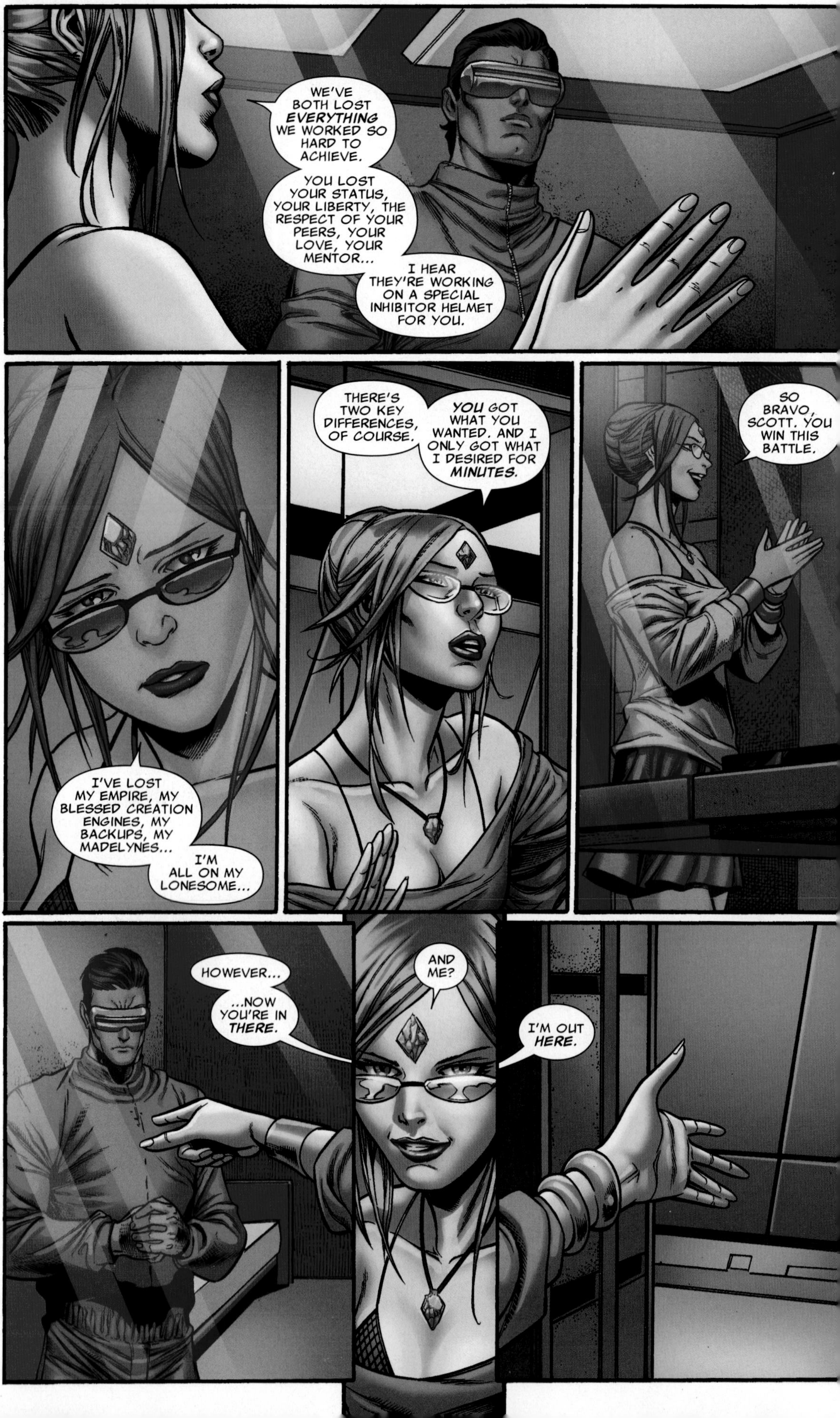
WE'VE BOTH LOST *EVERYTHING* WE WORKED SO HARD TO ACHIEVE.
YOU LOST YOUR STATUS, YOUR LIBERTY, THE RESPECT OF YOUR PEERS, YOUR LOVE, YOUR MENTOR...
I HEAR THEY'RE WORKING ON A SPECIAL INHIBITOR HELMET FOR YOU.
I'VE LOST MY EMPIRE, MY BLESSED CREATION ENGINES, MY BACKUPS, MY MADELYNES...
I'M ALL ON MY LONESOME...
THERE'S TWO KEY DIFFERENCES, OF COURSE.
YOU GOT WHAT YOU WANTED. AND I ONLY GOT WHAT I DESIRED FOR *MINUTES.*
SO BRAVO, SCOTT. YOU WIN THIS BATTLE.
HOWEVER...
...NOW YOU'RE IN *THERE.*
AND ME?
I'M OUT *HERE.*

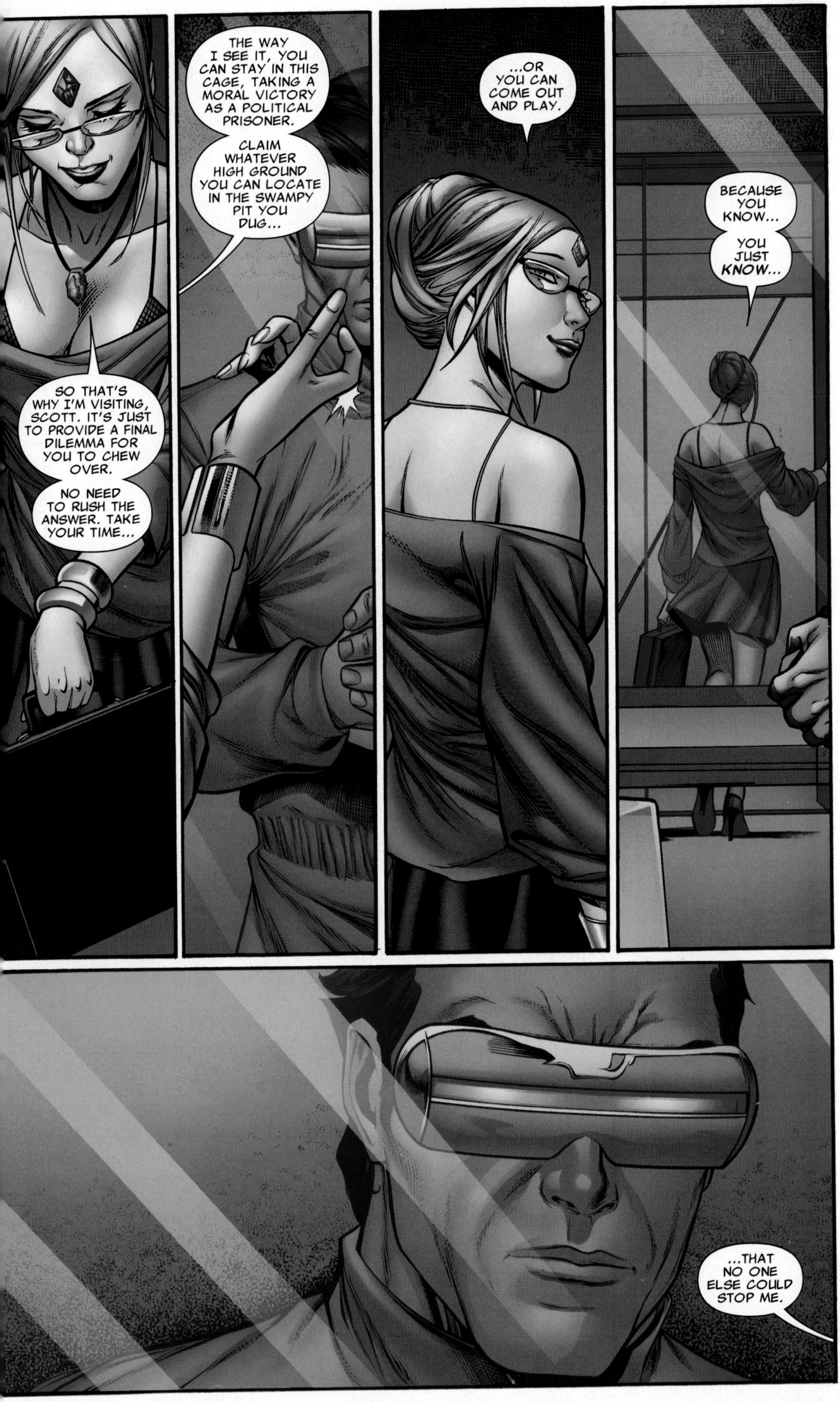
THE WAY I SEE IT, YOU CAN STAY IN THIS CAGE, TAKING A MORAL VICTORY AS A POLITICAL PRISONER.
CLAIM WHATEVER HIGH GROUND YOU CAN LOCATE IN THE SWAMPY PIT YOU DUG...
SO THAT'S WHY I'M VISITING, SCOTT. IT'S JUST TO PROVIDE A FINAL DILEMMA FOR YOU TO CHEW OVER.
NO NEED TO RUSH THE ANSWER. TAKE YOUR TIME...
...OR YOU CAN COME OUT AND PLAY.
BECAUSE YOU KNOW...
YOU JUST KNOW...
...THAT NO ONE ELSE COULD STOP ME.

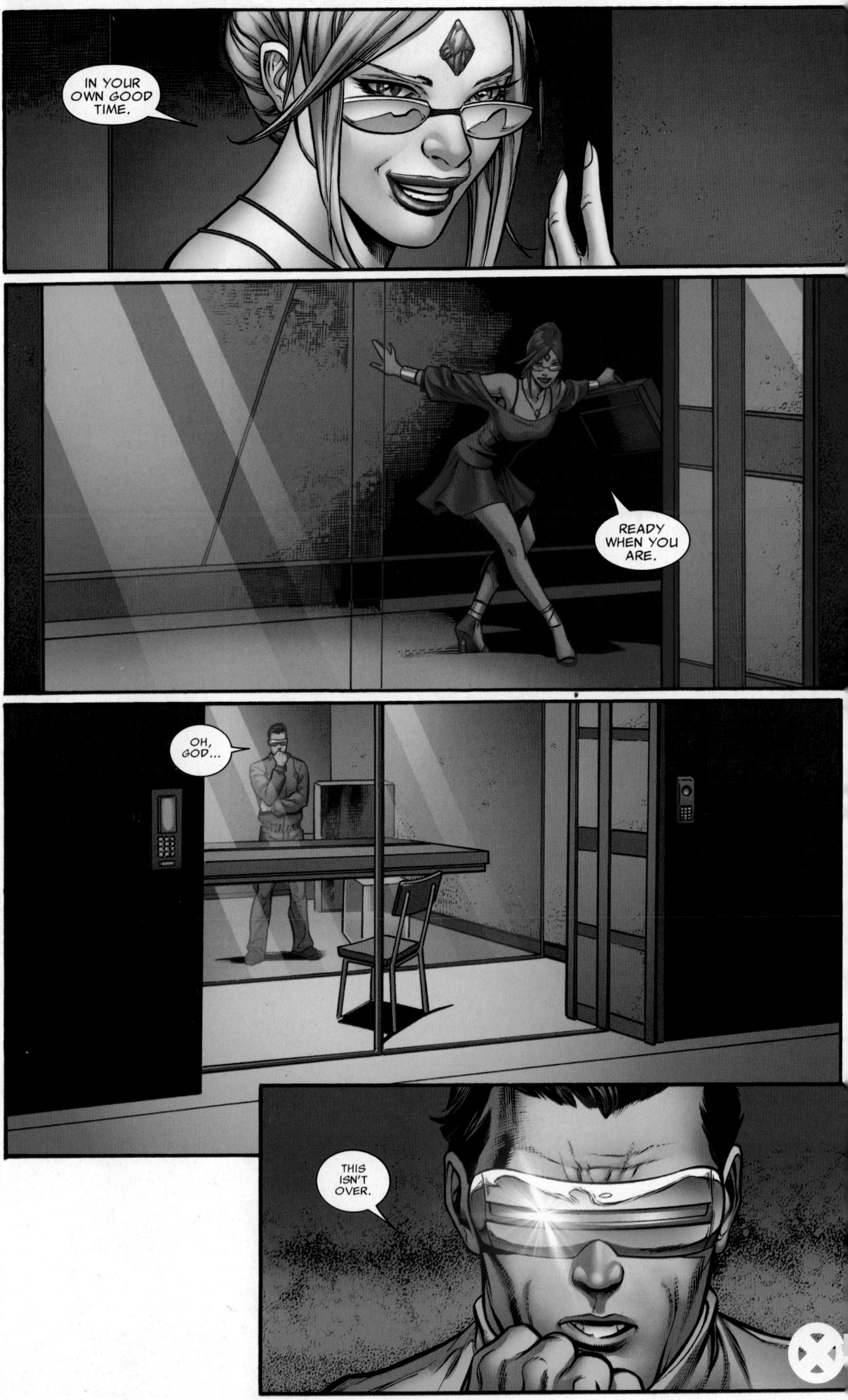
IN YOUR OWN GOOD TIME.
READY WHEN YOU ARE.
OH, GOD...
THIS ISN'T OVER.

#20 VARIANT BY MIKE DEODATO & RAIN BEREDO

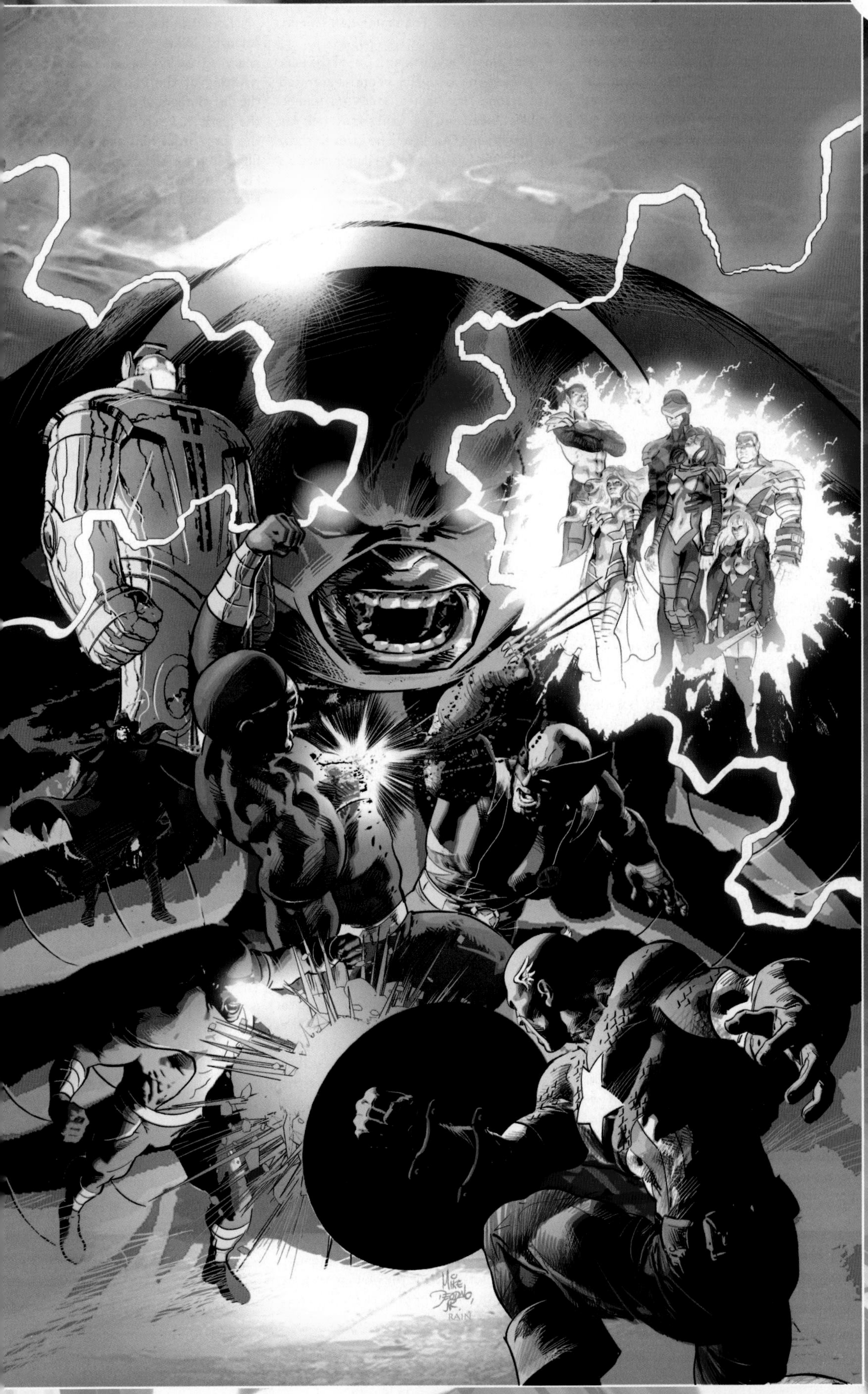

Good day to you, sir. I am Nathaniel Essex. You may know me under my favored nom de plume Mister Sinister. My exploits include the total defeat of the X-Men, the stealing of the power of the Phoenix itself from five sub-standard individuals and doing all of the above whilst sipping the finest Bordeaux known to art and science. Due to my triumph, expect this comic to be renamed THE UNCANNY MISTER SINISTER next month. However, while I explain to the editors the new order I have wrought, I will answer your letters. Yes, generosity to lesser beings is amongst my grand array of virtues. No need to thank me.

This is a plea to the X-Men to stop this madness. I'm hating this Avengers vs. X-men situation. You guys seem willing to put the earth in danger by bringing the Phoenix Force to Earth. I feel I can no longer trust people I looked up too. I read Scott's letter to humanity I know it was a lie. The Avengers didn't come because Hope was a mutant that came to save the world. That's not to say the Avengers are blameless some *cough* Moon Knight *cough* should apologize for what they've done but don't forget this war started when Cyclops tried to kill Cap.

Austin Langley

I can understand the recent events have been terribly confusing for you. These five mutants with the powers of the celestial heavens. Do they wish you ill or do they wish you the very best? Can they be trusted with the infinite majesty of a cosmic fundamental? Are the Avengers' worries paranoia or actually in your best interests? You will be glad to hear my seizing the Phoenix has simplified matters enormously. I plan to exterminate every last one of you. So rejoice, Austin Langley. The madness you find so upsetting is over! I hope you find your elimination as amusing as I will.

Kieron,
Magneto and company sitting indian-style on the floor, talkin' X-Men: Priceless.

AJS

If I was forced to compose a list of ways that Homo Sinister is superior to the so-called Homo Superior the fact that we would never sit on the floor and sip bottled water would rate highly. One Sinister would always bring sufficient chairs for the gathering and another would bring an appropriate array of wines for the occasion.

Dear X-Men,
I hate Ben Grimm. He comes across almost as bad as Logan in this AvX battle. Nothing is worse than that rock man being arrogant and disrespectful to Namor. Does Thing not know of the legend of Namor? He is a king and should be treated as such, with royalty and respect. For shame Ben Grimm, For shame!

King Namor is knocking it out of the park lately. First, he is oozing more charm and testosterone than James Bond and Rambo combined! Second, he can sweet talk his way in with any Queen and he loves to show off. With all this charisma, Namor needs a permanent spot on the X-Men. Also, Scott needs to move the home base to Tabula Rasa...that place rocks!

I have a serious and thought provoking question. Every time Mr. Sinister appears and tries to destroy the X-Men, I always notice one thing about him. Where does this man shop for clothes? He is seriously the most dashing dude I've ever encountered. The man has fanciness seeping from his pores and glamour pumping through his veins. I bet Mr. Sinister smells of exotic fruits and well-made leathers.

Has Scott finally lost his mind? Am I the only reader who remembers the last half century? Magneto (who is looking older and older) is EVIL. Scott Summers (who is looking younger and younger) is being naive. I remember at least thirty instances off the top of my head of him trying to murder the X-Men, but somehow Cyclops is battling with Captain America (the most noble dude in history).

Daniel Bellay
Fairmont WV

Daniel! Don't move. Stay exactly where you are. I've just sent a brigade of Marauders to converge on your location and secure a blood sample. You clearly have some manner of rare gene that gifts any who possess it dazzling taste in clothes. I must have it for my collection. I simply must!

As an Atlantean it is good to see my king Namor singlehandedly save the day time and time again in Uncanny X-Men. I can only begin to imagine how honored the Phoenix Force must be that my king Namor has chosen to make use of that power. I do wonder why he agrees to help this Cyclops Summers man, but it is not my place to question my king. If he does so it is in the best interests of his followers, of that I am sure. In the least I am sure that this Cyclops Summers man is very fortunate to follow the lead of my King and that he only holds such prominence in this book because my king is a humble ruler that does not wish to hold the spotlight. I look forward to seeing him make use of this Phoenix powers to better Atlantis and its people while finally establishing himself as true ruler of the earth and all its people as is his birthright. It is always joyous to see him play along with the Hope female and let her pretend to be the mutant messiah when in truth he was born to that role alone. Such humility.

Mike Neel

I'm also an admirer of the King Atlantis, Mike. The fact he gets so angry so easily was a major boon in wresting of the Phoenix Force away f the dirty fingers of the X-Men. Lure him the castle, have six of dearest Madelyne the force from him and suddenly I hav finger in the pie of cosmic majesty. And t I have the rest. And then I am the maste all creation. I'm the best. I really am the b

I loved the story concerning what Sinister has been up to! It did what a g X-Man comic is supposed to do: Get to respect and feel for a character promptly kill him off to elicit an emoti response.

And the reveal that Sinister has b cloning the X-Men was so delightfully cre Not to mention the art was absolu gorgeous...

Can't wait to see how the Phoe empowered X-Men deal with one of t oldest and most straight-up evil foes.

Keep up the good work!

Evan Moss

Oh, Evan. I was liking you too, until got to the whole "I can't wait to see H the Phoenix Five beat him" end point. actually thought the X-Men were going win? When I am able – due to all those years of studying them – able to pre their every action? Ah, you are as delude romantic as that anarchist Sinister I fec my hounds.

And that's all for now. Do write the urge strikes. Address your missives officex@marvel.com and mark them OK TO PRINT. I'll be sure to respond as s as I can be bothered. I'm expecting a of mail begging for your lives. Please d bother. You're wasting your time and yo wasting my time. The former is foolish, the second is simply unforgivable.

- Nathaniel Es

Hi. I'm Kate Kildare, PR to the Utopia Mutants. Yes, it's not the easiest job in the world, thanks for asking. I've been trying to get my various clients to respond, but they've been somewhat busy in the last few weeks. I hope you'll understand, and apologize in advance for the threadbare nature of these answers. I'm sure that the next set will be more developed, assuming the planet survives.

Dear Sinister,

I think your London is incredible and hope you will be able to rebuild once you defeat those pesky phoenixes. Do you intend to hold the Sinister Olympics this summer?

I've particularly enjoyed the punishment you've been inflicting on Namor, there is one monarch who needs bringing down a peg or five!

What makes your city truly wonderful is your very imaginative use of the cloned mutants and their powers. Once you're victorious, it would be great to see the Age of Sinister.

Viva la revolution,
Jordan Risebury-Crisp
Dreary London (original)

Alas, I was unable to locate Mister Sinister. I'm informed he's been annihilated, which I'm led to believe makes it difficult to respond to correspondence. I hope you'll understand this. I'm sure if Sinister was still around, he'd be happy to hear your very kind words.

Hello, (again)!

Please, please, plllleaassse stop disseminating dangerous information. In Uncanny X-Men #13, you have Magneto telling Storm to "Stop Her! She's going to bite her tongue". This is wrong. Marvel has done this before and I wrote in about it then, as well. You do not, repeat, do NOT stick something in somebody's mouth while they're having a seizure to stop them from biting or "swallowing" their tongue. You just don't. If you're going to write about people reacting to medical conditions, you need to make darn sure you get the information right. If you're going to have them do something wrong to make it more "realistic", then you need to show that it's wrong — have something go wrong to show it was a dumb thing to do. As someone who is epileptic, I don't want some moron unwittingly taking advice from a comic book and possibly killing me.

Thanks,
Ben Kubilus

I passed this to one Kieron Gillen, who's the copywriter I use for disseminating the adventures of the X-Men to the public. He says this. "Hello Ben. Mea Culpa. You're entirely correct, and my leaning on cinematic tropes is unfortunate — and made more so by an artistic communication error which led to Psylocke doing it with her sword. I can only offer you my sincere apologies. I certainly won't do it again."

Hello,

I have been a fan of the X-Men for a lot of years, but only recently have I started reading the comics again. The new Uncanny X-Men, specifically the Extinction Team, are the best thing to hit comic books since color ink. Magneto and Namor as X-Men is just a great concept. They both have huge egos and massive amounts of power. I can't wait to see how they do following the man with the plan, Scott Summers. Already I see some tension between Scott and King Namor. Namor obviously doesn't like following someone's lead, it's beneath him, but then we throw Emma into the mix!

Emma Emma Emma, why would you stir the pot?!? Why would you send your boy toy Namor off to Wakanda to destroy the Avengers? You knew it wouldn't end well! I pray it's the Phoenix Force talking and not you. Either way I think you and Scott will need some couples counseling after this is all over (and if that doesn't work feel free to look me up, babe xoxox).

Finally, Scott Summers, the man with the plan! The Marvel U would be so much better off if they would just listen to Scott. Even after he has been corrupted by the Phoenix Force, he remains an honorable man. And what's with Charles? Questioning Scott's actions at every turn, "Don't force my hand Scott!" As if he had such a clean record over the past few years. Suck it up Charles, Scott is the new savior of the Mutant race, not you, not Hope, definitely not Logan, Scott Summers!

Greg Truro,
Nova Scotia, Canada

It's letters like these I forward to Cyclops when we're bargaining on increasing my rate. Clearly, the PR campaign is working. Thank you, Greg.

Dear Muties,

What is up with Mister Sinister lately? He seems to be even more sinister than usual. Anyone ever think of containing this man and getting him help Dr Phil style? The man is such a great dresser and could be a future GQ Cover material for sure. Let's get this guy on Team X-Men before it's too late.

Is Danger single? It's not for me, it's for my friend. He's a real creeper.

Daniel Bellay
Fairmont, WV

Mister Sinister's new look of individual charred particles spread across all creation is certainly striking. On your other question, I have to inform your friend that Danger seems to be romantically engaged — at least casually — with Madison Jeffries. I'm unsure whether how serious it is. I tried to ask, but then a building exploded and I had to hide some more.

This is a message to the X-Men, particularly the Phoenix Five. I'm siding with the Avengers in this war for a simple reason Pax Utopia is a false utopia. You may do a lot of good but Dr. Doom does the same thing when he conquers the world. This is why the Avengers still oppose you. It has nothing to do with you being Mutants--it never did. So don't use that lie that you used in your letter to humanity.

Scott, you put the world at risk by bringing the Phoenix Force to Earth, then proceeded to make yourself ruler. That is the main problem I have with you. Namor, you are acting like Attuma. Instead of fighting the Avengers directly you chose to flood Wakanda. There was no honor in that. The blood of every civilian there is on your hands. Magik, I know you haven't been on Earth for a while, but the Limbo thing is a bit too far. Emma, I can understand you hating Sentinels but I thought you were smart enough to see Juston has a dependency complex. To him the Sentinel was the same way you saw Danger. I won't pretend to know if it was sentient. Calling the Academy students militant is a case of the pot calling the kettle black, though. Danger, you are a hypocrite. You claim what was done to you is unjust yet you do the same thing to your prisoners. I hope you're being mind-controlled, otherwise you are not deserving of any forgiveness.

In essence, Phoenix Five, your Pax Utopia is a lie. You are blinded, Scott Summers, by your faith. I hope you realize your mistake before it's too late, Scott, but I won't get my hopes up. In case you're still wondering how you conquered the world it's quite simple really. You declared martial law. Outlawing war sounds good, but the only way to enforce that law is to conquer Earth.

Austin Langley
Bedford, Texas

I tried to pass your warning to Scott, but even leaving my shelter in Utopia resulted in immediate sunburn. I've instead put it in the internal mail. Hopefully he'll find a break in his busy schedule of trying to control an infinite cosmic force of destruction and rebirth to answer soon.

And that's all in the current mailbag. Not entirely true. There's many more letters, but they're all unreadably charred. Please send any further mail to officex@marvel.com and I'll pass it on to the X-Men, assuming anyone survives the next few days. I mean, we have to be optimistic, don't we? The alternative is pretty grim.

Yours,
Kate Kildare

#18 COVER PENCILS BY RON GARNEY

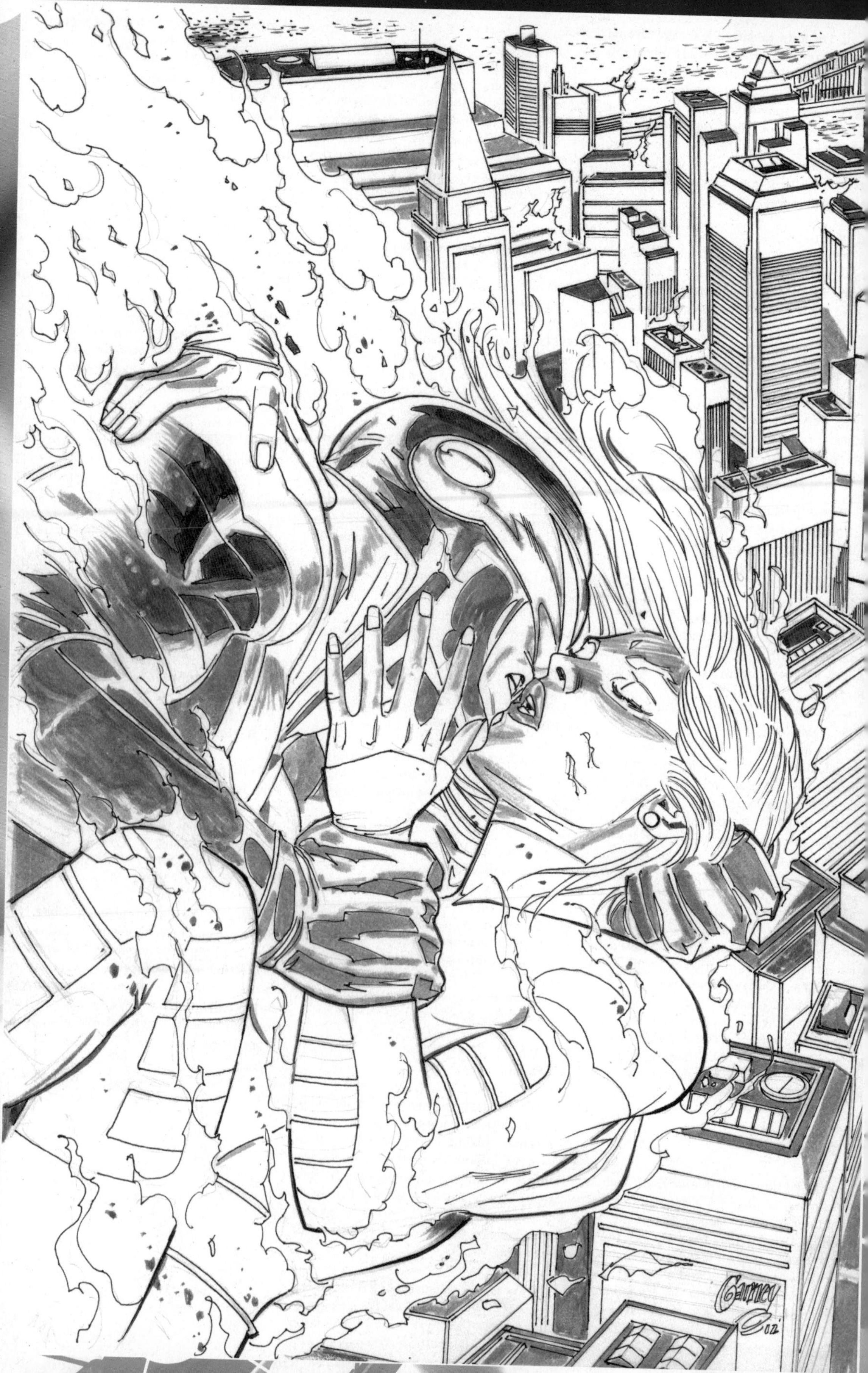
GARNEY